The Ethic of Traditional Communities and the Spirit of Healing Justice

The Ethic of Traditional Communities and the Spirit of Healing Justice

Studies from Hollow Water,
the Iona Community, and Plum Village

Jarem Sawatsky

Foreword by Rupert Ross

Jessica Kingsley Publishers
London and Philadelphia

First published in 2009
by Jessica Kingsley Publishers
116 Pentonville Road
London N1 9JB, UK
and
400 Market Street, Suite 400
Philadelphia, PA 19106, USA

www.jkp.com

Library of Congress Cataloging in Publication Data

Sawatsky, Jarem.

The ethic of traditional communities and the spirit of healing justice : studies from Hollow Water, the Iona Community, and Plum Village / Jarem Sawatsky ; foreword by Rupert Ross.

p. cm.

Includes bibliographical references (p.).

ISBN 978-1-84310-687-6 (pb : alk. paper)1.Restorative justice--Cross-cultural studies. 2.Healing--Psychological aspects. 3.Healing--Religious aspects. 4.Hollow Water Reserve (Man.) 5.Iona Community. 6.Village des pruniers (Buddhist community)I. Title.

HV8688.S39 2009

364.6'8--dc22

2008030207

British Library Cataloguing in Publication Data

A CIP catalogue record for this book is available from the British Library

ISBN 978 1 84310 687 6

Printed and bound in Great Britain by
Athenaeum Press, Gateshead, Tyne and Wear

Dedication

To Rhona, Sara and Koila
For your teaching, patience and partnership
on this journey into healing justice
and for the many journeys to come

Contents

Acknowledgements

All research is, of course, communal. In research we enter into a web of relationships, and even our observing changes their nature and our nature. What we see is not just dependent on what is there. We see through the lens moulded by those who have gone before. We cannot help but stand on the shoulders of our ancestors, our mentors and our enemies. Each shape what we see, how we see it and what meaning we attach to it. As I have learned from the communities in this study, acknowledging the gifts of those who have gone before is an important part of doing healing justice.

At the heart of this research are three wonderful communities. While each had grounds to be suspicious of academic university research, each agreed to participate in the research and to host me as I tried to learn as much as I could about their approaches to healing justice. I would like to thank the Elders and community of Hollow Water, Manitoba, Canada for agreeing to participate in this research. In particular I would like to thank Burma Bushie, Marcel Hardisty, Sharon Klyne, Jeanette Cook, Randy Ducharme, Gabriel Hall, Bernie Hardisty, Laura Hardisty, Marilyn Sinclair, Donna Smith and the rest of the staff at Circle Healing and Community Holistic Programme. In Plum Village I would like to thank Thich Nhat Hanh, Sister Chân Không, Pháp Liêu, Chân Tùng Nghiêm, Đào Nghiêminh Nghiêm, Mai Nghiêm, Nhủ Nghiêm, Tôn Nghiêm, Trish Thompson, Pháp Xả and the rest of the monks and nuns at Plum Village in France. In the Iona Community in Scotland (and beyond) I would like to thank Kathy Galloway, Graeme Brown, Ruth Burgess, Tom Gordon, Desirée van der Hijden, Nick Prance, Zam Walker, Richard Sharples and Biddy Sharples. It is a deep honour to enter into the imagination, stories, traumas and joys of another person and other communities. It is also a great responsibility. I have tried from beginning to end to conduct this research in respectful ways. I deeply thank these communities for sharing their ways, for being my teachers and for encouraging me to practise the habits of healing justice within the concrete fabric of my life.

I was also intrigued by his sense that he had found enough similarities between the approaches of an aboriginal community in Canada, a Celtic-Benedictine community in Scotland and a Vietnamese-Buddhist community in France to warrant deeper comparison, and I have been anxiously awaiting his findings. My wait has been rewarded, because he has discovered that, to a significant degree, the core beliefs of each community appear to flow from *common* understandings about the essence of creation, and the role of mankind within it. In the pages that follow, he gives voice to three distinct ways of expressing those shared, foundational beliefs, and each articulation adds to our understanding of all. I also suspect that each of the three communities will be interested to learn that they are not alone, either in what they are doing or in the world view that is manifested in their work. Other 'communities' will also find a resonance with these voices, and likely a deeper determination to forge similar paths.

I am also impressed by the way Jarem has articulated the many contrasts between the social paradigm that creates justice-as-healing approaches and the prevailing western paradigm that spawns our crime-and-punishment approaches – and keeps us trapped within them. Too-often even well-intended westerners jump into restorative justice processes only to cause *escalating* discord and dissatisfaction, simply because they failed to see that there really is a paradigm issue in play. Jarem phrases the challenge this way:

> Sometimes, in our zest for change, we become a mere reflection of what we resist. We change the coverings but not the underlying logic... We use an 'alternative' process, but we use it within the imagination and framework of the existing culture. Because of the way we use the alternative, it is not a genuine alternative at all. It does not challenge the basic logic, and thus actually entrenches the status quo. This research seeks to understand healing justice within the broader context of the conditions and factors which sustain such a justice.

Understanding what is meant by nourishing 'good relations' is thus the core challenge, and it is often difficult to understand how much time and courage it takes to bring them into being, and that they are neither created by, nor dependent upon, getting people to perform particular acts (like making restitution or uttering formal apologies). If Jarem's research only stands as a warning about how deeply different the two approaches to justice really are, that in itself will be of great service.

I also want to commend Jarem for his bravery, on several levels. First, it takes *professional* courage to break the rules about remaining at all times an impartial and objective researcher, and to suggest that these may in fact be *counter*-productive research strategies in this context. Second, these three communities required that he, too, act, speak and respond not like an objective researcher but like everyone else, as an engaged, uncertain and vulnerable human being participating in rigorous processes of self-examination. It demanded that he leave many of our accustomed safety nets behind, and that takes a high degree of *personal* courage. Third, it takes courage to *write* so openly about personal responses to the experiences gained; when Jarem writes that 'For me, entering the landscape of these communities was deeply inspiring, awakening and revealing', he is taking professional risks, and I salute him for it.

Finally, I want to congratulate Jarem for the way he has written this book. He has freed himself – and his readers! – from the professional jargon that so often characterizes research of this kind. He tells his story cleanly and smoothly, inviting everyone to join him in the ups and downs he encountered along the way. This is not the work of a cheerleader for 'justice-as-healing', but the informed reflections of a deeply curious human being who wonders if there might be better ways for all of us to behave towards each other. At the same time, he is not in the least hesitant to express misgivings or pose unanswered questions as he goes. Like all tales of penetrating explorations, this book leaves the reader more deeply intrigued and curious at the end than they were at the beginning.

It has been a pleasure sharing his adventures on these pages, and I commend them to anyone with an interest in the human condition and in the various ways human societies can either limit or nourish the potential for good in each of us.

Rupert Ross
Assistant Crown Attorney for the District of Kenora

Introduction: What if Justice is About Becoming Whole While Learning to Sing?

The Unbroken[1]
There is a brokenness
out of which comes the unbroken,
a shatteredness
out of which blooms the unshatterable.
There is a sorrow
beyond all grief which leads to joy
and a fragility
out of whose depths emerges strength.

There is a hollow space
too vast for words
through which we pass with each loss,
out of whose darkness
we are sanctioned into being.

There is a cry deeper than all sound
whose serrated edges cut the heart
as we break open to the place inside
which is unbreakable and whole,
while learning to sing.
(Rashani 1991)

What if justice is about becoming whole while learning to sing? How do we nurture the conditions where shatteredness might bloom into the

---

1   Reprinted with kind permission of Rashani (www.rashani.com). Copyright © Rashani 1991.

unshatterable? What imagination and support is necessary to sustain that journey into darkness where we are sanctified into being? How do we cultivate the ability to hear the cry that is deeper than all sound and to see the unbreakable in the broken? What if justice is meant to lead to joy, to emerging strengthened out of fragility, to finding our place in the song? What if many of our basic assumptions about justice are misguided? What if a more healing kind of justice is possible? What if it already exists?

In my work and life I kept hearing little hints that such a justice might already exist. I kept hearing stories from indigenous communities about 'people forgetting who they are', about 'taking offenders onto the land', about needing to 'return to their traditions' as part of sustaining a 'healing way of justice'. The more I listened, the more I learned that this 'alternative' voice comes not just from indigenous communities, but also from engaged Buddhists, fringe Christian communities and other communities. The questions they are asking, the language they are speaking and the cultural framework of their practise is very different from much of the literature of my chosen fields of restorative justice and peacebuilding.

So I set out to see if I could find concrete examples of this healing justice being practised in living communities. I wanted to see if I could show up in such a community and touch and taste this healing justice. What I was really curious about was that if one could find healing justice, would it offer sufficient breadth and depth to help address some of the dissatisfactions I was feeling with more mainline Western approaches to law, justice, conflict and peace? In other words, I wanted to test if there was substance to these claims about healing justice. I also wanted to examine how the discourses of law, restorative justice and peace might be transformed by a careful listening to, and examination of, such a healing justice. I thought that perhaps these communities could provide some insight into the kinds of social, cultural and even spiritual relationships that are necessary to sustain a more healing way of justice. This research, then, is a journey into healing justice and a quest to address those themes.

For many individuals, communities and states, justice has come to reflect the same ugliness as injustice: pain, loss of power, loss of identity, disorientation, loss of respect, becoming broken and, in the extremes, killing other people. Being 'brought to justice' is not something many seek in their lives. Sometimes it is the very seeking of justice, in both personal and international relations, which leads to deep experiences of injustice.

It is not surprising, then, to find the search for 'alternative' conceptions and practises of justice is alive and strong in many countries around the world. The rapid global rise of the restorative justice movement is, in part, symptomatic of this searching. The increased interest from individuals and even states in indigenous forms of justice is another part of this searching. The United Nations' declaration of the Decade for a Culture of Peace (2001–2010) and the World Council of Churches' Decade to Overcome Violence (2001–2010) are further attempts to find an alternative justice which might lead to deeper peace rather than to continue cycles of violence. An emerging alternative and response to this search is 'healing justice'.

This book is an exploration into notions of healing justice. Healing justice is related to both indigenous justice and restorative justice. It is used by a number of communities to point away from 'state justice' and towards justice of another kind. By state justice I simply mean the range of ways Western, and mostly modern, states approach and structure justice. While state justice has been the subject of much study, healing justice has not. In this study I have undertaken three tasks:

1. To identify who uses healing justice and to create three case studies of healing justice in action.

2. To try to understand the conditions and factors that sustain such practises and visions.

3. To explore what restorative justice and Western states might learn from the insights of these communities.

The first task in exploring the visions and practises of healing justice leads to an investigative account and the conclusion that a healing kind of justice is possible, and that it has been and still is practised by diverse communities around the world. I will counter the logic that current systems of state justice are the best that can be expected, and also the logic of last-resort thinking which is used to justify state violence in relationship to crime, to processes of colonization and to wars. Such last-resort thinking argues that some form of violence or punishment is needed and justified to make the system work and thereby makes violence and/or punishment part of the normative definition of justice. This argument will be picked up in more detail in the final chapter. In the end the reader may well choose the current state justice systems ahead of the practises of healing justice described here. The goal of this book is to make the choice a real contest and not permit the status quo to be accepted unthinkingly. In fact, the goal is not so much to convert readers to the practises described in this book as to spark more intelligent discussion and questions as to the cultural dynamics that sustain particular visions of justice. This brings us to the second task of this book.

The second task, understanding the conditions and factors that sustain such practises and visions, will force us to take a much broader view of crime and harm than is often taken within both criminal and restorative justice studies. Sometimes those looking for an alternative are too quick to see something interesting, extract the form and try to transplant it into foreign soil. As an example, note the spread of Family Group Conferencing around the world. This practise started as a way of transforming the New Zealand state system which the indigenous people and the system itself saw as institutionally racist (MacRae and Zehr 2004). By the time this practise travelled to Australia, it had become a tool to strengthen state (police) control over youth (O'Connell 1998). Sometimes, in our zest for change, we become a mere reflection of what we resist. We change the coverings but not the underlying logic. We see this in international politics where revolutionaries become the next dictators. Sometimes we also see this where restorative justice initiatives are institutionalized as mechanisms of crime control. We use an 'alternative' process, but we use it within the imagination and framework of the existing culture. Because of the way we use the alternative, it is not a genuine alternative at all. It does not challenge the basic logic, and thus actually entrenches the status quo. This research seeks to understand healing justice within the broader context of the conditions and factors which sustain such a justice. It asks not only how healing justice is done but if healing justice represents a challenge to the basic logic of Western approaches to law and justice.

In his classic book, *The Protestant Ethic and the Spirit of Capitalism* (1985), Max Weber sought to understand why capitalism grew in the West. The rise of Western capitalism, in Weber's analysis, was due to a partnership of four key dynamics: the development of science, the development of modern technology, bureaucracy and the spirit of the Protestant ethic. It is this last factor which readers find so fascinating in Weber's analysis – 'that modern economic and social development has been influenced by something that seems at first sight utterly distinct from it – a set of religious beliefs' (Giddens and Birdsall 2001). Much later, Richard Snyder wrote *The Protestant Ethic and the Spirit of Punishment* (Snyder 2001). He was looking for the ways that elements of the Protestant ethic similarly fuel an understanding of justice as punishment.

The question underlying my research topic has similarities to those of Snyder and Weber. However, the emphasis is different. I seek to understand, not capitalism or punishment, but healing justice. The focus is not the West, but the particular traditional communities in which healing justice is still found today. However, somewhat like Weber I seek to understand why healing justice continues to survive and to be practised and want to understand why healing justice is found in particular faith communities. For this reason, the second task of this book is to understand the kinds of relationships, conditions and factors that sustain such a justice.

The basic argument of this book is that there may be cultural dynamics which are more determinative of the kind of justice than the processes of responding to harm. If we want to learn in respectful and fruitful ways from these communities that practise healing justice, we need to focus less on the processes of healing justice and also less on how we might replicate them in our systems. Rather, we should focus more on what these communities might teach us about the conditions and factors that are necessary to sustain a vision of a justice that heals. Changing our own system in light of the fruitfulness of a different form of justice loses its transforming value unless we also learn how to nurture the conditions necessary to sustain such practise and vision. When we learn about the conditions and factors or the kinds of relationship and structures which sustain healing justice we can have more meaningful discussions on what supporting such dynamics might mean for our particular culture and community. Furthermore, for those of us engaged in the various alternative justice movements, an awareness of the kinds of relationships which sustain healing justice may provide fruitful insights for how alternative processes need to be linked to broader issues of systemic change.

A note on terminology. I have loosely called these communities 'traditional' to distinguish them from 'modern' and 'state' forms. This distinction is lost in part because while each community draws on pre and post modern imaginations, each community lives and operates in the modern world. So traditional is not the opposite of modern nor is it something that is essentially conservative or static. The traditions I am trying to point toward are particular traditions and narratives that equip a people to live creatively in the present by drawing on the wisdoms of the past. In this respect I follow a whole host of ethicists and traditional teachers who turn to such particular traditions as a means to know how to be in the present in ways that touch but are not determined by the dominant imagination. In the Christian tradition this approach is articulated by the likes of Stanley Hauerwas (Hauerwas 1981), and John Howard Yoder (Yoder 1972). In Aboriginal traditions it is often the Elders but also teachers like Taiaiake Alfred (Alfred 1999), Marie Battiste and James (Sa'ke'j) Youngblood Henderson (Battiste and Henderson 2000). In Buddhist traditions it is the Engaged Buddhist movement and authors like Thich Nhat Hanh (Hanh 2003b), Joanna Macy (Macy 2007) and Maha Ghosananda (Ghosananda 1992). Each turns to their own 'traditions' to find ways of being together, of co-existing, of inter-being in the present. Throughout this text 'traditional' is used to refer to this relationship of a people to past, present, stranger and neighbour.

The third task of this research is to explore what restorative justice and Western states might learn from the insights of these communities. For those involved in restorative justice and other alternative justice movements, the goal of this research is to present a new dialogue partner. Much of the development of restorative justice has taken place in dialogue with various state forms of justice. This dialogue comes in many forms: negotiating programme relationships, seeking funding, doing evaluations to sustain funding, seeking permission for programme and developing a flow of cases. Sometimes the dialogue has challenged state notions of justice, seeking to be an alternative to state justice. But whether the dialogue has been based on a partnership model or on an over-and-against model, dialoguing with the state has influenced the shape, imagination and direction of restorative justice. Chapter 2 on restorative justice will carry this argument further. One of the goals of this research is to present an additional dialogue partner for the restorative justice movement, that of communities practising healing justice. The goal of dialogue is not usually to convert wholesale but to gently influence each other. The argument that will be presented here is that the development of restorative justice would be greatly enhanced by seeing traditional communities as key dialogue partners. This of course is already happening in those areas of restorative justice where there is an especially keen interest in various forms of indigenous justice. However, the focus of the dialogue is usually over forms (e.g. circle processes) and, sometimes, over values. This research will challenge restorative justice to accept a much broader and deeper view of healing justice which would include an examination of the conditions, factors and imagination which sustain such a vision. This might well reshape the restorative justice perspective.

Part I begins with an overview of what healing justice is, who uses this language of justice and how they use such language. While this book does review some of the existing theory on healing justice and related topics, theory is not the primary source of exploration. I will review the theory and practise implications of restorative justice (Chapter 2) but the primary focus will be on traditional communities engaged in learning the best ways to survive together. In other words, in searching for alternatives to justice, I will leave the geography of theory and the geography of crime and enter into the geography of traditional communities to learn something about the geography of healing justice. I will return to this notion of how particular approaches to justice might be likened to different geographies. For now it is important to warn the reader that this journey invites us into perhaps unfamiliar lands or geographies. Our old assumptions about what justice is and how it works do not help us to see, identify and understand healing justice. Chapter 3 picks up these challenges of learning how to enter into healing justice. I have tried to design this exploration of healing to be ethical and respectful so that the means of research is consistent with the focus point. This chapter tells the story and highlights lessons relevant to *how* we can learn from communities which practise healing justice.

Part II gets us more deeply into the ethic of particular communities. Some readers may want to begin their reading here. Chapters 4–6 present the three case studies of healing justice: Hollow Water, an Aboriginal[2] and Métis community in central Canada; Iona Community, a Christian community on the coast of Scotland; and Plum Village, a Vietnamese-

---

2   I have used the word 'Aboriginal' as a respectful way to speak of the indigenous peoples of North America. What constitutes respectful and appropriate language is in flux. Here I have deviated from the Oxford Dictionary and public media usage which would use a lower case for 'aboriginal'. 'Aboriginal' denotes the name of a people, a nation. In a similar way the word 'Canadian' is capitalized.

inspired Buddhist community in exile in southern France. These case studies have been shaped from spending a short time living with each community, listening to their teachers and peoples, participating in their ways and reading what they and others have written about them. For two years, during my study, visits and writing I tried to immerse myself in their imaginations to see what I might learn about healing justice. One of the results is the case studies and this book of reflections. A brief history of each community is offered, but the bulk of each chapter focuses on the particular practises and visions of healing justice within that community. These chapters also highlight what these communities understand to be the sustaining factors and barriers to their particular approach to justice. While the words are mine, I have tried to work with each community in describing them. My goal in creating these case studies is that the communities themselves are able to recognize themselves and respect the telling of their own story. None of these communities are homogeneous; they have much diversity and complexity. Consequently it is important for the research that several members of each community were included in the verification of their story. The case studies explain how members of these communities understand their own approaches to healing justice.

Part III presents what has been learned about the spirit and phenomenon of healing justice. Chapter 7 presents the comparative analysis of the shared characteristics of healing justice derived from the three case studies. Even though the case studies were selected because of the multiple ways they differed from each other, this chapter finds many striking common characteristics of healing justice. The final chapter examines the meaning of this research for three target audiences: communities which practise healing justice, the restorative justice movement and those involved in Western state governance.

The search for healing justice in these pages may take a reader to some uncomfortable places. Healing justice does not neatly follow the logic, structure or purpose of criminal justice or social justice. The search for healing justice brings the reader face to face with communities and their more collective imaginations. Moreover, these communities are faith or spirit-based communities of three different kinds. Those who value a rationalist, secular, individualist approach will probably find this research most challenging. Those who are attracted to a restorative justice vision as a different paradigm of justice but have been disappointed with the depth and breadth of that difference may well find this research hopeful and enlightening. For those who have sometimes wondered why some spirit-based communities are so violent while others seem to be more peaceful this research presents many interesting insights.

The goal of this research is not to present a theory of healing justice. The goal is to demonstrate that healing justice exists within modern society. It is to learn about the shape of healing justice from the perspective of those who practise it. Finally, the goal of this research is to take seriously the meaning of healing justice for the communities with such a practise, for the restorative justice movement and for the broader discourse of Western state governance.

This research is not an independent, objective analysis of healing justice (as if such a thing could exist). It is my attempt to learn in a respectful way from three communities which practise healing justice, or are said to practise it. This is a very personal journey where the author is not absent or invisible. While I am not a member of any of these communities I have cultivated friendships in each. As a reader will soon learn, friendship, respect and personal journeys are very much a part of healing justice.

This research develops three case studies. These are not samples from which you can draw statistically valid generalizations. However, I believe this research has tremendous implications for others. This research uncovers powerful stories and insights which unsettle popular notions of justice even as they reveal the horizon of a different kind of justice, namely healing justice. The reader is invited on this journey into the geography of healing justice.

Part 1 – Overview

Chapter 1

Exploring Healing Justice

Justice as healing is an old tradition in Aboriginal thought and society. Now, after our experiences with colonialism, racism, domination, and oppression, we have returned to Aboriginal jurisprudence as a foundation for contemporary remedies. The systematic deprivation of Aboriginal ownership of land and resources, Aboriginal wealth and income, as well as our culture, human dignity and social position have placed difficult demands on our traditional values and rituals. We need to explore our vision of justice as healing in their totality.

James Sakej Henderson, Cheyenne Professor and Research Director,
Native Law Centre of Canada
(Henderson 1995)

Crime is often a symbol of woundedness within but so is the retributive concept of justice. The outer reality mirrors an inner reality, only love and compassion can remove such walls. Only respect for others and us can break the cycle of violence and revenge. Biblical justice is fundamentally respectful because people and relationships are central. We learn respect by being respected, not by being disrespected. A justice that heals is a justice that respects.

Howard Zehr, Mennonite Professor of Restorative Justice,
Eastern Mennonite University, Virginia
(Zehr 1994a)

The emphasis on non-violence within so much of Buddhist tradition is not because of some otherworldly preoccupations; it is based upon psychological insight that violence breeds violence. This is a clear example, if anything is, of the maxim that our means cannot be divorced from our ends. If there is no way to peace, the peace itself must be the way.

David Loy
Buddhist Professor of Comparative Philosophy
and Religion at Bunkyo University in Japan
(Loy 2001)

An Aboriginal, a Mennonite and a Buddhist...sounds like the start of an inappropriate joke. But this is the starting point of an inquiry into healing justice. Each author speaks by drawing on the wisdom of his own tradition. Each author critiques Western conceptions of justice. And each author tries to capture the spirit of his own tradition by pointing towards a kind of healing justice.

But what is this healing justice they are talking about? Is it possible to show up at a community and to touch and taste a healing kind of justice? Do these different communities which speak about healing justice have anything in common with each other? Are they talking about the same phenomenon? What is all the fuss about?

Our exploration into healing justice begins by tracing those who use the language of healing justice. It will continue by identifying communities that are said to have some conception of healing justice. However, we need to first understand who uses this language and how they use it. In light of those insights, I then lay out in more detail the purposes of this research and the potential implications for three audiences. Before going too far in an exploration it is important to understand some of the potential dangers. The final sections of this chapter focus on some of the objections to the notion of healing justice and also on some of the inadequate attempts to listen to these communities.

Genealogy of healing justice

Before we go further into the nature of this inquiry we must return to the Aboriginal, the Mennonite and the Buddhist. What are they really talking about when they talk about a justice that heals? What is healing justice? Where has it come from? Who uses it, how do they use it, and why?

Inquiries into both healing and justice go back thousands of years. Some would say they go back to the creation of the world. But where, when and for what reason did these two streams of inquiry join together in the term 'healing justice'? Or, perhaps, which communities kept alive a memory of a time when justice and healing were inseparably linked? A review of academic literature for the occurrence of this concept helps to trace the various usages of the term in academic circles. However the language of healing justice does not originate in academia and, therefore, a review is a survey of secondary usages. The primary usages lie in the everyday practises of various traditional communities. However, our search will begin by tracing the published uses.

I searched a number of sources for the use of the phrase 'healing justice' but also the related phrases, 'justice that heals' and 'justice as healing'.[1] According to the above search criterion, the first use of these terms is in the eighteenth century by an English poet, Charles Churchill, who cynically described 'perverse and deadly' state justice as healing justice (Churchill 1933). The terms do not appear again as a major theme until the 1980s.

In tracing the use of these terms I identified five streams of influence:

➤ Christians interested in Christian approaches to crime

➤ Aboriginal people interested in living traditional ways of justice

➤ restorative justice advocates describing the heart of justice and interacting with 'serious' harm

➤ governments responding to Aboriginal people and restorative justice advocates

➤ various other academic fields.

I will pick these up chronologically as they appear in the published literature.

---

1   I searched two copyright libraries, the Library of Congress and the British Library, for books that had such phrases in title, subject or keyword. I also searched 34 academic journal, research and dissertation databases covering approximately 20,000 journals from every discipline in the Arts and Humanities. In addition I searched for these phrases both with Google Scholar and, to a lesser degree, with Google search engine. I then tried to get in touch with some of the authors who were the first to write about this terminology (according to the criteria above). I asked these authors what they knew about the origins of this terminology. There are surely some uses of these terms that I missed, but I believe this survey fairly outlines the story of how and by whom these terms have been used, and it points toward why such a term is now coming into public use.

Christians interested in Christian approaches to crime

In the early 1980s, under the direction of Howard Zehr, the Mennonite Central Committee Office of Criminal Justice created a poster with the words 'crime causes injuries; justice should heal'. This language is picked up by Daniel Van Ness in an early publications which speaks of needing to heal the wounds of crime and its victims (Van Ness 1986).

In 1988 a Canadian, Morton MacCallum-Paterson, a United Church member, published a book called *Toward a Justice that Heals: The Church Response to Crime* (MacCallum-Paterson 1988). This book seems not to be widely used or cited, but it is listed in the Victim Offender Mediation Association's restorative justice library. In 1992 Arthur Paul Boers, a Mennonite, published a similar book entitled *Justice that Heals: A Biblical Vision for Victims and Offenders* (Boers 1992). And in 1994 Howard Zehr, the Mennonite in our opening quotation, wrote two articles which have been cited a number of times in restorative justice literature: 'Justice that heals: the vision' (Zehr 1994b) and 'Justice that heals: the practise' (Zehr 1994a). These were originally presented at a New Zealand conference, 'Making Crime Pay' and were subsequently published in *Stimulus*.

In these articles Zehr argues that both crime and criminal justice are fundamentally about disrespect. First, both the crime and the response of state justice to crime are a disrespect of victims. Victims are ignored. Their needs are not attended to. Zehr also argues that crime and the state justice response to crime are a disrespect of offenders. An alternative, Zehr argues, is a justice that heals, one that respects victims, offenders and the communities from which they originate. Zehr recognizes that Christianity has played a key role in the development of state justice. But this role, he argues, was a perversion of Christianity.

> Certain biblical concepts were taken from their context and grafted on to foreign Greco-Roman principles. The Bible was then reinterpreted through a hybrid lens that viewed God as a punitive and legalistic judge. The result: an obsession in the West with the retributive theme in the Bible. (Zehr 1994b)

Zehr argues that the more faithful reading of biblical justice is not one of a God of wrath but a God of restoration. Following Perry Yoder's interpretation (Yoder 1987) Zehr argues that biblical justice 'is fundamentally respectful because people and their relationships are central' (Zehr 1994b). From biblical justice rooted in right relationship, Zehr advocates for a justice that heals and respects. These two articles have often been cited in subsequent restorative justice literature. Zehr also continues to use these healing justice phrases as an equivalent for restorative justice (Zehr 1997a, 1997b).

Each of these four authors has tried to engage a vision of biblical justice with a response to crime. Each author differentiates between biblical justice and the criminal justice system. Each author uses the phrase 'a justice that heals' as a way to identify how the biblical vision of justice can bubble up, or become manifest, in the experience of harm. But where did the phrase come from? None of these authors are sure where the phrase came from, or who it was borrowed from, and none claim that they invented the term (H. Zehr, personal communication, 9 October 2005; A. Boers, personal communication, 11 October 2005; D. Van Ness, personal communication, 18 December 2007).

These terms seem to have taken hold in some Christian circles. The Canadian Church Council on Justice and Corrections now uses 'healing justice' to describe their work in restorative justice (Church Council on Justice and Corrections of Canada 2001). Similarly, Daniel Van Ness of Prison Fellowship continued to use 'healing justice' as a short-hand to summarize the content and spirit of restorative justice (Van Ness 1997, 1998). A number of other Christians have also used these phrases (Badali 1999; Burgess and Galloway 2000; Consedine and Bowen 1999; Forrester 1997; Marshall 2001; Shefsky 2000). It is significant to note that most of these Christian authors are writing in the area of restorative justice.

Aboriginal people interested in living traditional ways of justice

A second group that uses the term healing justice is Aboriginal people, mostly in Canada. One of the Aboriginal communities working at healing justice is Hollow Water, Manitoba, a small Aboriginal community whose internal suffering has been marked by extraordinarily high rates of sexual abuse going back generations. With roots going back to 1984 the Community Holistic Circle Healing Programme's approach was to respond to sexual abuse in such a way as to break the cycles of abuse. In Hollow Water's own literature about the history of their project they speak of undertaking the 'Development of Healing Process and Healing Contract' in April 1988. The Hollow Water approach gained national and international recognition and is surely one source from which the vision of healing justice has spread (Aboriginal Corrections Policy Unit 1997;

Bushie 1999; Couture 2001b; National Film Board of Canada 2000). Hollow Water is one of the communities included in this study.

In 1992 Rupert Ross, Assistant Crown Prosecutor in Ontario, was seconded to the Aboriginal Justice Directorate of Justice (Ross 1996) Canada and spent three years travelling across Canada, exploring various local understandings of Aboriginal approaches to justice. Ross's landmark publication on this research also explores this vision of healing justice (Ross 1996). In that final report Ross records the ways various Aboriginal groups approached justice as healing. Ross reports that Aboriginal people have been speaking of justice as healing, or being on a healing path, for as long as he has known them (R. Ross, personal communication, 13 October 2005).

In 1995 James Sakej Youngblood Henderson, Professor and Research Director of the Native Law Centre of Canada at the College of Law, University of Saskatchewan, became the founding editor of the Native Law Centre of Canada's journal, *Justice as Healing*. In the opening edition of that journal Henderson lays out a vision of justice as healing (Henderson 1995). His paper was quoted in the opening of this chapter. Henderson calls Aboriginal people to return to an expansive and whole vision of life. He is not trying to create some new theory of justice, but to point back to the wisdom of Elders.

The journal *Justice as Healing* is the most significant source of articles on this topic, as it repeatedly came up in various searches, and a wide range of authors cites its articles. Some of the articles in *Justice as Healing* reflect directly on the meaning of this term (Lee 1996; Yazzie 1995), but most are reflections within the spirit of this vision. Recently a compilation of various of the articles of *Justice As Healing* has come out in book form (McCaslin 2005c).

Henderson recalls that the term healing justice is constructed from various Algonquin languages and that the Elders have always used the term, as have Alex Denny, the grand captain of the Mikmaw Nation, Trish Monture, a Mohawk scholar, and Leroy Little Bear of the Blackfoot clan (J. Y. Henderson, personal communication, 7 October 2005).

Slowly Aboriginal understandings of justice as healing begin to enter the journals of academic literature. One of these early articles is by Margot Manson in a 1994 edition of *Canadian Lawyer* and is entitled 'Justice that heals: native alternatives' (Manson 1994). Wayne Warry uses the term justice as healing as the Aboriginal name for restorative justice

(Warry 1998). A number of other authors use this language to describe the justice practises of a particular Aboriginal community (Elder Hanlon 1999; Large 2001; Miller 2001; Ryan 1995).

While most of the examples cited above come from Canada, this kind of healing justice is found in other indigenous communities that are in the process of trying to respond to colonialism by returning to their traditional practises and teachings. Robert Yazzie and James Zion tell the story of the 1982 return to Navajo Peacemaker Courts (Yazzie and Zion 1996). On the other side of the world, John Pratt tells the story of recovering a Maori sense of justice in New Zealand (1996).

Terms like 'healing justice' are used by Aboriginal people for this dual purpose: on the one hand, to describe a holistic vision of justice which draws on the wisdom of the Elders and traditional teachings and, on the other hand, to distinguish their justice from state justice, from that justice which was anything but healing for their communities. This double usage is similar to the Christian usage of the term, but the Aboriginal use seems more expansive. The Christian view tends to draw on biblical teaching to respond to an issue (crime), whereas the Aboriginal approaches invite their people into a way of being. The Aboriginal use of these terms is less issue-focused and more identity-focused.

Restorative justice advocates describing the heart of justice and interacting with 'serious' harm

As is already clear from this review healing justice terms are rooted most fully in the field of restorative justice. As noted, leading international scholars of restorative justice like Howard Zehr, Jim Consedine and Daniel Van Ness have used 'healing justice' or 'justice that heals' as a way to summarize both what restorative justice is and what it is not. Describing restorative justice as a healing model of justice has become the practise of a number of restorative justice authors (Breton and Lehman 2001; Dolinko, Braithwaite and Tonry 1999; Pepi 1997; Salen-Hanna 2000; Sullivan and Tifft 2001; Thorsborne 1998; Wright 2002). Similarly, there are organizations like Rittenhouse, a Quaker organization in Toronto, Canada, that now describe their work in transformative justice as 'healing justice'. Most of these authors use some form of the term healing justice to summarize the heart of justice.

Some in restorative justice see healing justice as marking out a different paradigm of justice. Van Ness and Strong begin *Restoring Justice* with a story of a judge who through dealing with a rape case, comes to believe in 'the need for criminal law practitioners to see themselves as healers' (2006). They argue that the current paradigm of criminal justice is limited by patterns of thinking which 'filter out virtually all aspects of crime except questions of legal guilt and punishment'. For them healing justice is a different pattern of thinking which seeks to heal all the injuries revealed by an act of crime – the injuries in the offender and community that helped contribute to the cause of the crime and the injuries to the victim and community that came about because of the crime. They argue that a restoring justice works towards healing of such issues. They also argue or suggest that the current criminal justice system could be the agent for such healing if the patterns of thinking change from a focus on punitive to healing models of justice. Breton and Lehman (2001) take the concept of healing justice further. While also critiquing the punitive character of the criminal justice system they argue that our concepts of justice lie at the heart of everything we do in life, not just criminal justice. They argue healing justice explodes the categories of criminal justice from administering blame to cultivating well-being and joy, from heaping blame to cultivating relationships of compassion within every sphere of life. Within restorative justice the language of healing justice is sometimes used to point toward a paradigm which is contrasted with punitive justice.

As we saw in the case of Hollow Water, there are a number of restorative justice advocates who use various terms of healing justice within the context of abuse, usually sexual abuse (Coward 2000; Professor and Gaarder 2000) but also substance abuse (Braithwaite 2001). For those who feel that restorative justice has been sidelined to applications for petty crime, this usage should be quite interesting and, perhaps, instructive.

Governments responding to Aboriginal people and restorative justice advocates

As Aboriginal people and restorative justice advocates speak more of healing justice, governments have begun to respond. Some saw the creating of the Commission for Truth and Reconciliation in South Africa as a government trying to 'provide justice with healing' (Lewis 1995). In Canada, the Indian Residential Schools Truth and Reconciliation

Commission was commissioned by the Government of Canada with a five-year mandate (2008–2013) to work at 'acknowledgement of the injustice and harms experience by Aboriginal people and the need to for continued healing' (Government of Canada 2008). On the other end of the scale of involvement, governments have sometimes tried to coordinate and direct the uses of healing justice (Linton and Clairmont 1998). Sometimes governments have tried to draw lessons from healing justice, such as the United Nations report *Searching for Innovations in Governance and Public Administration for Poverty Reduction* (United Nations Department of Economic and Social Affairs 2004).

Clearly, the language of healing justice is starting to enter the realm of government. There is not yet enough literature to see how governments will use this terminology.

Healing justice in various other academic fields

The final stream of influence in the usage of these terms is that of other academic fields. We have seen that healing justice is used within Christian, Aboriginal and restorative justice circles. Those are the groups that use these terms most frequently. There are other areas where this terminology is also starting to take hold. One of these areas is feminist theory. Legge blurred the categories of healing and justice in a paper entitled 'Multi-dialogical spiralling for healing and justice' (1995). Jennifer Willging uses the term, healing justice, in her analysis of feminine anger (1996). Rosemary Radford Ruether uses 'healing justice' in her book, *Women Healing Earth: Third World Women on Ecology, Feminism and Religion* (1996). Carol Lee O'Hara Pepi uses the term when trying to develop a feminist intervention strategy which utilizes restorative justice (1997). Some feminists view the term healing justice as connecting with their worldview. This use seems to share a similar dynamic with most other uses in that the feminist use of the term is both a pointing toward a centre and a pointing away from the more harsh forms of state justice.

The term, healing justice, has also begun to creep into the academic literature of other disciplines: mental health (Herman 2003), anthropology (Marshall 2003), psychology (Drewery 2004), peace studies (Sawatsky 2005; Staub 2004), and communitarian philosophy (Crocker 2001; Smith 2001). Other emerging fields like trauma healing (Herman

1997) and therapeutic jurisprudence (Wexler and Winick 1996) are also exploring some relationships between justice and healing.

One other use of these terms which is noteworthy is David Loy's chapter 'Healing Justice: A Buddhist Perspective' in *Spiritual Roots of Restorative Justice* (Loy 2001), a segment of which was quoted in the opening of this essay. Loy argues that a Buddhist approach to crime is essentially based in ideas of compassion, mercy and love. This Buddhist approach tries to understand the roots of a conflict found both within the minds of the people involved and within the social systems involved. Within Buddhist understanding, all people, including victims and offenders, have the same Buddha-nature, that non-self which is whole, pure and interconnected with all of life. All people, including judges and lawyers, are usually dominated by greed, ill will and delusion, but within Buddhist belief it is possible for all people to change and outgrow these delusions. He argues, 'the only reason to punish is education for reformation' (Loy 2001). He does not argue that a Buddhist response to crime is free of all uses of punishment. What he argues is that the whole Buddhist response to harm is within a cultural community that seeks after right, compassionate living. Limited punishment in such extreme cases is of a markedly different nature than modern punishment that happens outside a community of compassion.

Loy sees this Buddhist view as very close to Zehr's biblical understanding of justice but in sharp contrast to state justice (Loy 2001). State justice is grounded in Hobbes' theory of the social contract that, Loy argues, makes fear the origin of the state. Fear is the opposite of love. Ultimately, Loy sees states' justice and Buddhist justice as offering two different paradigms of justice, one based on fear, the other based on love. He argues we must choose which kind of society we want to live in. Once again we see healing justice used to point away from state justice and towards the wisdom of traditional community conceptions of justice.

The terminology of healing justice does not seem to figure centrally in other Buddhist writing, but the spirit of this justice is definitely present in Buddhist communities. This is evident both in Thich Nhat Hahn's description of the Buddhist monasteries' process of dispute resolution (2003e) and in Rebecca French's description of the legal cosmology of Buddhist Tibet (2002).

Summary on the genealogy of healing justice

Seven observations from this survey:

First, it is only very recently (1980s) that such terms have come into academic literature. Those who use these terms tend to see them, not as a new movement, but as pointing toward ancient wisdom of traditional community.

Second, particular segments of spiritually-centred communities – Christian and Aboriginal, but also Buddhist and Quaker – have been at the forefront in articulating visions and practises of their own best sense of justice as healing justice.

Third, most of those who use this terminology do so to point away from state justice, which is characterized as colonializing, oppressing, violent and based on fear, while at the same time pointing toward the ancient wisdom of traditional communities, which is characterized more as learning, growing, loving and respecting. Moreover, healing justice, understood from its own context, is seen as something that may be able to decolonialize state justice.

Fourth, those groups who originally used this term were drawing on metaphors and wisdom from their own traditional communities. From within those traditional imaginations, the terminology of healing justice does not link two distant and conflicting fields, health or healing with justice. This is unlike the modern imagination, which specializes and fragments and makes healing something different from justice.

Fifth, even though many of those who use the term, healing justice, are pointing towards a community's way of life, much of the discussion of healing justice occurs in what we may call the 'geography of crime'. Such a narrow focus is problematic, if one really wants to understand a holistic vision of justice that is embedded in a way of life. A broader interpretative lens is needed if we desire to understand healing justice without corrupting it or doing violence to it.

Sixth, none of the people who use this term suggest that their own traditions were purely restorative, if that means lacking in all punishment, coercion and retribution. All argue, among other things, that healing, not pain, is the interpretive framework of justice. In other words, the healing justice described here does contain elements of pain and coercion, but these are small parts of a larger framework of healing.

Seventh, while there is growing interest in healing justice, there have been no comparative studies to see what similarities and differences exist between communities that use this terminology. Ezzat A. Fattah has made a similar observation noting that as the language around justice expands – restorative justice, peacemaking justice, transformative justice, informal justice, healing justice, satisfactory justice, real justice, relational justice, positive justice – what is desperately needed is 'sociological and cross-cultural studies aimed specifically at discovering the notions, the conceptions and the ideas of justice among various communities' (Fattah 2002).

Research focus

This study picks up on Fattah's challenge that which is desperately needed is cross-cultural studies aimed at understanding particular notions of justice from various communities. Given the growing and diverse use of the language of healing justice and given the absence of cross-cultural studies on the topic, this study stands as a first attempt to bring together such issues. The purpose of this inquiry is to explore, through comparative case study, that which sustains notions of healing justice for three traditional communities: Hollow Water, an Aboriginal and Métis community in Canada; Iona Community, a Christian community in Scotland and Plum Village, a Vietnamese Buddhist community in Southern France. These communities mirror the groups using the language of healing justice outlined above. Writings from each community surfaced in our genealogy of healing justice. Each community has, or is said to have, a vision and practise of healing justice. More is said in Chapter 3 concerning how I came to select these particular communities. This research is an attempt to see if it is possible to identify what constitutes healing justice in each of these settings and to identify what these communities see as necessary to sustain that kind of vision and practise of justice.

This research is guided by four central questions:

1. How do traditional communities describe visions and practises of healing justice?

2. How do traditional communities describe the general conditions that sustain and nurture healing justice?

3. How do traditional communities describe the general conditions under which healing justice is impossible?

4.   What similarities exist among the conceptions of healing justice in various traditional communities?

Sub-questions:

Working definition of healing justice

This research is designed to flesh out the meaning of this term from the standpoint of traditional communities. At the beginning of my research I found it helpful to have a very loose definition in order not to impose my conceptualization on traditional communities. In light of the review of the uses of the language of healing justice, I tentatively defined healing justice as:

➤ a collective paradigm or imagination, usually drawing on an ancient wisdom tradition, that seeks to find ways of surviving together

➤ by structuring life so that means reflect the end of respect for life and

➤ by treating harms as opportunities to transform suffering and root causes of harm and, at the same time, to cultivate conditions of respectful living within the interrelated aspects of self, other, communities, social structures, environment and Spirit.

I return to this definition in the conclusion of the book.

Research audiences and implications

One of the primary audiences of this work is the restorative justice movement. There are three ways this research offers transformative challenges to this movement. It invites restorative justice to expand its dialogue partners to include traditional communities understood within their own context. Restorative justice has been highly influenced by a dominant discussion partner, the state (Pavlich 2006). This argument began in the introduction and continues in Chapter 2 on restorative justice. We are changed by those we dialogue with and those we contend with. This research invites those in the restorative justice movement to enter a respectful dialogue with communities practising healing justice to see what transformation might unfold. Second, this research will challenge restorative justice advocates to shift the level of their analysis from a micro-encounter orientation to an orientation that includes more macro-perspectives by linking restorative encounters with restorative cultural dynamics. These cultural factors, or relational dynamics which sustain or act as barriers to healing justice, may be more determinative of restorativeness than the forums that are presently used in responding to harm. This research seeks to identify and respond to a gap in mainline restorative justice. The problematic gap is that the processes of responding to harm are separated from the broader cultural conditions and factors which can sustain visions and practises of either harm or of healing justice. Third, the goal of this research is to transform the basic logic or imagination of those engaged in restorative justice. The argument will be made that while restorative justice acts as an alternative to state justice, in some ways it does not challenge the basic logic of that justice deeply enough. By listening to communities which practise types of justice that are based on a different imagination, this research will challenge restorative justice to more deeply transform its basic logic or imagination of justice.

Restorative justice is not the only audience that might learn from this research. Traditional communities practising healing justice should be supported and challenged by this research. It is not easy to embody a different kind of justice, even when it is a healing justice. Communities that practise healing justice, like any other community, are dynamic communities which grow and change to meet the changing realities of the world. Yet, sometimes in the process of that change, we give away pieces we later realize were core to our identity, and we take on others which are incompatible with this identity. Taiaiake Alfred offers this kind of internal critique for Aboriginal communities in his classic, *Peace, Power, Righteousness: An Indigenous Manifesto* (1999). Often these insights are only seen in hindsight. Sometimes they can be learned by hearing others' stories. In hearing others' stories, we do not need to become like them but, rather, we are reminded of what is important and what is flexible within our own story. This comparative research, then, is for the benefit of traditional communities which practise various forms of healing justice as ways to survive together.

A third audience of this research is those involved in Western governance and justice. What might the Western legal system learn from practises of healing justice in traditional communities if those practises were understood in their own context? Perhaps the Western states have lost something that needs retrieving. Perhaps the way forward is through listening carefully to those rooted in an almost forgotten wisdom. Perhaps we need to return to those who still have the capacity to remember a way of justice where healing and justice are one. In hearing their stories we may learn something about the nature and trajectory of Western justice. We might find ways of opening up paths to return to or to cultivate anew some forms of healing justice.

As we saw in the literature, healing justice is often used to point away from state justice and towards some form of alternative justice. Therefore, this research is not directed toward enhancing a state justice system. However, there are many at various levels of state systems who might be interested in, and benefit from, this research. As notions of modernity are transforming, so are the ways we govern and organize societies.

To a sympathetic listener within Western governance systems, this research presents a number of interesting policy challenges. Some are along the lines of legal pluralism. For example, how do we create space for multiple distinct identities and notions of justice to co-exist within overlapping political spaces? Other challenges relate to the nature of justice itself. For example is pain and punishment a necessary and helpful part of justice? Should justice be state centric? Other challenges are along the lines of social engineering. By broadening our research to the factors and conditions that sustain healing justice we do not know what questions might arise. They might include questions like: have we designed cities that are too big to nurture caring? Have we created enough green space to cultivate identities where people can see their connections with the land? Some of the challenges and opportunities offered to the restorative justice movement might also hold true for justice systems.

An underlying motivation in this research is to demonstrate that justice is not the exclusive realm of the state nor does it need to be based on administrating retribution and revenge for it to be just. For hundreds of years, various churches have developed theologies that have supported the colonializing state's authority to act as violent judge (Cayley 1998; Gorridge 1996; Van Ness and Stronmg 2002; Zehr 1990a). Those within and outside of the state, both Christian and non-Christian, have inherited this legacy. This research pushes toward a different understanding of justice which flows from alternative views of Creator, land and political structures. While much work has been done in recent years to move to post-colonializing forms of governance, some debate remains as to how far we have come. Learning from communities practising healing justice is possible. Some of these communities have endured many attempts at colonialization and assimilation but have remembered or recovered their practises and visions of a justice that heals.

Objections to healing justice

Before we proceed too far on this search for healing justice it is important to be aware of some of the objections to such a study. Healing justice is quite an odd term, at least to those who have been brought up with Western conceptions of justice. Some argue that the Western conceptions of criminal justice see justice as requiring an adversarial fight according to prescribed rules, to determine blame and hand out pain or punishment. This is not far from the view portrayed on the nightly TV shows about crime and justice. The guilty party is determined and cornered in such a way that they can be 'brought to justice'. This metaphor, everyone understands, is an allusion to handing out pain, the pain of being locked up and sometimes even the pain of being killed. According to this view, justice is very quickly equated with pain. This justice-as-pain orientation is not confined to criminal justice but becomes part of the shared imagination and expresses itself in the home, in schools, in spiritual communities and in foreign policy.

For many who hold this view, pain is not delivered just for the sake of pain. Pain, it is believed, has a purpose. The guilty party is punished to show the victim and the community that justice has been delivered, namely, that the offender has received his or her 'just deserts'. Delivering pain, they believe, shows the offender that crime does not pay. It tries to decrease future crime by showing potential offenders that crime will not be tolerated. In fact 'just deserts' theory argues that punishment is the only legitimate goal of sentencing and that non-incarceration is preferable in most cases (Von Hirsch and Committee for the Study of Incaceration 1976). Just desert theorists sought to limit the reach of the state to administer only the amount of punishment an offender 'deserved'. They argued that punishing one offender to deter another violated the principles of just deserts. However, while they sought to limit punishment, they did concede that justice was still about punishment. The effect of this theory in practise and sometimes in legislation is to legitimate punishment (Singer 1979). For some, like Anthony Duff, pain or punishment is the means by which a community communicates with one of its members about a moral wrong the person has done (Duff 2001). For some, pain is delivered to satisfy a cosmic order or theological belief that God wants the sinner to be punished (Megivern 1997). In other words, Western conceptions of justice may use pain as a communication tool, as a therapeutic release, as an education tool, as a prevention device and as a spiritual rite. But in all such cases justice is pain. Healing justice would likely been seen to violate the fundamental purpose and approach of justice – not because healing justice is free of pain but because it sees justice as healing the causes of pain rather than administering more pain.

Others argue Western conceptions of justice are not all, or even mostly, related to pain. This argument might concede that criminal justice fits the adversarial perspective outlined above, although they would also argue that parts of even criminal sentencing which focus on rehabilitation and compensation do not fit a general analysis of pain. However their main point is that criminal justice is a particular subset of the larger social justice theories of liberal society. Social justice is seen here as a broad umbrella for a number of different kinds of Western justice which seek an equitable distribution of the benefits and burdens of life together. One category under social justice is correctional justice. Criminal or penal justice is a further subcategory under correctional justice. This way of categorizing Western ways of justice argues that while penal justice may mostly rely on pain, many of the other subsets of Western justice do not. In other words, some kinds of justice suspend the normative ethical standards in order to protect those same standards.

The point I am making is not that most kinds of Western justice are free from the logic of pain and violence evidenced within the criminal justice setting, but rather that Western conceptions hold that justice can be broken down into different categories and types and that each type may follow a different ethical standard. Furthermore, each category of Western justice follows its own ethical standard even though the standard may be in direct conflict with more normative ethical standards. For example it is ethical to administer pain in the criminal justice system, but it is a crime for the public to do so. Justice is seen to have many different types, spheres, ethics, some of which conflict.

Is it possible that healing justice offers a critique of both the particular ethic of penal justice and of the overall concepts of Western justice? Is it possible that healing justice reflects a different logic, one that does not know through categorizing and fragmenting? We must proceed in our exploration of healing justice knowing that it may challenge the basic conceptions of modern justice.

Another objection to healing justice is that the concept itself brings together two opposites. Is not healing quite a separate field, category or ethic from justice? Might not bringing together these conflicting paradigms corrupt both and achieve neither?

Following this argument, justice is of a different quality than healing. According to Clayton and Williams (2004) Western understandings of justice are focused on issues of social justice which 'arise when decisions affect the distribution of benefits and burdens between different individuals or groups'. In the early conceptions of modern justice, Locke and Hume saw justice as a respect for private property with a focus on developing rules that would benefit landowner and industry (Clayton and Williams 2004; Hume 2004; Locke 2004). John Rawls redirected the benefits of social justice. In *A Theory of Justice* (1999), Rawls indicates that justice is about mitigating the consequences of luck, or social lottery, such that those who are born into hard situations with limited choices are given more opportunities. Modern Western justice in this broad sense is about distribution of particular rights and responsibilities.

Mainline Western understandings of healing, on the other hand, are very closely associated with conceptions of health care and conventional medicine. There are some Western conceptions of healing which critique the dominance of the medicalization of healing over the last 150 years, but there is little doubt that conventional medicine has become the dominant discourse of healing within mainline Western understandings in the past century. Buckman and Sabbagh (1993) define conventional medicine as 'a body of actions and treatments that accords with the general philosophy and understanding of disease and therapy taught in established medical school, practised by doctors and licensed and regulated by their governing authorities'. This definition does reflect a number of similarities with Western conceptions of criminal justice in that it is problem-focused, regulation-focused, and specifies a realm of trained professionals. However, one of the central differences is that we turn to medicine to alleviate pain, whereas we sometimes turn to criminal justice to administer pain. Some modern forms of the Hippocratic Oath suggest that this kind of health care healing limits healing to the care for the sick and the prevention of disease. It is significant to note that most modern forms of the Hippocratic Oath (PBS Nova Online 2004) edit out the one original reference which does link healing and justice, namely the physician's responsibility to 'keep the sick from harm and injustice' (Edelstein 1943).

Even this editing-out illustrates that modern notions of health are seen as a separate sphere from modern notions of justice. As we saw within different categories of social justice, the two spheres of medicine and justice each have their own code of ethics. It is on this basis that some see healing justice as a dangerous mixing of opposites. Healing might be needed but shouldn't be mixed or confused with justice.

The failures of the rehabilitation model within criminal and penal justice is another basis on which people might feel that the mixing of health and justice is dangerous. Indeterminate sentencing which took root in the early 1900s in many Western states resulted from a medical model of justice where the criminal was seen as morally sick and in need of rehabilitation and healing. Those sentenced were to be held until those within the justice system believed that they were cured. Soon advocates of prison reform, among many others, started to reject a medical model of crime (American Friends Service Committee 1971).

In the case of healing justice, the fear that it might be mixing modern notions of health and justice misses the point. Those who use the term 'healing justice' tend not to draw from the modern imagination but on various non-modern imaginations. In these imaginations healing is justice and justice is healing. This is not a combining of opposites or a dialectic tension but an articulation of an imagination, paradigm or worldview in which healing and justice are one.

Inadequate attempts to listen to traditional communities

To enter fully into healing justice, we need to be aware not only of the objections but also of the troubled history of researchers and mainstream society learning from traditional communities. Much of the Western learning from such communities has been based on a mining model in which 'resources' are stripped from their home and exported to foreign lands (Kvale 1996). Adam Crawford has correctly challenged some of the restorative justice literature of case studies on traditional communities for following this kind of mining approach which he labels 'butterfly collecting'. Crawford uses this image to challenge the practise of 'extracting examples from the cultural and social environment which sustains them' (2002). Indeed, much of the restorative justice tradition could be told from the standpoint of what processes and techniques (Victim Offender Conferencing, Family Group Conferencing, Circles) are transferred and imposed on different contexts. Sometimes it has been assumed that if traditional communities have anything to teach those in justice studies, it is in the area of alternative forms of justice (e.g. processes of restorative justice) or in the area of nurturing general values which support good citizenship (e.g. *Religion, The Missing Dimension of Statecraft*, (Johnston and Sampson 1995). These tendencies make genuine dialogue very difficult. Fruitful dialogue cannot be based on importation/exportation models any more than it can be based on assimilative models. *How* this dialogue happens is very important.

This research seeks to resist such tendencies by focusing respectfully and holistically on those cultural dynamics – the relationships, conditions and factors – that sustain practises of healing justice. The goal is not to extract resources by breaking out interesting conflict resolution processes from the relationships and settings that make sense of them. The goal is to learn as much as possible about the nature of those relationships that nourish and sustain particular kinds of healing justice. Perhaps by identifying and learning about these broader sustaining relationships we might ask wiser questions, questions not based on replication but on how our relationships – with each other, the land, the known worlds and the unknown worlds – lead us towards particular kinds of justice. This research is for those interested in learning which kinds of relationships lead towards various kinds of healing justice.

Numerous inadequate attempts to understand more traditional communities have come from the field of legal anthropology and have resulted in much valuable learning. Legal anthropology developed as a practise of looking to such traditional communities in an attempt to understand our own systems of law by comparing theirs to ours (Nixon 1997).[2] At first legal anthropologists expressed clear colonialist tendencies. Sir Henry Maine's categorization of communities from primitive to Victorian demonstrates this Eurocentric evolutionary impulse to make 'them' more like 'us' (Maine 1906). Since this beginning legal anthropologists have tried shifting focus and methodology to find a more fruitful means to illuminate the ordering of society. Malinowski's *Crime and the Savage*

---

2   This section follows Nixon's analysis of some of the major developments and tensions within legal anthropology.

Society (1926) employed the methodology of ethnography and began to shift the focus from a set of laws to the cultural context of those laws. Similarly this research is interested in the cultural context of particular communities in their approaches to healing justice. Like Malinowski, it focuses less on rules than on the broader cultural context which seems to sustain that vision and practise of justice.

Another critical debate in legal anthropology set Bohannana (1957) against Gluckman (1969) over whether legal anthropologists need to use Anglo-American legal categories in the study of non-Western societies. Bohannan believed that the use of Western legal categories did not help to illuminate what was happening in a given community. He used native terms instead and believed comparison was nearly impossible. Gluckman believed that standard terminology, drived from Anglo-American legal categories, was needed for conducting sound comparative analysis. This healing justice research is a comparative analysis which does not use Western legal concepts as the basis of comparison and thus follows neither Bohannan nor Gluckman.

In the 1970s legal anthropology took further steps to shift the focus from rules to processes of dispute resolution. A number of legal anthropologists argued for this position (Comaroff and Roberts 1981; Roberts 1979). They were part of a broader movement within alternative dispute resolution and conflict resolution studies to find other ways to manage conflicts. Restorative justice arises, partly, out of this setting. A shift from rules to processes of dispute resolution helped to create more space to understand how conflicts were responded to within a given context. However, this focus also resulted in an expropriation of these processes from their context. Processes were seen as techniques which could be extracted and imposed in other areas. This research is designed on the premise that another fundamental shift in legal anthropology is needed: from processes to the factors and conditions, or cultural dynamics, which sustain particular visions of justice.

Post modern critiques have questioned the focus of legal anthropologies on case study, which Llewellyn and Hoebel had introduced with *The Cheyenne Way* (1941). Conley and O'Barr (1993) argued that a case focus, meaning a particular dispute focus, shifts the attention of anthropologists away from routine compliance with law and toward deviant behaviours and conflict. My research focuses on a broad view of healing justice. It is not full of exotic stories of how particular communities respond to particular disputes, although these are not absent. It builds on Conley and O'Barr's movement from a harm-focus to a focus on everyday practises. However, rather than focusing on everyday practises of compliance with law, my research focuses on everyday practises of healing justice as defined by the communities practising such justice. This broad focus for justice means that healing justice will take us into territories not normally considered relevant to some mainstream approaches to law, order and justice.

Mainline approaches to justice are constantly changing. Faced with pressures to change their own criminal justice system, some Western states are in small ways turning back to traditional communities to see what practises might be incorporated into their Western system. The rapid international rise of restorative justice and current interest in indigenous justice may, in part, be due to this kind of turning back to traditional practises.

Some people in these communities welcome such attention and partnership. Others see such initiatives as 'yet another form of state control and cultural manipulation' (Lee 1997). They argue that such interest is a form of neo-colonialism which, rather than outlawing traditional practises, absorbs them into the system, thereby distorting and destroying them. Many now think that a focus on transferring techniques, programmes and processes will always favour the momentum towards institutionalization at the expense of both the context from which they were taken and the new context into which they are transplanted.

Another attempt to understand traditional communities has come from criminologist Nils Christie who looked to more traditional societies to find ways to decrease what he saw as an immoral over-reliance on pain within Western systems of justice. He describes the goal of his book *Limits to Pain*: 'On the basis of experiences from social systems with a minimal use of pain, some general conditions for a low level of pain infliction are extracted' (1981). This research has significant overlap with Christie's work but it shifts the focus from pain to healing; it is not an inquiry into what is wrong with Western justice but rather an inquiry into what is working in communities that are living a justice that heals. Implications for the Western justice system will not be sidestepped, but neither will it become the interpretive framework for understanding healing justice.

Many have tried to approach traditional communities in order to understand their own sense of justice. This research differs from many of those attempts in methodology and in focus. The focus of this research is not on the Western justice system, nor on narrowly understood legal traditions, nor on pain. The focus is on listening to communities that are said to have a practise of healing justice.

Summary

This research turns to traditional communities to learn about healing justice. The hope is to find respectful ways of learning from their stories. The goal is not to extract and replicate knowledge found in those contexts. Nor is it just to describe and identify their practises of healing justice and the factors and conditions that support them. The hope is that a respectful reading of these cultures will raise many troubling questions for how society is organized in other cultures, especially our own. The implications of this research lie not in expanding a repertoire of techniques and processes, or even in the deepening of understanding for the sake of understanding. This research has a transformative purpose. The stories we listen to feed and transform our imaginations and our actions.

Before jumping into the case studies, we explore further what has already been learned about healing ways of justice. We turn now to the fields of restorative justice and Aboriginal justice, to examine what they have learned about the kinds of conditions, factors and relationship that sustain a restorative kind of justice.

Chapter 2

Searching Restorative Justice

Introduction

There is a growing trend from the mid-1990s on to speak of restorative justice as healing justice. In our initial overview of the use of the term healing justice in Chapter 1, we saw that this term is used by several restorative justice scholars to summarize the heart of restorative justice. Many other restorative justice authors explain that restorative justice is a healing model of justice. Furthermore we saw that some of the most developed literature comes from Aboriginal communities where the practitioners speak of doing both restorative justice and healing justice.

Yet few of these authors delineate why they use the term healing justice, or how they hope such language will contribute to the field. Clearly healing justice marks out a different arena than punitive justice or criminal justice. But just what is this different arena? One way of marking this arena is to inquire about what kinds of broader relationships in society are needed to sustain a more restorative view of justice. On this question, however, the restorative justice literature is strikingly vague. This vagueness leads to a central contradiction within the literature of restorative justice.

The contradiction is this: if restorative justice is so interested in healing models of justice, why does restorative justice have so little to say about the kind of relationships which sustain such a vision of justice? The field of restorative justice is not without reflection on the kinds of relationship which sustain particular kinds of justice. Where they exist I will highlight them. However, it is important to identify this contradiction in the literature because I think it highlights significant, often unexamined and somewhat troubling, assumptions within the literature of restorative justice. My research seeks to address that gap. Through the study of three communities that have developed practises of healing justice I will show how it can be sustained over time.

After a brief overview of restorative justice, I will demonstrate how the literature of restorative justice is overdeveloped in the area of case-management and highly underdeveloped in the area of socio-systemic analysis. Then I will highlight some troubling assumptions within the field of restorative justice which have led to this contradiction by examining the field of Aboriginal justice and its relationship to criminal justice.

Overview of restorative justice

I begin with a brief description of the field of restorative justice. An overview to this field will help to better understand and locate the significance of the case studies that follow. A number of restorative justice authors either begin or conclude their books with a statement suggesting that there is no agreement as to what restorative justice includes (Bazemore and Schiff 2004; Roche 2001). It is even difficult to determine a starting date of this movement. Some suggest the starting point is the development of Victim Offender Mediation Projects by Mennonites in Canada in the 1970s (Alper and Nichols 1981; Peachy 2003; Umbreit 1989). Others go slightly further back to the Alternative Dispute Resolution (ADR) movement of the 1960s–1970s (Wright 1991). Still others suggest that restorative justice is an ancient form of dispute resolution drawing on various cultural-spiritual and non-state traditions (Braithwaite 2002; Hadley 2001; Weitekamp 2003). In a recent chapter entitled 'The Meaning of Restorative Justice', two leading restorative justice scholars, argue that restorative justice is a contested term for which there can be no clear definition (Johnstone and Van Ness 2007). They explain the meaning by identifying three overlapping conceptions of restorative justice, each claiming to be doing restorative justice but with slightly different visions, goals and sometimes methods. These three groupings are: encounter conception, reparative conception and transformative conception. We will return to these three conceptions later. What is important here is that Johnstone and Van Ness present restorative justice as an array of perspectives which share some concepts but contest other key concepts. The closest Johnstone and Van Ness come to a definition is to identify six ingredients and to say at least one must be present if any particular perspective is to be credibly described as part of restorative justice. These include:

1. There will be some relatively informal process which aims to involve victims, offenders, and others closely connected to them or to the crime in discussion of matters such as what happened, what harm has resulted, and what should be done to repair that harm and, perhaps, to prevent further wrongdoing or conflict.

2. There will be an emphasis on empowering (in a number of senses) ordinary people whose lives are affected by a crime or other wrongful act.

3. Some effort will be made by decision-makers or those facilitating decision-making processes to promote a response which is geared less towards stigmatizing and punishing the wrongdoer and more towards ensuring that wrongdoers recognize and meet a responsibility to make amends for the harm they have caused in a manner which directly benefits those harmed, as a first step towards their reintegration into the community of law-abiding citizens.

4. Decision-makers or those facilitating decision-making will be concerned to ensure that the decision-making process and its outcome will be guided by certain principles or values which, in contemporary society, are widely regarded as desirable in any interaction between people, such as: respect should be shown for others; violence and coercion are to be avoided if possible and minimized if not; inclusion is to be preferred to exclusion.

5. Decision-makers or those facilitating decision-making will devote significant attention to the injury done to the victims and to the needs that result from that, and to tangible ways in which those needs can be addressed.

6. There will be some emphasis on strengthening or repairing relationships between people, and using the power of healthy relationships to resolve difficult situations. (Johnstone and Van Ness 2007)

Here, restorative justice is presented mostly as a decision-making process (points 1, 3–5) which empowers (point 2) and may use or help build relationships (point 6). Rather than being crime and rule-of-law focused, the focus is on harm (point 1). Rather than responding to harm by blaming offenders and ignoring victims, the focus is on the offender's responsibility and restitution to meet the victim's needs (points 3, 5). What distinguishes restorative justice processes and outcomes is a change of values from those of state justice systems to those of respect, non-violence and inclusion (point 4). Rather than focusing on fact-finding and rules of procedure, restorative justice is a relationship-centred approach to justice (point 6). Johnstone and Van Ness are not trying to establish new ground here but to find ways of describing all those who see themselves as participating in the restorative justice movement. Therefore the conclusions here echo much of the restorative justice literature.

Howard Zehr's classic book *Changing Lenses* provides one of the early and most systematic presentations of restorative justice (1990a). In 2002 he wrote *The Little Book of Restorative Justice* which tries to update some of these opinions and to offer a short description or overview of restorative justice (Zehr 2002b). For Zehr, restorative justice begins by focusing on the needs of victims, offenders and the community. He outlines what he calls the three pillars of restorative justice which create a principled response to injustice:

1. Restorative justice focuses on harm.

2. Wrongs or harms result in obligations.

3. Restorative justice promotes engagement or participation.

Like other restorative justice authors, Zehr realizes that definitions by themselves are highly inadequate, but he does offer what he calls a 'skeletal outline' of restorative justice. 'Restorative justice requires, at minimum, that we address victims' harms and needs, hold offenders accountable to put right those harms, and involve victims, offenders and communities in the process' (2002b).

Zehr's overview is quite consistent with Johnstone and Van Ness's work. Both present restorative justice as an alternative to criminal justice, although in this more recent work Zehr distances himself from his earlier viewpoint that restorative justice is the polar opposite of retributive justice. Both see restorative justice as a principled process for empowering and meeting the needs of those involved in harm. Both see an interplay of victim, offender and the broader community.

We will return to these two definitions in the conclusion of this chapter. First we turn to the literature of restorative justice to explore two key questions: What are the kinds of relationship which sustain restorative justice? Why is there so little written on the relationships which sustain this vision of justice?

A critical contradiction in the literature and imagination of restorative justice

To address these questions I will use the basic thesis of James Gilligan's *Preventing Violence* (2001) to cast light on the state of the field of restorative justice and on this gap in the literature on sustaining relationships. Gilligan has been on the faculty of the Harvard Medical School since 1965 and for 25 years has directed the provision of psychiatric services to the Massachusetts prisons and the prison mental hospital. In *Preventing Violence* he outlines what he calls a medical model to preventing violence. Avoiding what he sees as the trappings of legal and moral models of violence prevention, Gilligan explores how preventing violence would look if the lessons learned from the medical community on preventing disease and promoting health were taken seriously. He suggests that the key frame of reference is to learn the difference between tertiary, secondary and primary care. Tertiary care is the response of last resort. It is the emergency response of treating patients who are in need of urgent medical attention. It is the act of trying to rescue someone in the process of having a heart attack. This level of care, Gilligan argues, is the most expensive and the least helpful in stopping the spread of disease. He does not argue that it is not needed but, rather, that because it waits until there is harm and then focuses on individuals, it does not have the capacity to deal with the root problems, with the spread of disease or with the contributing factors which are causing or enabling the disease to grow.

Secondary care focuses on groups whose members are not yet in need of urgent care but are at risk for developing harmful conditions (e.g. overweight men at risk for heart disease). The object of this kind of care is to help people manage the various environmental factors that could reduce the risk of disease. Like tertiary care, secondary care is a problem-focused response but is less of an emergency response.

Primary care is neither problem-focused nor patient-oriented. Primary care focuses on developing healthy patterns whereby people do not need to enter the realm of secondary or tertiary care. Following the medical example, a healthy food guide is an example of primary care which can prevent overeating, thereby preventing some heart disease.

Gilligan relates this framework to violence. He argues that humans cannot live with shame. Those who are forced to live with shame become 'living zombies', alive but unable to feel and therefore capable of committing great violence on themselves and others. To prevent violence, then, is to establish the conditions which minimize people's exposure to shame and maximize their access to non-violent mechanisms to undo shame. Gilligan argues that these conditions are often social and psychological, but some of the most significant are economic. He claims that the larger the gap between rich and poor, the more murders a society will experience, arguing that the gap between rich and poor is the best indicator of homicide rates. Addressing this gap is an example of primary care which is the most cost-effective way to stop a huge amount of violence and shame. For Gilligan, the kinds of relationships which help to sustain a more restorative and less violent approach to justice include the economic structures.

What is interesting about Gilligan's work is how it shifts the focus from the logic of problem-focused incidents (tertiary care) to the logic of healthy societies (primary care). Through this shift we must make the very hard journey from a focus on the exotic violent behaviour of 'the criminal', the exotic other, to a focus on how we structure our life together. The media feed on the exotic, the violent, the crisis, the episode. Government funding is also focused on these same characters. However, as long as these capture our attention, we remain blinded to how we and our socio-economic structures are part of the story of that violence, that offender, that victim. Gilligan's three units of analysis help us to survey the literature on restorative justice in order to find the kind of socio-cultural relationships which sustain that vision of justice.

Tertiary care and restorative justice

Applying Gilligan's medical analysis to restorative justice we find that most of the practitioners within the restorative justice field are content to do tertiary care.

Johnstone and Van Ness' overview of restorative justice demonstrates this orientation to tertiary care. They outline their three overlapping conceptions of restorative justice (encounter conception, reparative conception and transformative conception) of which the first two conceptions could be termed tertiary care conceptions as the process does not begin until the bleeding starts and then seeks to find a way to repair the harm. The encounter conceptions group puts emphasis on creating space for victim and offender to come together. The reparative conception group emphasises what is needed to make things right for the victim and community. Both conceptions 'kick in' after the harm takes place.

We see the same focus in the Johnstone and Van Ness list of six restorative ingredients. Arguably five out of the six are directed at the tertiary care level, the stage where harm has already occurred (2007). The six are as follows: participating in a process aimed at repair and future intentions; empowering those affected by crime; focusing on responsibility and reintegration of offenders rather than punishment; being guided by principles or values like respect, inclusion, non-violence; focusing on victim injury and needs; strengthening or repairing relationship and building healthy relationship. As this final ingredient focuses, in part, on healthy relationship, it may go beyond the tertiary care approach, but the vast majority of 'restorative ingredients' come from and lead to a tertiary care approach.

Many describe restorative justice as certain processes of encounter – Victim Offender Conferencing, Family Group Conferencing and Circles (Bazemoore and Umbreit 2001; Johnstone 2002; Maxwell and Morris 2001; Van Ness and Strong 2002). This encounter focus tends to be related to repairing harm, even as it may deal with future intentions. In fact, much of the literature of restorative justice focuses on building, advocating, evaluating and implementing these processes of encounter:

➤ Victim Offender Conferencing (Umbreit 1994; Wright 1991; Zehr 1990b)

➤ Family Group Conferencing (MacRae and Zehr 2004; Maxwell and Morris 2001; Pennell and Burford 2000)

➤ Circles (Aboriginal Corrections Policy Unit 1997; Hamilton 2001; Pranist, Stuart and Wedge 2003)

The first section of Sullivan and Tifft's *Handbook of Restorative Justice* focuses almost entirely on tertiary care, although subsequent sections move well beyond. In McLaughlin's *Restorative Justice: Critical Issues* (2003), over half of the chapters are devoted to understanding and improving particular processes and techniques of restorative justice. We see this tertiary care focus in Wachtel's call to replace criminal justice processes with restorative justice processes (1997). Strang defines restorative justice as a process which restores damaged relationships between victims, offenders and community (2002a). All of them, in different degrees, share a focus on a tertiary care approach to restorative justice.

This tertiary approach to restorative justice is so strong that the Supreme Court of Canada uses it in its attempt to define restorative justice as any attempt to:

> [r]emedy the adverse effects of crime in a manner that addresses the needs of all parties involved. This is accomplished, in part, through rehabilitation of the offender, reparations to the victim and to the community, and the promotion of a sense of responsibility in the offender and acknowledgment of the harm done to victims and the community. (*R. v. Proulx* [2000] 1 S.C.R.61)

In fact, many of the broad approaches to legislating restorative justice focus on this level of process and tertiary care. Canadian Bill C-41 and the New Zealand 1989 Young Persons and Their Families Act are both examples of mandating restorative justice measures after a crime has happened. A crime-focused restorative measure usually is a tertiary measure as it is not applied until after an incident of harm, a 'crime', is committed. Only then is a restorative response sought.

I would estimate that at least 90 per cent of the literature on restorative justice fits this first category of tertiary care. While some argue that restorative justice is more cost-effective and efficient than court and penal systems, Gilligan argues that a major focus on tertiary care leads to a very expensive system which does not have the capacity to stop the spread of disease. Literature in this category tends to focus on refining restorative justice techniques and processes for harm response. Thus, there is little consideration for asking broad systemic questions concerning what cultural dynamics sustain a restorative vision and practise of justice.

Secondary Care and Restorative Justice
Secondary care is one of the least developed areas of restorative justice theory. Within the health-care model, secondary care is a step toward

preventative care in that it identifies people who are at high risk of needing tertiary care in the future. The goal is to work with them and their environmental factors in such a way as to prevent future harm and the need for tertiary care.

In restorative justice most programmes work on a case-by-case basis. When evaluation does happen it happens by evaluating the 'success' (or otherwise) of the cases by considering factors such as 'stakeholder satisfaction', recidivism rates, and contracts completed. The focus of this kind of evaluation assumes that by doing tertiary care well you are doing preventative care. In other words, you can break the cycle of victimizing and offending by following best practise for restorative justice encounters. There is clearly some truth to this assumption. There are victims, offenders and facilitators who will testify with great strength to this fact. Restorative justice can contribute to crime prevention (Roach 2000; Van Ness and Strong 1997). These stories do need to be celebrated, but they should not blind us to seeing how the stories are connected to the larger communities and systems, and how the various cultural dynamics within communities and systems lead to certain kinds of stories (e.g. Gilligan's analysis that where there is a large gap between rich and poor there will be increased violence and victimization).

The insight of secondary care is that simply by dragging people out of the river, tertiary care, you do not gain the capacity to prevent harm in the first place. Very little work has been done within restorative justice to move upstream to see how and why people are being thrown into the river. This is the lens of secondary care.

There are some hopeful signs. The New Zealand Family Group Conferencing model itself, by involving extended family, seeks to understand 'the case', or the harm within the wider relational dynamics of the family. Circles approaches, which involve this wider community, sometimes also share this focus. When groups address not only the harm to the victim, but also the roots of what leads a person to harm another, then restorative justice starts to move into a more preventative role. With a community present in the circle, it is possible to see in a harm both what those who did the harming need to take responsibility for and, at the same time, the various systemic influences which the group needs to take responsibility for.

In parts of New Zealand, facilitators of Family Group Conferences have started to 'conference the conferences' (MacRae and Zehr 2004).

Where facilitators notice that they have clusters of cases where the young persons involved share a geographic location or a school, the facilitators host a conference. They gather various people from within the system, such as from the school, social services and police, to see what is going on in a particular area, and to see if there can be some plan that addresses why young people in that area are choosing to offend. This is an example of linking a case-focus to a system-change focus. A similar development is happening in the South African Peacebuilding Forum within the Zwelethemba model (Froestad and Shearing 2007) which has developed *Peacemaking Forums* to respond to harms as they arise and *Peacebuilding Forums* to work structural issues. The Zwelethemba model is also a good example of creating an economic system for allowing funds to shift from crisis-response to system-change. By not paying facilitators, they funnel money into mini-grants for peacebuilding, thereby enabling a form of secondary care.

Another example of a form of secondary care in restorative justice is some of the programmes on restorative practise within schools. One convicted armed bank robber in Canada tracked his beginning with crime to a time when he had been expelled from school, was bored, and needed some cash to have a good time. He has become a leader in restorative justice, and he claims that if you figured out how to keep children in school 'you could save a thousand victims' (Durocher 2002). This is an example of secondary care. Young people who are expelled from, or even in frequent conflict at, school are at risk of becoming offenders. The rise in restorative justice programmes in schools is an initiative in secondary care (Amstutz and Mullet 2005; Compton and Jones 2003; Hopkins 2004; Morrison 2002).

Notice that where restorative justice moves towards secondary care, it does so by leaving the landscape of crime and moving further upstream to schools, to family history and to socio-economic patterns within a society. However, the literature is limited in this regard.

Primary care and restorative justice
Whereas secondary care consists of problem-focused preventative actions for high risk groups, the primary level of heath-care focuses on care for the whole society. This is the arena of asking how to live in ways that lead to health and to avoid becoming 'at risk' in the first place. This is

the arena of asking what cultural dynamics sustain a particular vision of justice. However, as with the secondary level, so here also the restorative justice literature is strikingly quiet. Many writers have grand visions of restorative justice, an imagination guided by values and principles, but few address what kind of socio-cultural relationships are needed to sustain that imagination. Some identify this as a significant gap in the field of restorative justice (Daly 2003; Dickson-Gilmore and LaPrairie 2005). However, the gap they identify is often between promise and theory on the one hand (which are generally seen to be positive but overstated), and practise on the other hand (which they see as unclear as to whether it does deliver what was promised). The gap I am addressing here is a different gap. It is the gap between a vision and practise of restorative justice and knowing what background of primary care relationships support that vision and practise.

Within restorative justice there are some who work at issues of primary care. Johnstone and Van Ness identify them as advocating a 'restorative justice as transformation conception' (2007). These scholars and practitioners do not focus narrowly on crime policy but on the larger realms of life, namely, institutions (Braithwaite and Stang 2001), imagination and paradigms (Sawatsky 2003; Zehr 1985), language (Ross 1996) , meeting needs (Sullivan and Tifft 2001), punishment-free societies (Redekop 2008) and structural analysis (Dyck 2000).

Some of these come to restorative justice, not through alternatives to crime, but as a way of living in faithfulness to what they have learned about life, identity and spirit. For many of them, restorative justice draws on the rites of various ancient cultural-spiritual contexts (Braithwaite 1997; Marshall 2001; Roach 2000; Strang 2002b); Van Ness and Strong 1997; Weitekamp 1993; Zehr 1990a). In this same spirit much of the writing on Aboriginal justice presents a conception of justice as a way of life.

In this section on primary-level approaches to restorative justice we will examine four key approaches: restorative justice as paradigm shift as outlined by Howard Zehr; restorative justice as social justice approach to institutional change as outlined by John Braithwaite; restorative justice as needs-based justice as outlined by Dennis Sullivan and Larry Tifft; and transformative justice as systemic change tool as outlined by Ruth Morris.

Howard Zehr suggests that restorative justice might represent a paradigm shift. As we have already seen in what Zehr calls his 'skeletal outline' of restorative justice, his focus is on restorative justice as an alternative approach to crime, and his language is that of victims and offenders. By these markings we might consider his approach to be a tertiary approach because it seems to assume that we wait until the harm has happened and then figure out how to respond. However, Zehr is drawing on a biblical imagination and understanding of justice. He outlines this quite clearly in *Changing Lenses* (1990a). According to Zehr, the covenantal justice of the biblical understanding of justice is rooted in *shalom* or all rightness. Here justice is connected with relationship to God, to land, neighbour and stranger. Zehr argues that such an approach can not be equated or merely 'plugged in' to a modern paradigm. In a chapter entitled 'Justice as Paradigm' Zehr notes that paradigms create a kind of common sense through which the world is interpreted. He cites the change in science from the Ptolemaic worldview to a Newtonian worldview as an example of paradigms and paradigm changes. He notes that such changes were resisted as adherents to the old paradigm did whatever they could to patch up its dysfunctions and maintain stability. The Ptolemaic view that the sun orbited around the earth could not account for newly observed astronomical anomalies. Rather than accept the proposal that the earth revolved around the sun they proposed that the sun performed a series of epicycles while maintaining its orbit around the earth. Faced with dysfunction the typical reaction of scholars and practitioners is to propose superficial change without changing the fundamental assumptions. Radical new proposals are co-opted into keeping the old system alive. Paradigm change is about changing the fundamental assumptions. It does not mean that everything in the old system is rejected but it does represent a fundamentally different imagination.

Building on Randy Barnett's work (1997), Zehr suggests that the justice system is showing symptoms of a paradigm change and that while restorative justice initiatives advocate a change in paradigms, their initiatives and programmes often function as epicycles, being co-opted into supporting the old paradigm. The old paradigm he names retributive justice and the new paradigm is restorative justice. He recognizes that retributive justice and restorative justice share some goals and might even use some similar methods. However he distinguishes between how the two paradigms use these goals and methods. The restorative paradigm is a journey through tragedy and trauma to belonging and identity (Zehr 2002a). It is a journey from the destruction of meaning to the re-creation of meaning. It is a journey from humiliation to honour, from disrespect to respect. The retributive paradigm, Zehr claims, is a symbol of woundedness and alienation, often leading victim, offender and community in the wrong direction on this journey. Zehr uses the journey metaphor to articulate the fundamental imagination or paradigm shift from retributive to restorative paradigms. Since the early 1990s at least 55 papers have been written on restorative justice as a paradigm.[1] This focus on paradigm raises the important issue of whether healing justice represents a fundamentally different imagination or whether it is being used as an epicycle, proposing an alternative but being used in the way of the old paradigm. Since we have already tentatively described healing justice as a different imagination, this connection to paradigm shift in restorative justice is very important.

Whereas Zehr focuses on how restorative justice represents a different imagination, Braithwaite focuses on applying restorative values to institutional change. Braithwaite starts by trying to articulate the fundamental values and ideas that should be at the centre of a restorative theory of criminal justice. Together with Pettit, Braithwaite argues for a republican ideal of freedom as non-domination as an explanatory and normative theory for criminal justice. They list three features of such a republican system of criminal justice:

1. a preference for parsimony (if in doubt, intervene less in peoples' lives)

2. whatever power is shared is subject to checks and balances

3. an orientation to reformation and reintegration. (Braithwaite and Pettit 2000)

Braithwaite and Strang call for a linking of restorative values to wider public issues of social justice and give the examples of reduction of homelessness, reduction of school expulsions and transformation of corporate systems that are in need of such attention. In other words, they suggest that the kinds of relationships which help to sustain restorative justice include economic structures to reduce homelessness, increase compassionate school policies and establish ways of holding corporate systems accountable. However, they offer very little information on how that is done. In fact, they claim that very little research has been done in

---

1   The website www.restorativejustice.org lists 55 restorative justice articles with paradigm in the title. Accessed 4 June 2008.

this area, but that it is one of the biggest research questions in the field (2000).

In other writings, Braithwaite explores the relationship between restorative justice and social justice. Rejecting the position that 'restorative justice is unimportant to struggles of social justice' and arguing against the necessity of the position that 'restorative justice risks the worsening of social injustice', Braithwaite advocates the position that 'restorative justice can be an important strategy for advancing social justice' (Braithwaite 2003b). He writes:

> The most important way restorative justice may be able to reduce social injustices involves reducing the impact of imprisonment as a cause of the unequal burdens of unemployment, debt with extortionate interest burdens, suicide, rape, AIDS, Hepatitis C and potentially most important, the epidemic of multiple-drug-resistant tuberculosis. (2003b)

He also suggests that restorative justice can give a voice to dominated groups such as Indigenous peoples, women and children suffering abuse. Furthermore, by dealing with corporate injustices such as fraud, insurance fraud and tax fraud restorative justice might turn around 'some of the stupendous advantaging of the rich over the poor...'. (2003b) His focus is on how restorative justice can contribute to social justice. This is an important focus shared by other scholars (Crawford and Clear 2003). What has been missing, however, is any analysis on what kinds of relationships are needed, within social justice institutions or otherwise, to contribute to a vision and practise of restorative justice.

Some of Braithwaite's earlier writing includes this focus. In an essay entitled 'Social Conditions Conducive to Reintegrative Shaming' Braithwaite argues that 'the fundamental societal conditions conducive to cultural processes of reintegrative shaming are communitarianism and interdependency' (1989). These are potential conditions for sustaining a more healing approach to justice. Healing justice cannot be assumed to be the same as Braithwaite's theories of reintegrative shaming because Braithwaite advocates a leading role for the state in shaming, and for the divorcing of the act of shaming (done by the state) and reintegration (done by the community) (1989). Healing justice, on the other hand, tries to distinguish itself from the state and, as will become clear from the cases of healing justice, where shaming happens, it happens through the same community of care which also reintegrates. Braithwaite is trying to draw on the wisdom of communities and societies with deep traditions of restorative justice. It may be that his conditions conducive to reintegrative shaming can be seen in communities with a healing justice practise. However, it is in Braithwaite's application of these theories to the modern state systems that he departs from understandings of healing justice.

Braithwaite sees communitarianism and interdependency as interrelated. Braithwaite sees three elements to communitarianism: '(1) densely enmeshed interdependency, where the interdependencies are characterized by (2) mutual obligation and trust, and (3) are interpreted as a matter of group loyalty rather than individual convenience' (1989).

Equally interesting is Braithwaite's account of the erosion of communitarinanism in individualistic societies in the West, which, he argues, corresponds to a rise in crime control and greater reliance on the state. The source of this erosion by individualism, according to Braithwaite, is ideology, urbanization, industrialization, declining intensiveness of agriculture and increasing residential mobility (1989). These, too, might be seen as barriers to the sustaining of a healing justice vision and practise.

Another attempt to broaden the scope of restorative justice to include social-structural justice issues comes from Dennis Sullivan and Larry Tifft in their book *Restorative Justice: Healing the Foundations of our Everyday Lives* (2001). They criticize restorative justice for its 'lack of concern over the structural conditions, the political-economic foundation that determines whether the personal integration and reintegration of a person into his or her community will be possible' (2001). They build on restorative justice theory by proposing a needs-based justice which can respond to the social-structural harms and institutional conditions while at the same time responding to interpersonal harms and harmony. They contrast needs-based justice with the economies and paradigms of rights-based and deserts-based conceptions of justice. Rights-based conceptions of justice are problems for Sullivan and Tifft because they distribute power according to one's social position or social location, positions largely determined by the lottery of birth. Deserts-based conceptions of justice are deemed problematic for distributing power according to efforts, talents, achievements and failures. They see both these conceptions as violent conceptions of power. Rather, they suggest, we should meet the needs of all parties as those parties define their own need. The goal here is not equal distribution but 'equality of well-being'. By focusing on the satisfaction of needs they are creating space for victim, offender and community to participate in a justice practise where they state their own needs and work together to meet the needs of all. They are also creating the space to criticize those 'power-based social arrangements and hierarchically-ordered relationships that by definition deny the possibility of the satisfaction of the needs of all' (2001). They argue that 'success as a healing community will depend upon how needs-oriented our primary social institutions are' (2001). Sullivan and Tifft present other conditions and factors that are required of just communities if they are to be rooted in restorative justice. These include:

➤ a commitment and continual action 'to dissolve the self' (2001). They see the self as a power-based entity that is the source of violence as it creates distance between people and allows for hierarchical ordering. This is a necessary step to developing a concern to meet the needs of all

➤ some form of communal, corrective process which includes opening oneself to the whole community for confession, self-examination, forgiveness and/or reconciliation (2001)

➤ a 'political economy that protects, nurtures, supports and accommodates the growth needs of all' (2001)

➤ a restorative way of being in the earliest relationships. 'The process of creating restorative communities begins with our intimates and in our child-care and parent-care relationships' (2001). They believe that a restorative way of being cuts across all relationship and action. Beginning close to home creates a way of being that spills over into all other areas. So from home relationships, Sullivan and Tifft move to school and work relationships

➤ a seeking for justice through restorative process

➤ an effort to meet the needs of the natural environment. This is part of a needs-based justice and therefore part of a restorative community's political economy.

These are all conditions and factors which Sullivan and Tifft claim need to be present in a restorative community which extends a needs-based justice into every sphere of life. Sullivan and Tifft offer perhaps the most comprehensive overview of the kind of relationships that are needed to sustain a more restorative way of life. Their list comes from applying a form of basic human needs theory. This research has a different starting point, not theory but three communities practising healing justice. If

Sullivan and Tifft are correct in their analysis, we may well see their features mirrored in these three case studies of healing justice.

Another field of study which examines connections to social justice is transformative justice. Ruth Morris explains that the development of the language of transformative justice came about because restorative justice 'still accepts the idea that one event now defines all that matters of right and wrong – it leaves out the past, and the social causes of the event' (2000). Transformative justice seeks to transform relationships in ways that support social justice and equality rather than simply restoring community and individuals (Cooley 1999; Martin 1999). It goes beyond the process emphasis of restorative justice to challenge the assumptions of the current economic, environmental, political, judicial and social systems (Muhly 2001). Rather than seeing the problems beginning with the crime, as retributive and restorative justice do, Ruth Morris argues that transformative justice begins with the causes of crime (1995). These causes may lie within individuals but more likely are also intertwined in the socio-economic systems which create the conditions that individuals must grapple with. To understand causes one must have both micro and macro-perspectives working together.

There have been other attempts to see restorative justice as a primary response. Some authors have attempted to design restorative systems. However, most of these pay little or no attention to cultural dynamics which sustain a restorative vision. They focus on other issues such as how much punishment and constraint is allowed (Dignam 2003), or on becoming the primary response to crime (Van Ness 2002), or on marketing restorative justice to state justice administrators (Harland 1996).

In this section we have been using the framework of a health-care response to disease to explore the literature of restorative justice and in particular the gap in the literature on cultural dynamics which sustain such a vision of justice. I have argued that restorative justice is a discourse which offers itself as a significant alternative to notions of Western justice. However, restorative justice in practise is heavily focused on crisis care without developing sufficient links to more systemic issues.

These arguments are not entirely new. Gerry Johnstone challenges restorative justice not to focus too much on criminal justice reform, for such a focus hides wide systemic issues of harm (2004). Elmar Weitekamp rebukes scholars in the field for beginning their analyses with state systems rather than non-state systems because such a beginning point 'tak[es] for granted the existence of political power and state law' (2003). George Pavlich charges restorative justice with supporting the status quo and not providing a deep enough alternative, but rather creating dependency on the existing state system (2005). Pavlich is supported by Martin Wright, who argues that restorative processes have done little to surface or engage the factors conducive to crime (2005). Ovid Mercredi, former Grand Chief of the Assembly of First Nations in Canada, clearly says that systemic change for Aboriginal people will not come from a case-by-case focus (2001). A number of scholars have identified the difficulty of moving from a case-by-case approach to resolving systemic problems. However few have shown a way of bringing these together or explained why restorative justice has been prone to the more individual view.

Before explaining the reasons for this gap I need to make an important clarification. I have used the health-care categories of tertiary care, secondary care and primary care to try to highlight this gap. Now I would like to address some limitations of applying the metaphor of primary care to restorative justice, especially in light of a study on healing justice. Models of primary care usually rely on teams of experts to analyse the complex relationships within the environment and then on the basis of 'sound scientific analysis' to provide guidance as to what constitute healthy habits. These in turn usually become part of an educational programme which is a means to impose scientific health standards on the larger community. The community, who do not have the expertise of the scientists, are expected to give up their habits of living and follow the expert advice. Healing justice is not analogous to a foreign expert-driven, reductionist imposition. In practise, restorative justice sometimes is. The metaphor is helpful to identify a significant gap in the vision and practise of restorative justice but it is not helpful in structuring the imagination of what restorative justice should look like, if the goal is to learn from healing justice. Primary health-care focuses typically draw on the modern scientific perspective which tends to reduce, break apart, rationalize, separate ends and means, and relies heavily on a cause-and-effect and technological imagination. Both restorative justice and healing justice, at least in their argumentation, would move in different directions. Healing justice tends to criticize modern Western approaches to both justice and medicine and so should not be interpreted through the lens of a health-care approach.

Reasons for the contradiction

One way to understand why restorative justice has an imbalance between case and systemic foci is to note how restorative justice is related to Aboriginal justice. I will try to give a brief overview of Aboriginal justice and show how it contrasts with criminal justice. Then I will examine if restorative justice is more like Aboriginal justice or criminal justice. The reasons for the contradiction will unfold as we see how restorative justice does not sufficiently challenge many of the key characteristics of criminal justice. This is an argument I have expanded on elsewhere (Sawatsky 2008).

Aboriginal authors' writings on justice featured very strongly in our survey of the usages of healing justice. It is difficult to give a helpful overview of Aboriginal justice as there is no pan-Aboriginal understanding of justice and some Aboriginal authors are clear they do not seek to create a single theory of Aboriginal justice (Henderson and McCaslin 2005). Aboriginal groups are many nations with different languages, traditions and cultures. However there are important common themes which connect the approaches to justice of many of these groups. A second difficulty in such a brief overview is that some Aboriginal authors object to Aboriginal justice being equated with restorative justice (Austin 1993; Jackson 1992; Jackson and Rubin 1996; Monture-Angus 1995; Roach 2000) while others equate restorative justice and Aboriginal justice (Yazzie 2005) or suggest that they are similar approaches (Lee 1996). This overview will not try to reconcile these different voices. What all of them have in common is that they see Aboriginal justice and, sometimes, restorative justice as a way of being in the world. Aboriginal justice therefore represents one of the most important primary-level approaches to justice.

Aboriginal justice tends to have a double focus. On the one hand it seeks to return to ways of justice that are natural to and healing of Aboriginal communities and, on the other hand, it seeks to decolonialize the Western system (McCaslin 2005c). Reflecting this double goal some communities have even flirted with shifting their language from healing to 'decolonialization healing' (Lane et al. 2002). These two tasks are bound together in a search for identity. Aboriginal identity has been shaped by the long-term attempts of the dominant culture at colonialization, assimilation and even genocide. Hence, a return to traditional understandings of justice cannot be pursued apart from engaging in the transformation of the political systems and imagination which facilitated and continue to facilitate such colonialization.

Aboriginal justice begins within an understanding of the many relationships within the created world (McCaslin 2005a). It therefore also begins with the Creator. The Elders are the ones who pass on the teachings originally passed down from the Creator (Lee 1996). Gloria Lee claims that 'the way a person relates to the Creator and to all creation determines how they perceive justice and view restorative justice' (1996). The first sustaining factor of Aboriginal justice, then, is having the right relationship with the Creator and all of creation. Aboriginal justice is an ecological and spiritual vision of justice which is lived in the traditions, stories and ceremonies of various distinct groups. Spirituality is one of the primary ingredients of such healing justice (Lane *et al.* 2002). It is not surprising that most successful programmes of Aboriginal justice-as-healing are 'built on empowering Aboriginal languages, ceremony, traditions and values' (Henderson and McCaslin 2005). Aboriginal justice is not based on equality but on difference and developing distinct identity.

A justice rooted in relationships with the land and with all of creation leads to a concern for the healing of all, including those who have harmed others – both 'offenders' and 'colonializers'. Justice as healing is here a justice that does not accept the paradigm of winners and losers. Similarly, it does not accept the notion of individual guilt. Aboriginal justice is a communal sense of justice which does not shy away from holding persons responsible for harms. Rather, it sees such acts as an opportunity to strengthen the person, the community and the nation through a healing process (McCaslin 2005b).

When an Aboriginal community gathers to do justice it seeks holistic ways of responding to a harm in its entirety (Melton 2001). Western systems which fragment, compartmentalize and limit the kind of information which is admissible hold little weight in these circles. For them a key part of the healing process is speaking the truth. This means looking deeply at a situation to determine the web of forces which contribute to harming behaviour. Such a holistic approach is not limited to the one incident of harm. It seeks to speak the truth of the root causes of harming while, at the same time, nurturing the key dynamics of belonging and balance (Lee 1996; MCaslin 2005b). The Navajos describe someone who harms as one who 'acts as if he has no relative'. Chief Justice Robert Yazzie asks what one does with someone who acts as if they have no relatives? His answer, 'You bring in the relatives' (2005). Aboriginal justice is about being a good relative (Henderson and McCaslin 2005). Involving the family is the way to get past denial in someone who has harmed others. (Yazzie 2005) This kind of justice is about making families and communities strong again (Lee 1996; MCCaslin 2005b; Pranis *et al.* 2003). Therefore this justice is about being part of a people and seeking self-determination as a people.

Aboriginal justice tends to use heart-thinking more than head-thinking (Zion 1997). Emotions are a central part of healing justice. The values of justice include respect, dealing with each other in good ways, strengthening families and communities and returning to traditional teachings. These values are learned and taught by experiencing them and practising them. Hence, the methods of justice reflect the virtues of justice: respect, love, engaging family and community, changing one's relationship with land, Elders and Creator, coming together with the community.

It is not surprising that many Aboriginal people speak of Aboriginal justice as a paradigm which contrasts with Western justice (Lane *et al.* 2002; Cousins 2004; Henderson and MCaslin 2005; Melton 2001). From listening to a range of Aboriginal authors, I've created Table 2.1: Western and Aboriginal Paradigms of Justice to illustrate the range of contrasts within these conflicting paradigms. Of course, in reality this relationship is much more complex, lively and messy than any table can communicate, but Table 2.1 highlights how some of the basic assumptions about justice different between Aboriginal justice paradigms and Western ones.

Where would restorative justice be located in Table 2.1? As we have seen, the discourse of restorative justice often is that of being an alternative to the state criminal system. There are clear ways in which restorative justice does challenge the criminal system. Restorative justice sees justice more as repairing harm than punishing offenders. It challenges the state-centric models of justice by calling for a more central role for victims, offenders and sometimes communities. However there are also ways in which restorative justice mirrors the criminal justice process. Both restorative justice and criminal justice have a case orientation which begins with someone breaking the law or harming someone else. A case or incident orientation tends to focus on the micro rather than the systemic or more macro issues. While restorative justice challenges the criminal justice system to move from a rules focus to a 'who's been harmed' focus (Zehr 2002b), waiting for harm and focusing on response to harm is part of the reason why restorative justice has an inadequate systemic focus. Symptomatic approaches will always have trouble addressing systematic problems. This

Table 2.1: Western and Aboriginal Paradigms of Justice

Western Paradigms of Justice	Aboriginal Paradigms of Justice
Justice begins with law/rules and the system	Justice begins with the Creator, the natural world and the Elders
Order is state-enforced	Natural order already exists which demonstrates how we are all related
Justice is/should be a universal system/process	Ways of justice are rooted in local knowledge, language, experience
Justice is separated from the spiritual	The spiritual is essential to justice
Linear, time-bounded way of thinking	Holistic, cyclical way of thinking
Equality seen as sameness	Equality seen as honouring distinct identity
Win/lose paradigm in disputes	All need healing, all need each other
Individualist conception of guilt	Communalist (co-responsibility in guilt and also in nation building and personal healing)
System fragmented, compartmentalized	Holistic approach to responding to harms in their entirety
Colonializing and assimilative goal of making everyone good citizen	Healing as being a good family member and seeking self-determination
Majority rules minority	Seeks consensus
Authority, rank, obedience valued	Rooted in relationship, traditions, emotions, dealing with each other in good ways
Justice as responding to rules (which are the mechanism of social control)	Justice as making families and communities strong again
Reliant on experts and states responding for the community	Reliant on own ways of doing justice by the community
Incident-focused	Complex system oriented
Focused on symptoms	Focused on root causes and creating balance
We are individually responsible	All are related and co-responsible; harms are signs of imbalance in community
Justice through intellectual debate	Justice as heart-thinking and balancing the physical, spiritual, mental, emotional
Offender needs punishment	Offender needs good relations
Proving case by arguing facts	Confronting denial in offender through family and community participation
Using force, coercion and guilt as methods of justice	Using talking things out, respect, solidarity, interdependent relationships, and love as methods of justice
Justice as identifying the guilty	Justice as knowing who you are, finding identity within the community
Justice as a discreet act	Justice as a way of life
Justice as punishment	Justice as healing the root causes of imbalances

harm focus sometimes means focusing on symptoms. Restorative justice has developed few means to dig to the roots of conflict, especially if the roots lie outside the immediate participants as in the case of system or structural conflicts. By waiting for harm, restorative justice also tends to rely on the state to refer cases. Here justice begins with the state. While restorative justice has criticized the adversarial criminal processes of justice some restorative justice advocates seem just to substitute one process for another. They rely on Victim Offender Conference or Family Group Conferencing or Circles as key aspects of what makes their work restorative. However the logic is still the logic of processes, that if we can get people into the right process we will get an acceptable outcome. Finally, focusing on the harm done sometimes narrows the focus to individuals, the ones who have been directly harmed. Here is another characteristic shared with the criminal justice system. This narrow focus sometimes blinds restorative justice advocates to both the broader problems and the resources which lie outside the individuals who have been harmed.

Summary

By not sufficiently challenging the underlying logic of the criminal justice system, restorative justice sometimes gets caught in a short-sighted cycle of crisis and case management which is similar to the criminal justice system.

Any exploration into the kind of relationships which sustain healing justice is an exploration into territory which has traditionally been, at least partially, outside the field of restorative justice. Most of restorative justice has focused on tertiary care rather than primary care. Focusing on traditional communities and on healing justice will challenge some of the basic logics of both the criminal justice system and the restorative justice movement because healing justice may not work according to the logic of crimes.

However, one should not assume that the foci and challenges presented by this research would not be welcome in the field of restorative justice. In many ways this is a young movement which began by grassroots practise rather than comprehensive ideological vision. Many of those working in the practise of restorative justice are interested in it as an alternative way of doing justice. Many of them may welcome the challenge to deepen and broaden the implications of the 'alternative' praxis. Some desire such a transformation but struggle with just how to do it. This book addresses an important gap in the field.

Chapter 3

Learning How to Enter into Healing Justice: Research Methodology

Introduction

How one goes about a quest often determines where one goes and what one finds. We understand that an airplane ride is not a good method for bird watching. But the *how* strategy also determines what we see once we get there. What did the European settlers to North America first see when they encountered indigenous peoples? How we approach life and research determines what we see, but our approach has a lot to do with assumptions that we often leave unarticulated.

This chapter outlines how this research was carried out. It is about searching for the *how* that would both take us in the right direction and help us to see what we needed to see once we got there. This was no small task. Three research challenges lay at the heart of the development of comparative case study methodology utilized in this research. The chapter will examine each of the following challenges:

➤ How to conduct respectful research within traditional communities which tend to be highly critical of many Western modes of research.

➤ How to conduct research into healing justice which will not be subject to the same limitations of restorative and criminal justice outlined in Chapter 2.

➤ How to compare holistic cases in ways that respect their particularity while still looking for interconnections.

Research challenges
Researching those suspicious of research: Learning respect

A second research challenge was to find a research methodology which might offer internal validity from the perspective of the communities being studied, while at the same time offering external validity according to accepted norms of research practises. From the review of the literature we have seen that healing justice is not simply a modification of Western justice, that is, correctional, retributive or procedural justice. If this were the case, deriving a methodology might be more straightforward. To find a way of researching communities that tended to be suspicious of Western methods, it was important to understand and be attentive of their perceptions, especially as this research was designed to understand those perceptions. I needed to find a methodology that was respectful of the communities involved, respectful of their ways of knowing, of their cultures and beliefs. Some of the people who advocate for healing justice also warn against the colonializing effects of social science research as it has been experienced in these communities (Smith 1999). Others have argued that Western systems of knowing are too problem-conceived to be able to comprehend the nature of the wisdom of these communities. Indigenous communities are suspicious of some forms of western research, in part because of the unethical and demeaning ways in which some western researchers have treated these communities. Two obvious examples are biotechnological research and the patenting of life (Lewinski and Hanh 2004; Posey and Dutfield 1996) and Napolean Chagnon's study of the Yanomami tribe in Venezuela (Borofsky and Albert 2005; Tierney 2001). However, the more harsh criticism is that the very ways of Western knowing and, therefore, the ways or methodologies of doing research are embedded in a worldview of cognitive imperialism, a colonialist worldview. For example, a search for universal truths hides the fact that there are different ways of knowing. The search makes superior one way of knowing by calling it 'normal', 'natural', 'general' or 'universal'. All other ways of knowing, whether indigenous, Buddhist, Christian or whatever, are either ignored or demeaned in some form for being archaic, religious, primitive or uncivilized.

The obvious challenge for me was to see if there was some way to find a non-colonialist way of researching into the cultural dynamics that sustain traditional justice. My standpoint was that any research into healing justice must use respectful and ethical means. It was not possible to learn deeply about a practise of respect without respectful research methods. For this reason, my methodology had to take very seriously the arguments about what constituted ethical research in various traditional or indigenous communities. Battiste and Henderson (2000), in a chapter entitled 'Ethical Issues in Research', make a number of important suggestions: indigenous peoples should be able to exercise control over information relating to them; indigenous people should have direct input in to the development of research projects; ethical research must replace Eurocentric prejudice with new methodologies that value diversity over universality and synthesis over negative exclusions; researchers cannot rely on colonial language to define indigenous reality; non-indigenous research can be helpful but cannot speak for communities; research must consider the collective interests of the group, not just relying on informed consent of individuals or even of leaders; researchers must respect the cultures they are working with; research should be conceptualized and conducted in partnership with the indigenous group. These guidelines significantly shaped my research.

Many Buddhists also find fault with Western modes of research. These criticisms follow a similar logic to the Aboriginal criticisms but emphasize that the Western research approach often relies on a separation of subject and object which is deeply problematic. Rejecting this dualistic way of thinking, then, also leads to rejecting observer-oriented research. For Buddhists such indirect experience does not, and cannot, contain truth. Truth requires direct or pure experience without concepts. In fact, knowledge and concepts are seen as the biggest obstacles to awakening. 'To reach truth is not to accumulate knowledge, but to awaken *to the heart of reality*' (Hanh 1995, empasis on original).

The challenges of these traditional communities to modern research are not without precedent within academia itself. Many postmodern academics share the suspicion of the neutral observer who watches his 'subject' in some neutral way. In parts of quantum physics, anthropology, religious studies, feminist studies and many others, there is a growing rejection of modern notions of dualism and neutral observer status. These researchers recognize that not only the community, but also they themselves become a part of their research. This kind of research is based more on developing relationships than on being a neutral observer. In fact my research follows the spirit of anthropological studies and action research studies in which the modern notions of subject/object have been rejected.

In the area of comparative studies, however, there is less development of ways of conducting research by non-modern methods. Comparative study tends to be the creating of categories of knowledge, or fundamental concepts, which can be observed in diverse areas. In some ways, this is exactly the kind of logic the Buddhists warn against. So I needed a particular kind of comparative methodology to conduct this research in a way that was respectful and attentive to the communities involved.

Researching without the process-technique fixation: Looking wider and deeper

The first challenge in finding an appropriate methodology was to find a way of conducting research into healing justice which would not be subject to the same limitations of restorative and criminal justice outlined in Chapter 2. Part of the criticism of restorative justice offered in Chapter 2 is that proponents have borrowed practises from traditional communities but have not fully understood the environments that sustained those practises. Furthermore, that by focusing on a dialogue with a state government to accept their alternative practises, restorative justice proponents overemphasize the practises and poorly understand what broader dynamics are needed to sustain the vision of justice from which they were derived. I knew I needed to do research which was not primarily interested in harms response practises. The healing justice literature clearly was talking about something broader, and I knew I needed to frustrate the usual appetite for extracting processes from their context. Therefore my focus would include, first, the description of what is healing justice from the standpoint of the communities and, second, an inquiry into what kind of relationships the communities saw as necessary to sustain such an approach. I suspected that if the communities themselves were to define healing justice, it would include, but not be limited to, the way disputes were handled. I also suspected that if I did a study of just one community that their ideas and processes might quickly become equated with healing justice. Examining three diverse communities simultaneously might demonstrate diverse processes with perhaps some kind of a shared logic. I also thought that by asking the communities directly about the kinds of relationships that sustain healing justice the dialogue would be pushed well beyond the techniques of tertiary care discussion which, as we found in Chapter 2, typifies much of the restorative justice literature.

Comparing holistic systems

A third challenge was comparing diverse communities in such a way as to respect the particularity of each community while, at the same time, looking for common dynamics and interconnections which might help sustain healing justice. This challenge was, of course, related to the second. I knew I needed to avoid the kinds of legal anthropology that uses Western legal language to understand a 'foreign' community. Some of the comparative methodologies of political science which use highly rationalistic and reductionist methods of comparison had to be excluded in favour of methods which would not reduce the stories and insights of the communities to fundamental concepts. In response to these challenges I developed a particular kind of comparative case study methodology where the communities participated in telling their own story and in examining possible interconnections with the other stories.

Developing a comparative case study methodology

In the end, I used a comparative case study methodology that borrows from the tradition of participatory action research by engaging the community in the describing of the case and in the analysis of the meaning of the case.

Initially I turned to macro-causal comparative history as a possible methodological approach. Theda Skocpol uses this approach in *States and Social Revolution: A Comparative Analysis of France, Russia and China* (1979)and so does Barrington Moore Jr. in *Social Origins of Dictatorship and Democracy* (1967). The approach utilizes a small number of cases to develop general explanations of causes and outcomes while, at the same time, paying close attention to the particular context of each case. At first this seemed to be a good way to hold together a small number of cases with integrity while building the capacity to recognize some common patterns and factors. However, the method is built on the modern rationalist scientific imagination which is based on John Stuart Mills' *System of Logic* (1884). It requires the breaking apart of a community into component parts to seek causal factors. Eventually it became clear that this methodology was too much in tension with the worldview of the communities I was going to study. These communities valued holisms, interconnected dynamics, and listening to many kinds of wisdom, not just intellectual wisdom. It made little sense to use a methodology they would find highly dubious.

Instead I chose a case study methodology as defined by David De Vaus in *Research Design in Social Research* (2001). Such case studies are common to social and legal anthropology and to many other forms of social and educational research. De Vaus claims that case study methodology is

> particularly appropriate when we need to investigate phenomena where it is not possible to introduce interventions... Case study designs are particularly useful when we do not wish or are unable to screen out the influence of 'external' variables but when we wish to examine their effect on the phenomenon we are investigating. (2001)

Yin, one of the leading scholars of case study methods, states the purpose with a slightly different emphasis:

> A major rationale for using [case studies] is when your investigation must cover both a particular phenomenon and the context within which the phenomenon is occurring either because (a) the context is hypothesized to contain important explanatory information about the phenomenon or (b) the boundaries between phenomenon and context are not clearly evident. (1993)

In my view my research met all of these criteria. I was trying to research a phenomenon, healing justice, within its natural setting of complex internal and external variables. I was trying to examine what variables affected or sustained healing justice. I was focusing on healing justice from the standpoint of traditional communities in the expectation that within the communities was contained important explanatory information about the phenomenon of healing justice. As these communities' valued holisms and interconnection, the boundaries between the phenomenon and the contexts were not clear.

I needed a research methodology which would help me move below the surface to gain a detailed understanding of the praxis of healing justice within the community. I was looking for a methodology that would work with a small number of cases and would help me to understand the imagination, behaviour, attitudes, motivation and relationships of those who are said to practise such a justice. Because I was going to partner with three very different communities I also needed a methodology which would give flexibility in the ways research was done. Because the communities I needed to research were often suspicious of the 'objective external researcher', I needed a methodology which allowed me to use myself as a research instrument. These features which I was looking for are all common features of qualitative research. After examining many forms of qualitative research, I decided that the case study approach was the best fit, but I was not content with just any kind of case study.

The particular kind of case study I was developing had a number of distinguishing characteristics as outlined by De Vaus (2001). This research was indeed to be a multiple rather than single case research. There were a number of reasons for creating a multiple case analysis. Multiple cases would provide more compelling evidence that healing justice was not the domain of one particular ethnic group but was practised in diverse ways across diverse contexts. Further, showing diverse ways of doing healing justice should help resist the temptation to reduce healing justice to a single process or technique. Multiple cases would also allow me to identify commonalities of patterns, insights and conditions across contexts.

De Vaus distinguishes between parallel and sequential cases. Parallel cases are multiple cases done at the same time by different researchers. Consequently, the cases have little opportunity to shed light on each other. Sequential case studies are done one after another, often by the same researcher, opening up the double advantage that cases can inform each other and that space is created for inductive theory-building (2001). My research was done in parallel but by the same researcher, which then opened up the advantages of cross-fertilization which De Vaus sees in sequential case studies. By creating multiple stages of case study development with cases which are pursued in parallel, the cases did inform each other on multiple levels.

Case studies are usually bounded by time in some manner. My case studies were retrospective rather than prospective. In other words these cases did not try to anticipate future change but rather looked back at the community and took a snapshot of the past. A different observer, in a different time or place, would no doubt see differently (Bradley and Cownie 2000). It was important, therefore, to indicate that slice of time in which the communities had been observed, namely 2006–2007.

In the end these cases were designed to be both descriptive and explanatory. As descriptive cases, they were presented as whole cases so that readers can build up a clear picture. An in-depth chapter is offered for each case. As explanatory cases, the goal of this investigation was to explain how healing justice was sustained from the perspective of communities that practised such a justice.

Another defining characteristic of my case study design was that these cases were focused on theory building rather than theory testing. Theory-building case studies begin with the context and the case, and then move to theory. In this way, the process has significant overlap with grounded theory process. My goal was to find commonalities between cases with the same phenomenon and to use comparative case analysis to highlight conditions and contexts under which healing justice can be sustained. While it might have been possible to also conduct theory testing with these cases, I decided that such a focus would detract from the goal of carefully understanding the communities' approach to healing justice from within.

De Vaus also suggests that some studies are holistic while other studies are embedded units of analysis. An embedded unit of analysis looks at one part of a system, whereas a holistic case study strives to understand how the whole system functions. Because these case studies examined healing justice within the various contexts that contained them, they are considered to be holistic case studies. In other words healing justice is not an embedded unit as we might consider most forms of Western justice to be. These case studies are not based on tracking particular dispute resolution cases but look more holistically at the whole system of the community to understand what meaning community members attach to healing justice and how it functions in their community. As healing justice is part of holistic communities, these case studies also had to have a holistic approach.

While there is no complete cataloguing of the case study methodology, De Vaus suggests that there are 64 different kinds of case studies depending on the combination of the characteristics outlined above. This case study research had the following characteristics: a multiple rather than single case study, a modified parallel study which has the characteristic of a sequential study, a retrospective rather than prospective study, a theory-building rather than theory-testing study and a holistic rather than an embedded units study. It also used the tradition of ongoing analysis and participation that is central to much qualitative research.

Site selection

I used a purposeful mixed type sampling to choose cases as outlined by Creswell (1998) and more fully by Miles and Huberman (1994). Cases were selected first because of a phenomenological criterion: they seemed to be examples of healing justice. The goal was to find operating communities which claimed to have some practise of healing justice.

Cases were also selected to create maximum variation or difference. The goal was to find communities that differed widely on various criteria but still shared the phenomenon to be studied, in this case healing justice. In this way common patterns across different contexts related to healing justice could more easily be identified. For site selection in this research, the following key factors of difference were used:

➤ *Different ethnic groups* – Rupert Ross closes his study of Aboriginal justice in Canada with a retelling of the teaching of the four colours (1996). The teaching goes that there are four different colours of people on this earth. Each colour group is a different ethnic group. Each has a different age and a different gift that was given to it by the Creator and vitally needed by the other three groups. The story suggests that we need each group to have a full picture, to use all the gifts we were given. Including difference in ethnic groups would give a fuller pictures and test if healing justice was specific to a particular ethnic group.

➤ *Different language structure* – If imagination is encoded in language, as ethnographers and indigenous people claim that it is, finding communities with different original languages is a key method of adding difference.

➤ *Different faith or spirituality traditions* – Faith is often used to exclude or to separate out. Diversity of faith or spirituality traditions can demonstrate how the particular view of justice is intimately connected to, and transcended by, its faith tradition.

Furthermore, the case selection utilized snowball or chain sampling (Cresswell 1998) that identifies cases of interest from people who know people who know which cases are information-rich. Part of my process of case selection was to ask various people engaged in restorative justice which communities they thought I should study.

Other factors that were considered in site selection:

➤ Was there a large primary literature resource, including writings by the community and/or research conducted in a participatory and holistic manner, such as is sometimes done in ethnographic and participatory action research studies?

➤ Would I likely be given access to the group?

➤ What would make a fruitful mix? John Paul Lederach argues that the key to fruitful peacebuilding initiatives is not so much focusing on *what* but on *whom*. He calls this the 'strategic who' and the 'critical social yeast'.

> Who, though not like-minded or like-situated in this context of conflict, would have a capacity, if they were mixed and held together, to make other things grow exponentially, beyond their numbers? (2005)

➤ What were the identity and interests of the researcher? I am a white Canadian Mennonite scholar-practitioner of peace. My identity and interests clearly factored into this activity, both consciously and unconsciously.

➤ What fitted the ethos of the overview of healing justice literature from Chapter 1? In the reviews of healing justice and restorative justice, three communities kept appearing: Aboriginal communities, sub-sections of Christian communities and sub-sections of Buddhist communities. This gave weight to the final selection.

The selection of cases was not an attempt to find typical cases of healing justice. Nor was it an attempt at random selection or at some kind of probability sample. Cases were purposefully selected according to mixed methods of accepted practises outlined above.

My first step was to search for communities which practised some form of healing justice for which there was adequate literature available. Many of these communities are reported on in the previous chapters. The second step was to dig deeper by applying the above grid to rate the suitability of various communities to this research. That process led to the selection of three communities:

Hollow Water – This is an Aboriginal and Métis community in central Canada. Hollow Water's Community Holistic Circle Healing process had been recognized as one the most mature healing programmes in Canada. Theirs was a startling story of working with an approximately an 75 per cent sexual abuse rate going back through generations and finding a way of working at community healing which disrupted this generational pattern and rebuilt a healthy community. That they did it without focusing on incarceration and by keeping victim and victimizer in the same community had made them well-known nationally and internationally. That one report estimated their recidivism rate at 2 per cent, well below any other programme in Canada, had also caught public attention (Couture 2001b). Rupert Ross and the journal *Justice as Healing* were identified as key voices in the healing justice movement and both of them had highlighted favourably the work of Hollow Water. All this attention had made Hollow Water one of the most studied programmes, thus providing sufficient literature. Aboriginal communities feature as one of the main groups that use the language of healing justice. This study could not have been done well without including at least one Aboriginal group. To include the most mature programme in Canada would aid the task of this research. While Hollow Water came from my home province, I had had no previous contact with the programme. As a lecturer in peace and restorative justice, I knew and respected their story and had taught it to some of my classes, but I had had no prior connection with the community.

The Iona Community – This is a European ecumenical Christian community in Scotland. The current leader had recently used healing justice to describe the nature of the Iona Community's work and vision (Galloway 2000). The community had its own publishing press and had written extensively on its own practises. It welcomed 'outsiders' to visit in the form of retreat. According to my review in Chapter 1, the second leading stream of influence in the literature of healing justice is a loose grouping of various Christian voices. It made sense to find a Christian community to examine its practises. Many of the Christian voices of healing justice are scholars. One of the voices was that of the leader of Iona Community. On further investigation I had found that their interest and experience in healing justice extended well beyond the reach of the leader, going back to the start of the community some 60 years earlier. Previous to this research, I had met several of the Iona Community's members and had known of it for about 20 years but never had had a very close connection. I chose this group in part to test two disturbing ideas I had come across in teaching restorative justice. First, I had heard some white people suggest that practises like those of Aboriginal justice would never work in white circles. Second, I had understood why Aboriginal people wanted and needed and had distinct justice systems. I was disturbed that white communities, by and large, did not see the same need to develop distinctive justice responses that respected their particular identity and imagination. If there was a mostly white community which practised a form of healing justice, I wanted to see it and look into this provocative idea.

Plum Village – This is a Vietnamese-initiated Buddhist community in exile in the south of France. Its leader, Thich Nhat Hahn, is a world-renowned Buddhist peacebuilder and one of the key leaders of the Engaged Buddhism movement. David Loy, in a chapter on 'Healing Justice: A Buddhist Perspective', points towards pre-exile Tibetan Buddhism as an example of healing justice (Loy 2001). Plum Village is not based on Tibetan Buddhism but does share much in common with it. Plum Village includes both a monastic and a lay order. Thich Nhat Hahn has written extensively on Buddhist peacebuilding and on the practises of Plum Village. Like Iona Community this community has a practise of receiving 'outsiders' for retreats. I had had no real connection to this group but had read many of the books by Thich Nhat Hahn and respected them.

A different researcher might have chosen different communities, but these three communities kept resurfacing as I did my searching and reviewing of possible sites and measuring them against the purposeful selection criteria.

Research methods: Ways of listening and engaging
This research was not done in a straightforward liner way. Rather multiple cycles or stages were needed – in part so that I could digest what I was learning and in part so that I could see the communities for multiple angles and different seasons. So my data collection and analysis happened simultaneously in a three-stage process.

Stage 1: Selecting sites and developing tentative profiles
The first task was to find communities that fitted the criteria for site selection, purposefully selecting a group of cases and then working to

gain a welcome access to the group. To gain access I sent a personalized letter to each community asking for the community's permission to conduct research alongside them. In those letters, I tried to be clear about who I was, what research I wanted to do, and my motivations in doing this research. I also tried to make clear for them what costs, dangers and opportunities this research could offer them. At this stage of initial contact, I also invited the community to read and comment on anything I had written – including methodology – concerning the case. I made the commitment to offer what I wrote back to them for comment and correction, offering to record their disagreement if there were corrections I could not make in good conscience. I tried to demonstrate my respect for their communities and my desire to find a path together on how to conduct this research in respectful ways. I also made myself available to discuss any questions they had. Each community took between one and two months to discern and decide together if they wanted to participate in the research and, in the end, they agreed. After I had secured funding for the field visits, I proceeded to work out a research protocol with each community as to how to conduct respectful research within the community. The second task of this stage was to work with the literature available, 1. to develop a 'thick' (Geertz 1973) profile of each community (profiles included a general description of the community, a review of healing justice vision and practises and a review of possible dynamics that might be relevant to sustaining such a vision) and 2. to identify existing theories of what sustains healing justice within each community. Data collection focused on primary literature written by members of communities that practise healing justice, together with participatory research that had been done in partnership with the communities. Through careful reading and analysis I drew out descriptions of their visions and practises of healing justice as well as summarized factors and conditions that seemed to function as their barriers or sustainers of healing justice. As many of these sources were not focused directly on healing justice and the dynamics that sustained healing justice, I had to draw those out and weave them together.

Once I had completed all the tentative profiles of the communities, I turned to the final task of this stage, to conduct a preliminary comparative analysis to identify what seemed to be the common themes. Data analysis was an ongoing task. I relied on inductive identification of emergent themes, patterns, and questions. This strategy is called analytic induction.

Denzin (1978) outlines it as a strategy for finding commonalties across diverse cases. It is a method to achieve 'descriptive generalizations or to arrive at causal explanations. It is a strategy that moves from individual cases and seeks to identify what the cases have in common. The common element provides the basis of theoretical generalization'. (De Vans 2001)

Denzin (1978) summarizes six key steps in the process of analytic induction:

1. Specify what it is you are seeking to explain (the dependent variable).

2. Formulate an initial and provisional possible explanation of the phenomenon you are seeking to explain (your theory).

3. Conduct a study of a case selected to test your theory.

4. Review (and revise if necessary) your provisional theory in light of the case or exclude the case as inappropriate.

5. Conduct further case studies to test the revised proposition and reformulate the proposition as required.

6. Continue with case studies, including looking for cases that might disprove the proposition, and revise the proposition until you achieve a causal proposition that accounts for all the cases.

Denzin's process is clearly developed for theory testing rather than theory building. Furthermore, the final step of looking for negative cases is an attempt to prove that the findings have universal standing. As universal application was not a goal of this research and, in fact, offended the nature of healing justice, the final step was dropped. The process would have to be modified for use in the participatory style of theory building. The steps used were similar to Denzin's process of analytic indication for theory testing as stated below:

1. Specify what it is you are seeking to explain (in this case, healing justice).

2. Find diverse cases that share the phenomenon but differ on as many other factors as possible.

3. Conduct a study of each case and draw out the community's theories concerning the phenomenon.

4. Test the community's theories and practise against the other communities.

5. Review (and revise if necessary) your provisional theory in light of the cases.

6. Continue looking for common trends in the case studies until you achieve a set of shared patterns that are present in all cases.

This research followed a standard practise in much qualitative research, which is to make data analysis an ongoing task with data collection rather than a sequential task (Cresswell 2003; Maxwell 2005). This last task of comparative analysis resulted in a set of tentative ideas on the conditions and factors that seemed to sustain healing justice vision and practise. These tentative ideas were then used in the second stage, the field research, in part as an interview matrix. Conducting such data analysis early opened up two main advantages which would be realized in the next stage of field research. First, it allowed the cases to inform each other, as sometimes happens in sequential case study methodology. I could use the tentative findings from one case study to shed light on the experience of another community. This was one way that data analysis prompted further data collection and, in turn, further analysis. Second, building on the ethos of participatory research and grounded theory-building research, the communities were involved in data analysis and in validating or contesting my findings. Such community participation at every stage was encouraged by the ethical guidelines for research for indigenous people. It also fitted my desire for the communities to play a guiding role in understanding, explaining and analysing their approaches to healing justice. By conducting an early round of tentative case studies in my research I could use my field research to test if what I was hearing was really what was happening on the ground. I could also test where I might be misperceiving their ideas. Also I had opportunity to see if ideas that were clearly important in one case study had any equivalent or resonance in another case study.

Stage 2: Field research
A second means of collecting data was through field research, where I used field notes from structured observation of healing justice activities and tape-recorded interviews with leaders and community members. The

interviews followed a topic guide developed out of the general questions of this research, out of a survey of primary literature and out of a comparative analysis of the tentative profiles of the community developed in Stage 1. The topic guide was then made site specific to follow up on missing data, comparative areas of inquiry and to connect more meaningfully with the particular context.

Comparative research often compiles other people's research and brings to it a fresh focus, adds additional insights and brings it into dialogue or tension with other cases. It is often not cost-effective or even possible to do field research in each site. My own research followed this pattern, drawing heavily from other research and writing on these communities. However, I knew that if I could get to each community, the research would have so much more life and spark. Further I would have to engage more deeply and respectfully as I would now be accountable to the very people I would be studying.

Field research was not used as the primary mode of research, as this was not feasible for these multiple case studies. Since the field research was used for deepening and testing existing ideas, shorter field visits provided sufficient engagement. Interviews focus on understanding the community's story with healing justice. Sometimes I told bits of the stories of the other communities as a way of teasing out anything that functioned in a similar manner in their community. Previous researchers had found that individual interviews are more helpful than surveys and group interviews when researching Aboriginal people (Couture and Couture 2003). I knew the individual interviews would be important. Each field visit included various modes of data collection:

> individual interviews (ranging from 38 minutes to 2 hours and 20 minutes, the 28 interviews averaged just over an hour per interview)

> participant observation and non-participant observation of community events and places

> collecting of local written resources and quantitative material relating to healing justice.

My original aim was to spend about two weeks at each community to conduct interviews, observe and participate in the community's life. My plans were shaped by the needs and ethos and practical realities of each community.

The Hollow Water community, Canada, field research occurred over ten days in October–November 2006. I attended a two-day workshop at Hollow Water on envisioning healing in the community, did ten in-depth interviews with the staff, Board and Elders of CHCH in Hollow Water, spent a day collecting medicines with some community members, collected some community documents and had many informal conversations and walks with people at Hollow Water.

The Iona Community, Scotland, field research was conducted between November 2006 and January 2007. Field research included an interview with the Leader of the Community done at the headquarters in Glasgow, Scotland, observation at the Isle of Iona, and a structured email dialogue of seven dispersed members from Scotland, England and the Netherlands. Because their members are not part of a geographic community, I utilized email to conduct a two-month-long conversation which covered every aspect of the case study. In this dialogue I both asked the kinds of questions I asked in interviews and gave them readings from the tentative profile to collect their responses. Interview questions were done before responses to readings so that my tentative profile would not over-influence the language or direction of their responses. Email respondents were given the choice to send messages directly to me or to the whole group. Most sent to the whole group which also provided some very illuminating interaction among community members. This proved a rich data collection method.

The Plum Village, France, field research was conducted over two site visits to the community. The first visit was in the summer of 2006 where I, with my family, attended part of the Summer Retreat, and the second visit was in January of 2007 when I went to the Winter Retreat to interview the monks and nuns at Plum Village. When I requested the community's consent to develop this research they agreed to participate on the condition that before conducting any interviews, I come and learn to practise with them for a week during their Summer Retreat. Both visits were eye opening. In the second visit I was able to interview a diverse collection of nine monks and nuns, and one Order of Interbeing member (a lay order based in the community's teachings). I practised with them and attended many teachings by Thich Nhat Hanh and two by Sister Chân Không. I participated in all of their practises of Sitting Meditation, Walking Meditation, Beginning Anew, Touching the Earth, and Working Meditation. Informally I was able to interact with hundreds of people as the first retreat had about 650 guests and the second retreat about 100 guests.

These visits were designed to be relatively close together, allowing some time for digestion between visits but keeping them close enough together to facilitate the synthesis of ideas. The visits happened between July 2006 and January 2007. The tentative ideas on common themes developed in Stage 1 were significantly refined in this stage and eventually became the basis of Chapter 7, 'Shared Characteristics of Healing Justice'.

The in-depth interviews I conducted were a kind of qualitative interviewing designed to understand the meaning structure of the respondent. In such qualitative interviewing the interviewer must create the conditions for the respondents to open up and reveal their own understandings and experiences, without imposing too many of the interviewer's assumptions and structures on the respondents. I chose such qualitative methodology because of this focus on understanding things from the inside out.

Part of my preparation for interviews was to develop a consent-and-respect form. This form was derived from the individual consent form which is common to many forms of research. In a communal context, following established protocol, the first consent I asked for was communal permission to do the research. I also asked communities to help me develop a research protocol that would draw from their particular ways of knowing and past experience in designing what respectful research would look like in that particular community. Another step in this process was to seek the permission of the particular person to do research with them. As some of the communities questioned the helpfulness of confidentiality, I avoided that term, focusing rather on defining respectful research which included most topics typically covered in a consent-and-confidentiality form.

Stage 3: Drawing connections and checking results

The final stage of this research was to outline the results. The first step was to redraft the case studies of healing justice for each community. Near-to-final drafts of these chapters were sent back to the community (to interviewees who agreed to participate) to invite feedback and response. This verification process was done with the community, as the goal of the research was to try to understand their meaning and approach to healing justice. Only the community really knew if what I was writing actually described them. To respect the fact that I had received a gift from them, I wanted to subject my writing to their scrutiny. I also thought that such a verification process would help to moderate and correct any 'fringe' ideas I had picked up in individual interviews and any unhelpful bias on my part which came into the profiles. I continued to work at redrafting the case studies until I received positive feedback through this verification process. I continued at revisions until I heard comments from the communities like, 'You did a super job, almost so as to think you worked with the team for many years' (S. Klyne, Hollow Water, personal communication, 5 January 2007); 'you have grasped in a very profound way what we are on about' (G. Brown, Iona Community, personal communication, 26 January 2007) or 'I think it's very good… Thank you for your beautiful work' (C. T. Nghiem, Plum Village, personal communication, 19 July 2007). Final changes were made in the light of comments from the verification process.

The second step was to outline and provide argumentation for any common characteristics of healing justice. This involved repeating the 'Denzin's modified comparative analysis procedure', as outlined above, with the completed case studies. The results together with some interpretation are offered in Chapter 7.

The third step was to point towards the meaning of these results for three audiences: those interested in communal practises of healing justice; those interested in restorative justice and those involved in Western governance and justice. This analysis forms the content of the final chapter.

Ethical issues

My whole methodology is in part a search for an ethical way of doing research. I tried to develop a way of doing research that would be seen as ethical by the communities involved, by myself (the researcher) and, it is hoped, by other researchers examining this work. The ethical issues did not function as a safety check tacked onto a project. Ethical ways of research were integral to the whole of the research.

Nevertheless, I did have to wrestle with some ethical questions. Could my research harm the communities and individuals involved? Informed consent was requested both individually and collectively. Furthermore, research protocols were developed in advance and in collaboration with community leaders in such a way that how the research was done and what it focused on was known and agreed to by all parties. Part of the original request to a community to participate included a commitment that I would offer my writing back to the community for comment and that concerns and differences would be either addressed or noted if there was a clear difference between researcher and community. This research was being conducted with the full permission of the community and in each step of the process the attempt was made to conduct research that was respectful of the community. Because this research focused on an area of ethical concern, namely healing justice, it was important that it be conducted in ways that the communities recognized as ethical.

Validity issues

The language of validity is sometimes used in social science research to prove that your research is right. In that research the test of such validity is that a different scientist could repeat the experiment and the results would be the same. Again, this is a throwback to a modern approach not used in this research. Such a modern approach assumes a neutral observer status and a static object position. Neither was assumed in this research. Yet this research was still concerned that wisdom be pursued with integrity and in a way that respected the communities involved. So a number of issues of validity as integrity needed to be addressed.

How do I know this research did not simply reflect my own bias? To deal with bias, I brought to my awareness my personal perceptions about healing justice, and constantly monitored how this might affect how I analysed data. Such purposeful awareness of bias is one accepted practise for responding to bias (Cresswell 2003). Furthermore, as I tried to see how a community understood itself in relation to healing justice, I invited the community to validate or contest my findings. I also reread the transcripts to see where they supported or conflicted with my findings, thereby searching for discrepant evidence.

How do I know that a community was offering good quality information? Again I used a variety of tools. I substantiated claims in interviews and primary sources through participant observation and included only those aspects I could corroborate from at least two sources. I used triangulation methods to see if various methods of data collection pointed in the same direction. By discussing the findings with the community I got help to sort what might be more marginal views from more central views. Furthermore, I compared my findings with existing theory identified in my literature review. But the hardest test was giving what I wrote back to the community to invite response and critique.

How do I know that cases were dealt with consistently? The scientific way to create this validity is to use predetermined categories to try to understand diverse contexts. This approach has often been taken in legal anthropology. However, there have been many who have declared that using such modern scientific grids to understand communities that don't share the same assumptions as modern science does not allow us to fully understand those communities. The standard of consistency was not that of sameness. In fact, the research was done differently at each community. I lived at Plum Village for two one-week visits, whereas I conducted an email dialogue with dispersed members of the Iona Community and only made shorter visits to their headquarters in Glasgow and their retreat centre on the Isle of Iona. I learned very quickly that what worked well to collect rich data in one setting was completely unhelpful in the next. If I wanted consistently rich data, I needed to gather information differently. Consistency in the cases was developed by engaging the communities firsthand in description, comparative analysis and verification of the cases.

Last words

I set out to find respectful, non-colonializing ways of doing research with three diverse traditional communities. I found that such research was both possible and highly rewarding. Respectful research builds not only high quality research outputs but also friendship and lasting connections. The people I met in these communities became my teachers and, in some cases, friends. They are inheritors of old traditions of living life in more healing ways. And they live those traditions in many new and fresh ways. My research set out to try to reflect those ways within the pages of a case study. Through taking the time to develop and keep modifying a methodology based in respect and partnership and through creating multiple cycles of listening and interpreting, I was slowly able to understand how these communities approach healing justice. For me, entering the landscape of these communities was deeply inspiring, awakening and revealing. We now turn to their stories.

Part II – Case Studies: Seeing Healing Justice

Chapter 4

Hollow Water Community

Introduction

The sun peaks over the horizon and a thick fog clings about five feet above the level of the ground. As I drive the two hours north of Winnipeg towards Hollow Water I enter through gates of golden aspens and evergreens. It's an early October morning and the fall of 2006 is in full colour. I know that I come at a time of a change of seasons, not just for the land, but also for the community of Hollow Water that I am going to meet. Hollow Water commonly refers to the four neighbouring communities of Manigotagan, Ahbaming, Seymourville and Hollow Water First Nation in central Manitoba, Canada. Hollow Water First Nation is an Anishinabe or Ojibway community.[1] The other three communities are Métis communities. Together the four communities total about one thousand people.

In significant parts of the restorative justice movement Hollow Water has become almost a mythic story, a story of inspiration to many (Braithwaite 2003a; Cormier 2002; Dickson-Gilmore and LaPrairie 2005; Hadley 2001; Judah and Bryant 2004; Lindon and Clairmont 1998; McCold 2006; Ross 1996). Today Hollow Water is seen as 'the

---

1   Anishinabe (also spelt Ahnishinabe) and Ojibway are used interchangeably in the literature. Ojibway is the more widely understood term but as Hollow Water uses Anishinabe to refer to themselves, I will use this term, unless quoting from a source which uses Ojibway.

most mature and well-accepted of any healing programme in Canada' (Couture 2001b; Dickson-Gilmore and La Prairie 2005) and there are a number who proclaim its success (Aboriginal Corrections Policy Unit 1997; Couture 2001b; Dickson-Gilmore and La Prairie 2005; Jackson and Rubin 1996).

This particular story has grabbed attention for many reasons. First, Hollow Water faced a depth of harm and destruction that startled human sensibility and disturbed the stereotypes of friendly Canadian living. In the 1980s the community was reported to have an alcohol abuse rate of nearly 100 per cent, unemployment over 70 per cent (Couture 2001b), and there was a severe shortage of appropriate housing. As they started to work at community healing they discovered that alcohol abuse and unemployment covered other abuses hidden in the dark corners of Hollow Water, particularly sexual abuse. The community had chronic sexual abuse problems going back three generations and estimates were that 66 per cent–80 per cent of the population had been victims of sexual abuse (Couture 2001b; Dickie and MacDonald 2000; Ross 1996) and 35–50 per cent of the population had been victimizers (Couture 2001; Ross 1996). These harms covered the whole range of sexual abuse. Not just men had victimized others but so had women, children, Elders, parents and extended family members, and all of the victimizers had previously been victims (Bushie 1997c). During this time the community rated its own community health at 0 (having no health or wellness) on a scale of 0–10 (Couture 2001b). Hollow Water was a broken community.

But international attention and inspiration does not come from brokenness alone. In the 1980s Hollow Water and the surrounding communities initiated a healing movement to respond to this brokenness. As sexual abuse lay at the root of many problems, not least of which was harm to children, sexual abuse would, at the beginning, become the focus of a healing movement. Over time the community developed a new partnership with the Western systems of justice and social service based on the needs of the community, a partnership called Community Holistic Circle Healing or CHCH. Hollow Water rejected incarceration as the main mode of dealing with sexual abuse and sought to keep victims and victimizers in the community and to support them on a healing path. To do this they began the long road of returning to some of the traditional teachings and ceremonies. They also developed a 13-step process and protocol for responding to sexual abuse disclosures. Eventually researchers, government officials, and other Aboriginal communities started to notice what was happening. In 2001, after several positive studies, the government commissioned an economic analysis of Hollow Water which showed that in their practise of working at sexual abuse through healing forms of justice only 2 out of 107 victimizers were found to have re-offended, a recidivism rate more than six times lower than the national average rate for sexual abusing (Couture 2001b).[2] The economic analysis also concluded that for every $2 the provincial and federal governments spent on this local healing practise, they received at least $6.21–$15.90 worth of services (Couture 2001b).

I was driving toward a legend. When I decided to learn about healing justice from communities, I expected that I would need to visit Hollow Water. This was confirmed by my review of the healing justice literature in which the Aboriginal communities of Canada featured among the leaders of this movement. Rupert Ross and the journal *Justice as Healing* were presented as two major catalysts in the Aboriginal healing justice movement. Both sources used Hollow Water as one of their key examples of justice as healing. I had to go to Hollow Water.

Not having had previous contact with the community, I explained my motivation for wanting to come to learn from them. The CHCH workers, Board and Elders work by consensus and so my request had to be approved by a wide circle of community members. They did not bother much with my CV or academic background. They wanted to know why I wanted to learn, what I would do with the information, and if they would have space to tell their own story. Most of all I think they wanted to get a sense of who I was to see if they could trust me. Eventually I got word that I could come.

As I drove into the community I came with some fear and trembling. I knew I would be walking next to those whose ability to find healing in the midst of brokenness had inspired people from around the world. I knew I would be walking next to victims of sexual abuse and next to their victimizers. I was going into a culture for which I had deep respect, but which was very different from my own. Would it be possible for me to learn the touch and taste of healing justice?

---

2   Couture reports that Hollow Water has a 2 per cent recidivism rate while the national average for sexual abuse offending in Canada is 13 per cent and the average for all other kinds is 36 per cent. Hollow Water is known for its work with sexual abuse but they also deal with a wide range of other offences.

What I discovered when I arrived in Hollow Water was quite different from what I had read in the books and studies. The Community Holistic Circle Healing organization and the healing momentum in the community were at a low point. In some ways the healing movement had been declining over eight years and just as I arrived CHCH staff together with representatives of the community were beginning to examine what had happened and to re-envision what could happen with healing at Hollow Water. In my interviews hardly anyone mentioned the 13-step process which had inspired the world. As I listened to workers and community members, many of whom had 20 years of experience in the ups and downs of healing, I learned that the story and practises of Hollow Water were not confined to sexual abuse or processes to decrease recidivism. Even while some key outward signs of health were in decline, a much broader and deeper vision of healing justice was emerging. This vision was not based on naive idealism but was rooted in the experience of a 20-year path of working at and, sometimes, failing at holistic healing across the whole community.

First, a word on form. The people I interviewed would not speak in terms of what healing justice means to Hollow Water. They limited their comments more specifically to what it meant to them, or what experience they had had with healing justice. This aversion to speaking of one general, objective story of Hollow Water was instructive for me. Location matters to them. Space for others to see different things matters. Space for change matters. So if I follow their example, I cannot try to tell the general story of Hollow Water which anyone would find. I can only tell of what I experienced and of what had impact on me. I have tried in my analysis to stay close to their words while reporting on what I heard as emerging themes, but I cannot displace myself from who I am and from my experience. My friends at Hollow Water would only laugh at such a thought. Those at Hollow Water have discovered that abuse is about losing one's identity and that the healing path is about rediscovering identity. To write in a way consistent with this insight, I will not try to erase myself from the story. I will share what I heard from the people of Hollow Water in ways that I hope they can recognize. And I will share in a personal way. Perhaps such an approach can help restorative justice researchers to use modes of research which better reflect the visions and values of restorative justice (Ioews and Zehr 2003).

When quoting the people I interviewed I have not given their names. In this I have followed their cultural norm and the practise of other researchers into Aboriginal justice (Ross 1996). Their names are listed in the Acknowledgements and I am very grateful to have had them as teachers. Aboriginal cultures do not tend to have a strong sense of the ownership of words. A person might speak certain words to a particular person at a particular time. Repeating them in a different context may have a very different meaning. Moreover the practise of not quoting names should remind the reader that they see their wisdom as collective and not as individual. Also the people I interviewed might well have chosen different words for the reader than the words they chose for me.

To understand healing justice in Hollow Water it is as important to tell the story of the ups and downs of the healing movement there as it is to describe their vision, practises and ideas. I will try to weave these together as I tell this story in six phases. While these phases follow a somewhat linear timeline, they would be better understood in a circle, where the first phase begins and the last phase ends in the same place, where moving through the phases does not mean leaving the past behind but, rather, that each point in the circle is held in tension with the rest. This is not a straightforward historical account but a way of trying to explore and shine light on the community's collective memory and present practises.

Phase 1: We had everything we needed to live and be connected to Creator[3] (Creation–1860S)

'At the time of contact we had our own structures, healing and language. We had everything that we needed to live and be connected to Creator.'

Elder at Hollow Water

Some begin the story of Hollow Water in 1984 when a group began to meet to talk about what they could do to support healing in their community. That group used whatever they could find that might help, turning first to working at healing in themselves and finding support from Western therapy models. However they eventually discovered that

---

3   'Creator' without the definite article is common language usage for Canadian Aboriginal peoples. Perhaps this usage identifies a closer relationship, like a name. Perhaps it also leaves room for other ideas – not claiming to be the (the one and only) creator.

healing, for them, meant recovering a traditional path. This meant trying to learn what life was like before the abuse took hold, and before colonialism disrupted life in Hollow Water. To really understand what Hollow Water is up to now, we must go back to the beginning, to Creator and to Creation.

Their memories of those pre-colonial times are sketchy. Colonialism actively interrupted the handing down of traditions. Christine Sivell-Ferri (1997) and Basil Johnston (1976) have laid out some of the Anishinabe heritage. Hollow Water is working to bring back their traditions by engaging Elders from inside and outside their community to come and help them learn their traditions again, and by sponsoring projects like a research project into the clan structure to recover whatever they can about how life had once been organized.

Their goal is not to return to some golden age of perfection. Several people told me they do not think life was perfect before colonialism. People have always harmed others, but before colonialism there were ways of structuring life that made harm less likely and there were ways to heal from conflicts as they arose. They want to recover this structuring of life.

One Elder put it this way:

> Some time ago we didn't have the need to have jails, police, mental institutions...all the things that are currently out there that we have to go to for help. We didn't have those things before. We didn't need them. We have to get back to that way of living, that way of being again, so that we don't need those systems.

Those at CHCH seem to believe that healing is about a community returning to their former way of living in which justice and social service systems were no longer needed.

The language of justice does not seem to figure strongly at Hollow Water. They speak of holistic community healing and sometimes wellness. They speak of respect and truthfulness and other virtues. I asked one Elder about this lack of focus on justice, and he said that the whole traditional system working together is justice. Another said that their way of healing is their way of justice. What is clear is that they do not have some prior concept of justice as punishment, or justice as anything which is later balanced against or held in tension with other virtues. To understand what healing justice is at Hollow Water it is necessary to understand their pre-colonial vision and practises.

As best as I can understand the traditional vision of healing justice, that teaching includes a few key dynamics:

➤ Healing justice embodies the Seven Sacred Teachings and 'Living a Good Life'.

➤ Healing justice recognizes you are the land.

➤ Healing justice interconnects and balances.

Healing justice embodies the Seven Sacred Teachings and Living a Good Life

Hollow Water is significant because it is rooted in the Anishinabe way of being (Bushie 1997d; Couture 2001a; Ross 1996; Sivell-Ferri 1997). As Burma Bushie, one of the original leaders of CHCH, says, 'The spirit piece is at the very core' (quoted in Couture 2001b). The Seven Sacred Teachings were given by Creator and handed down through the generations by the Elders. These teachings form the seedbed for healing in Hollow Water. The Seven Sacred Teachings of the Anishinabe include: courage; spiritual knowledge; respect for others, the earth, and for oneself; honesty; humility; love and truth (Bushie 1997d; Couture 2001b). An Elder told me that they form the basis, not just of how to relate to each other, but also to Creator, to the land and to social structures.

These teachings are the law of the Anishinabe. They are not primarily prohibitions against certain behaviours. They are teachings about how to attain what they called *p'mad'ziwin*, translated Living the Good Life. (Couture 2001b; Sivell-Ferri 1997) Hallowell, an American anthropologist, describes *p'mad'ziwin* (Hallowell 1955) as 'life in the fullest sense, life in the sense of health, longevity and well-being, not only for oneself but for one's family. The goal of living was a good life and the Good Life involved *p'mad'ziwin*'. Living the Good Life is expressed by the community in a related concept called *w'daeb'awaewe*, 'the truth as we know it'. Couture claims these two concepts are Hollow Water's guiding core energy (2001b). My research confirms these findings. When asked how to explain healing in Hollow Water to outsiders, one CHCH worker said 'Healing is living'. Numerous respondents said that healing was about learning to be Anishinabe.

Healing justice recognizes you are the land

Creation, meaning the land, the animals and all the many interdependent relationships within it, is central to understanding the Anishinabe approach to life and healing. This theme surfaced in every interview I conducted. For them healing justice is not possible without the right kind of relationship with Creation. They are clear that humans do not live above Creation. They are Creation. Some even suggested that trying to live above, or be stronger than something else, is the root of abuse. For them, change toward healing comes from staying close to Creation. They realize they are dependent on it. One Elder gave me this explanation:

> Once you recognize that as a human being you are the air, the water, the plant life and the animal life, and we take this in to sustain your physical being, once you can see that, understand that, recognize that, I think you are on a good road of learning and becoming complete and being on a healing way.

This primary role of Creation within the Hollow Water approach to healing is supported by other research on the Anishinabe. In describing the Anishinabe worldview Sivell-Ferri says that they see Creation as Creator's gift of beauty and mystery in which humans are the last and most dependent of all creatures (Johnston 1976; Sivell-Ferri 1997). Many of the Anishinabe practises of healing, such as sweat lodge ceremonies, smudging ceremonies and prayers, come out of these teachings of the connections within Creation.

Healing justice recognizes and cultivates interconnection and wholeness

Healing justice flows out of this understanding of creation and of Living the Good Life and, therefore, it follows the laws of interconnectedness and wholeness. For those at Hollow Water healing is about learning how you are connected to yourself, your family, your extended family, your community, your Elders, strangers and the land. All of these are from Creator and as a person at Hollow Water quipped, 'Creator don't make no junk.' Their way of justice works on the logic of connection. Western methods like incarceration work on the logic of disconnection. For those at Hollow Water incarceration only removes people from what they need to heal – the land, the community, the Good Life. Their focus on connection is a double focus. On the one hand, abuse can be understood as harmful experiences passed down through the generations and, therefore, to heal it is important to understand the kinds of abuse present in your family tree. On the other hand, interconnection is about learning about good and healthy connection. It is about learning to see the gift and beauty of each person and how he or she is needed by all the rest. In this way healing understood as expanding positive interconnections creates a holistic community which has members who know who they are and which is compassionately connected to all of creation.

Pre-colonial practises of healing justice

As I understand the traditional vision of healing at Hollow Water, it is embedded in the traditional practises that structured day-to-day life, in particular in the lodges, ceremonies and the clan system.

Ceremony structured the life and imagination of the Anishinabe in pre-colonial times. One Elder told me there was a song for everything, from the daily task of cutting down trees to the special gatherings of a particular ceremony. All of life was ceremony. When asked if these songs were part of justice practises, the Elder immediately agreed. 'Creator is the one who gave us everything. So anytime we use anything on the land we have to acknowledge Creator for gift.' Acknowledging Creator seems to be a major function of much of the ceremony. When I went out with several women of Hollow Water to pick medicine from the river, there were ceremonies an Elder had to perform before we set out and prayers given through tobacco offerings as we picked. They do not see these prayers as magic but as acknowledging Creator. They seem to believe that when we stop acknowledging Creator, negative things start to happen and healing decreases.

Similarly there are a number of different lodges set up in different places for ceremony and for teaching the people the best ways to survive together. These are the sweat lodge, the moon lodge and the Mindowin lodge, to name a few. These lodges, in their very structure and organization, teach about how to live a full life of respect. The Elders are responsible for explaining to people, when they are ready, the meanings of the lodges.

One story that I was told regarding the moon lodge was that traditionally women were held in great respect because they were the only ones who could carry life within them. When women live in the bush in close quarters their menstrual cycles (called their Moon Time) tend to get synchronized. So when their Moon Time was coming, the women would go to the moon lodge. This was a place off in the bush where they would live apart from the men. There would be ceremonies done at these lodges to give thanks to Grandmother Moon and to Creator for the gifts of life. When the moon time was over, the women would return. Some would be pregnant, others not. The men believed that the ceremony made them pregnant. Accordingly the women were held in sacred esteem. When science taught them that the sperm, not the ceremony, made the women pregnant, women became more like objects. Creator was not needed. Respect and sacred esteem vanished. Women and children were abused. Of course there were many other factors involved in the rise of abuse, but those at Hollow Water have learned through the worst kind of experience that not acknowledging Creator for the gift of life has dire, and often unintended, consequences. So the ceremonies and lodges teach them how to live a life of respect and acknowledgement for all the sacred gifts of Creator.

Before colonization the Anishinabe relied for survival on the clan system as a way of organizing life so that each person was cared for and had clear responsibilities to care for others. I was told a number of times that when you are assigned a clan the clan represents a responsibility to yourself, to the community and to the world. Families are not necessarily all in the same clan, so the clan system has a cross-stitching effect of connecting various sections of the community with a responsibility to work together for the benefit of the whole. An Elder explained the purpose of the clan system to me.

> In the clan system, each specific clan has a responsibility. Each person has a clan and each family has a kinship base, gender and family roots. You all know what that responsibility is. Along with knowing your clan and your responsibility you are also taught the Good Life. That's a lodge we don't have a home for yet – the Mindowin lodge. In that lodge you are given teaching on the good life, how to live the good life, and how you are connected to the rivers, to the wind and to all elements. All that is explained in the lodge. And everything in the lodge is significant to living the good life. If you follow that way and if you follow the clan responsibility, you learn the teaching of the law. Those are the basis of what keeps you centred and grounded in your walking… That means everything that you do is important in living the good life, not just responding to abuse… You grew up and you knew exactly what to expect if you didn't follow. If you harmed someone it was not just harming him,

but yourself and your whole clan… If you harm someone from another clan, your whole clan is responsible.

In this first phase of pre-colonial contact, Hollow Water Community had visions and practises of traditional law which led to but also embodied the Good Life.

Phase 2: We lost everything over the last 130–140 years (1860s–continuing)

The ceremonies which were always there and always used for wellbeing were put aside by an external system that saw that this is what maintains these people. Our people were seen as being in the way of progress. As long as we maintained that the land is sacred, the resources of Mother Earth are sacred, that they need to be protected and used in a sustainable and responsible way, we were seen as being in the way. And that was the main idea of colonialization – a breakdown of a system that protected the people and the source of life…so that capitalism could gain momentum.

That is how one Elder explained colonialism to me. Many others also have come to see that the forces of colonialization and assimilation lay behind the extraordinarily high rates of abuse.

In Hollow Water what was clear is that the many systems that were supposed to be helping the community – the penal, social service and education systems, the local community supports and the churches – were actually failing the community (Community Holistic Circle Healing Hollow Water 1996). The arrival of these systems caused far-reaching loss of cultural values. Here are some of these losses:

> language in which is embedded the sacred teachings and the imagination of how to survive together

> connection to land which taught them about Creator and about how to structure life together

> traditional ceremonies and ways of healing and cleansing

> transfer of parenting and survival skills (which was broken by the residential school system)

> relationships between Elders and youth

> respected place traditionally given to women

➤ traditional governance traditions as the Indian Act forcibly sidelined traditional leadership for new short-term elected leadership

➤ worldview and relationship with Creator

➤ knowledge of how to respond to conflicts, as justice and social
services and churches tried to take control of community problems

➤ economic well-being

➤ traditional employment

➤ sense of identity

➤ awareness of the sacredness of life.

These losses of the sacredness of life found expression in a most unsacred
way: sexual abuse of women and children, the very symbols of sacred
life. The sexual abuse epidemic in Hollow Water began with colonialism.
Colonialism destroyed the social order and traditional mechanisms which
taught a practise of a life based on sacred respect. Other effects of these
losses were family violence, alcoholism, oppression of each other and
internalized anger.

The devastating effects of the policies of colonialism and assimilation of Canadian Aboriginal peoples have been well documented by
other studies (Battiste and Henderson 2000; Dirks 1992; Jackson and
Rubin 1996) and do not need to be repeated here. In the 130 years of
the second phase the Hollow Water community lost everything through
both the attempts at assimilation and the attempts at helping that came
from various parts of the Western communities.

Phase 3: Hitting bottom and initiating healing (1984–1993)

In 1984, a group, later named the Resource Team, started to meet to
see how they could support community healing. The group consisted
of about 24 people, mostly women, and included representatives of
many of the service sectors of the community: Native Drug and Alcohol
Programme, Welfare Administrator, Child and Family Services Director,
community volunteers, Catholic and Mennonite church representatives,
chief and council, mayors, school representatives. The group was open
to anyone and met every two weeks. Their focus was to create a healthy
community. Significantly, the initial focus was not sexual abuse. They

looked at alcohol abuse and many issues to do with their youth (Bushie 1997a; Ross 1995). They could see complex problems in the youth and the tried to find ways to intervene and support.

However, they quickly learned that the first step was to work at healing for themselves. Most of the members were alcoholics. They knew they had to be on a healing journey themselves if they were to assist in the community healing. A core group went to the New Direction Training at the Alkali Lake community. Eventually this group, and others in the community, started to understand that part of the roots of their alcoholism and the problems the young people were having lay in sexual abuse. They hosted a community workshop entitled 'Nutrition and Health'. At this workshop a survey revealed that nine out of ten people in attendance had been sexually abused or had abused others or both. The group started to see attention to sexual abuse as the necessary beginning to reclaiming community ownership of their problems and the broader issues of community health.

Around this time a young girl disclosed that she had been molested by an uncle. The uncle went to jail and the girl began a long road of drinking and drugs. Many wondered how this kind of justice served the girl, the uncle or the community. The community decided they could no longer sit by and watch what the system was doing to their community. However, they needed help.

In 1989 they organized a two-year training course on sexual abuse and recruited people from each of the surrounding communities. Some of CHCH current workers are still from the first group of 12 who took this training. They learned about the signs and symptoms of sexual abuse, and for many of them this training opened up secrets of abuse they had hidden from even their own awareness. Supported by the Resource Group these people began to take a number of initiatives to spark healing in the community.

A lot of sexual abuse would happen at drinking parties, so when those working at healing heard of such a party going on, they would start to march in the streets of the community and carry signs saying, 'No more abuse'. They wanted to state publicly that this kind of abuse was happening and was unacceptable.

To try to break through the silence and taboos against talking about sexual abuse they got 24 people who were ready to share their own stories. They mapped out the community and set out in twos or threes to speak to everyone to share their story of abuse that had happened in this community. They did this over seven days. Their stories opened the floodgates. Many disclosures followed, especially among the youth. This was an exciting but very fragile time. Victims were often blamed, and some tried to commit suicide. Many of the victimizers were in power positions in the community. The Resource Team had to figure out what to do with disclosures, how to confront victimizers, how to relate to the Western systems of justice and social services and how to keep the community in the driver's seat of a holistic community healing movement.

The Resource Team recognized that the justice system was failing them on many fronts. When victims did disclose, charges were often dropped because when the police came to investigate no one would talk to them due to a lack of trust. When victimizers were sent to prison they often came back more violent and less responsible. When the victims, often children, did go to court, the justice system seemed to re-victimize them. The Resource Team saw it as their job to protect the victims and the community, especially the children, from the justice system. So they made a new partnership with the justice system based on the needs of the community. One of the leaders of this new model called the partnership at this initial stage, the 'combination of the law and the will of the community'.

> Inherent in the Hollow Water model is the combined power of the law and the will of the community confronting abusers with the hard choice of following a healing path or facing serious consequences... (Bushie 1999)

This partnership, named the Community Holistic Circle Healing or CHCH, developed a 13-step process to confront abuse within the community and a protocol with the various arms of the justice and social service systems for how this would happen.

CHCH 13-step process
In each case the team as a whole works through the 13-step process. They believe this helps to work at wholeness and to resist the fragmented and compartmentalized approach so common in Western methods.

1. *Disclosing* – The CHCH process receives disclosures and, unlike most restorative justice initiatives, the workers investigate and work with offenders even as they are denying responsibility. At the disclosure stage, the goal is to start to attend to the needs

of the victim. In two cases the victimizer disclosed abuses they committed without a victim coming forward. If the victim is a child, the police are informed immediately. An intervention team consisting of representatives from the justice system, the child protection service, the community mental health service and the community conducts an initial investigation. They try to determine what actually took place. Generally CHCH workers do their own police work as they have developed a better trust relationship with the community than the police have. They use their own relationships with, and knowledge of, the people involved to aid in the healing process.

2. *Establishing safety for the victim* – This is done by caringly recording their story. Generally victim's stories are believed. If the victim is a child and the victimizer is a direct family member, the child is usually taken out of the home and is placed in another home within the community. This home would be a home in which the family has been trained in issues of victimization and healing (Bushie 1997b). The CHCH team tries to work toward healing at every step of the process. Providing support for a victim is critical to creating the conditions to break the patterns of unhealthy relationships and to create or strengthen healthy ones. Victims always get a worker assigned whether or not they want to work at things. This is done so the victims know they always have someone they can call.

3. *Confronting the victimizer* – The first step is for the whole CHCH team to meet and plan the intervention and the confrontation of the offender. Confronting can be a long process, and the victimizer is expected to deny the offence and to use what power he or she has to control or manipulate the situation. Often people who have previously been victimizers have the greatest potential to confront victimizers and call them to account on their denial issues (Bushie 1997c). Even when victimizers admit guilt they are not fully believed, since, at the beginning, they often only admit to small parts of the story to avoid jail. Ultimately the CHCH team want to make sure victimizers are serious about doing the hard work of the healing journey (Bushie 1999). The

initial confrontation may take place in the person's house, a community place, a church or sometimes out on the land where you can 'let nature do its work' (Bushie 1997a). Again, the goal is to make victimizers feel safe enough to acknowledge their responsibility. The initial confrontation can take several minutes or several hours. The goal is to get the victimizers to acknowledge their problems. They are encouraged to admit the charges as this initiates the healing journey. Pleading guilty means that children do not need to take the stand if a case were to go to court and protects the victim from the harm of having to testify. Victimizers are given four days to decide whether to go with CHCH down the healing path or to go through the Western court system. When someone confesses they are taken to the Royal Canadian Mounted Police (RCMP) to give a voluntary full statement about the incident and also about any other abusive behaviour. The RCMP charge the person just on the initially disclosed abuse and then, after having been seen by the magistrate, the person is released back to CHCH custody.

4. *Supporting the victimizer's spouse or parent* – When the victimizer is confronted the CHCH team fans out to those most connected to the harm. Their goal is to give everyone the same information, to begin to break the patterns of silence and manipulation and to offer as much support as possible to those involved. The spouse naturally finds such disclosures very difficult. Some participate, consciously or not, in supporting systems of denial. Some simply need the care of the community as they learn such disturbing information about their spouse.

5. *Supporting the family and community* – The goal of healing is to strengthen the family and the community. The families of the victim and the victimizer are often dealing with multiple layers of harm involving both more victims and more victimizers. Hence, dealing with abuse can trigger all kinds of other trauma. The team makes sure that each family member has someone they can call after the circle closes. This, they say, is key for the healing process (Bushie 1997a). Confronting the victimizers is only the beginning of the process of getting the families to shift from a blame response to a healing response that is guided by the Seven Sacred Teachings (Bushie 1997c).

6. *Meeting of the assessment team with the police (RCMP)* – The CHCH team has negotiated an arrangement with the justice system that charges are laid, but the community is given time to confront victimizers. CHCH wants to encourage victimizers to take a healing path and to demonstrate that they are serious (Bushie 1999). This process can take anywhere from several months to a couple of years. Victimizers can choose to go through the court process and face jail (in which case, CHCH still tries to support them and the victim) or they can commit themselves to work on a process towards healing (Healing Contract) with CHCH, an option which does not include incarceration. When a victimizer commits to the healing process the CHCH asks the courts for at least four months to determine that the victimizer is serious about healing and not just wanting to avoid jail.

7. *Conducting circles with the victimizer* – Victimizers are expected to tell their stories and work at dealing with their problems with multiple groups of people. They are also seen as out-of-balance and in need of educating about what it means to be Anishinabe, to live in balance and to live a life guided by the Seven Sacred Teachings. The staff worker who does the initial confrontation becomes the victimizer's worker if he or she decides to work on a healing path. The first circle focuses on confession to the CHCH workers and on taking responsibility. The second circle is with the whole nuclear family and focuses on taking responsibility in this wider group. Sometimes the second circle with the family is used to help a person move to full responsibility. The power of the relationships within the family may be enough to pull a victimizer out of denial into full responsibility (Bushie 1997a). The third circle is the final circle and consists of the whole extended family. It is used to encourage the victimizer to admit guilt, if he or she has not already done so, and to listen to the wider community. Each circle is a time to remind people of the Seven Sacred Teachings which underline much of the healing work. In this way they encourage healing by rooting people in a sense of who they are as a people. A treatment plan and Healing Contract is drawn up for the victimizer. CHCH workers report that in the last ten years they have been using more and more traditional ceremonies as part of the plan.

8. *Conducting circles with victim and victimizer* – By the time the victim and victimizer meet in a circle they and their families have been working at their own speed through a long process. When the time is right they come into a circle together. Initially this is not a time for the offender to speak, but for the victim to speak to the victimizer and to say what was done to them and how it has affected them. The circle is guided by the victim's pace. The circles are usually small, comprising two workers, the victim and the victimizer. The CHCH team is there to 'support them, pray for them, and use the medicines' (Bushie 1997a). A treatment plan is also drawn up for victims to aid in their path of healing.

9. *Preparing the families of the victim and the victimizer for the Sentencing Circle* – Beginning four days before a Sentencing Circle happens, each night there is a sweat ceremony in the sweat lodge. The victim and family are invited and told that the victimizer and family are also invited. If for religious reasons someone does not want to participate in the sweat they are invited to come and sit outside the sweat lodge as others sweat for them. Traditionally sweats were used for cleansing of the body, the mind, the emotions, and the Spirit; people came to bring complex conflicts and to connect with Creator (Bushie 1997a).

10. *Preparing the victimizer's family for the Sentencing Circle* – The victimizer's family also is invited to participate in the sweats in preparation for the special gathering. The victimizer has a number of roles in preparing the sweat lodge building and in participating in traditional activities such as 'smudging' the building to prepare it for healing activity. Smudging uses the smoke of sacred herbs for spiritual and emotional cleansing before the Creator and is often performed before a significant gathering.

11. *Conducting a Sentencing Circle* – Initially sentencing happened in the Western court, but since 1993 the community has held its own Sentencing Circle. Here sentencing happens by court judge but through dialogue with the community. On the day of the event there is a sunrise pipe ceremony, flags are hung and the building is smudged. This is done to ask the Creator to come and help. As one worker said to me:

> You are not the one that makes the offenders change. It's Creator. It's the circle. It is not us. We are just there to facilitate. I

can't heal. I'm not the healer. Every time we have a circle we asked Creator to come and help us. We always start with a prayer and end with a prayer.

Everyone gathers in a circle. An eagle feather has high spiritual significance. In special gatherings only the person who holds it has permission to speak. The eagle feather goes clockwise around the circle the first time, and everyone introduces themselves and says why they are there. The second time around those that want to will speak to the victim in an attempt to absolve them of guilt, to build them up and to celebrate their courage. They may also wish to transform the views of the community which sometimes blames the victim. In the third circle of the eagle feather the focus is on the victimizer. People are invited to share how the offence made them feel and what expectation they have of the victimizer to put things right for the victim. The fourth circle is for giving recommendations as to what needs to happen with all the people involved, for the victimizer, for the victim and for the community. The team gives recommendations to the judge based on the whole process, but the whole community also is invited to give recommendations. In three Sentencing Circles which have occurred so far, the first of which involved 200 members of the community and the second and third involving about a 100 people each time, only one person recommended jail. The first Sentencing Circle prompted other victimizers to spontaneously and publicly confess to the community what they had done and to start a healing path. The purpose of this form of gathering is to encourage community healing and to allow the court to hear from those most affected by the victimization (Hollow Water Community Holistic Circle Healing 1995). The sentence comes in the form of a Healing Contract to be completed under the supervision of CHCH. Elements of that contract are spelled out in detail. Working at a Healing Contract is usually a three–five year process which includes counselling, support groups and multiple community circles where victimizers have to take responsibility for their efforts to date, try to understand the causes of their behaviour and how their behaviour affects others and try to work toward healing with victims, extended family and the broader community (Bushie 1997b). Often traditional ceremonies are included as part of the Healing Contract. Hollow Water's Sentencing Circle differs from some others in that it is not an attempt at community involvement at the end of a foreign process of establishing guilt. Hollow Water's Sentencing Circle is one step in a long journey of healing for the whole community. This journey started long before the Sentencing Circle and it will have to continue long after. Here the community marks a significant step in a healing journey for victim, for victimizers and for the community or, alternatively, to mark the failure to try to walk a healing path. These gatherings end with everyone, including victim, victimizer and judge, taking part in a feast.

12. *Sentencing review* – Every six months for the duration of the Healing Contract there is a review circle. These were started after workers realized that after sentencing victimizers tended to backslide and workers did not have the resources to keep them on track. In the sentencing review the community circle is reconvened and victimizers have to answer to the broader community for their actions, rather than to the worker. The workers find this is really helpful in keeping people on track (Bushie 1997b).

13. *Cleansing ceremony* – Before this ceremony and feast can be held the circle of the community is reconvened to update the community on progress, to check if there are any outstanding issues or reasons why they should not see this process as closed and to work at issues of reintegration and of strengthening the community. The successful conclusion of the Healing Contract is marked by ceremonies.

Over the five years of this phase, Hollow Water worked at youth issues, alcohol abuse, sexual abuse and designed a healing programme in their community which worked in partnership (including funding) with various arms of the provincial and federal government. More importantly they started to heal from within.

They developed a process that recognizes the victimizer as a member of the community (rather than some Western processes which suspend the victimizer's rights as a member of the community). As one CHCH worker put it, you just can't give up on people. Speaking of a victimizer she said:

He's always going to be here. His kids are here. Don't give up on this person. Keep at him or her until they understand that our focus is to one day have a healthy community.

Upon reflection on this phase, it seems to me that Hollow Water developed this process after stumbling on a number of key healing insights:

➤ Communities need to deal with their own harms rather than having them diverted to foreign systems.

➤ Healing starts with the self. Those wishing to support holistic community healing must themselves be on a healing journey. CHCH workers are included. They have to stay sober, have to share their own stories of abuse and need the circles of support as much as the victims and the victimizers.

➤ Healing is a communal journey. Individualistic methods of health and justice never made sense or bore much fruit in Hollow Water. As one CHCH worker told me:

> When you go to the therapist you walk out alone. At CHCH you don't walk out alone. We all go with you. We are all healing. When one is hurt it affects all. Like a family.

➤ Healing must shift from symptoms to root causes. The Resource Team began by focusing on a number of symptoms having to do with youth issues and alcohol abuse. To respond meaningfully to those symptoms they had to dig to the deeper root causes. These had to do with sexual abuse, often in childhood, and with a community journey disrupted by colonialism. Holistic community healing must create the space for victims and victimizers to work at healing their own childhood harms and, at the same time, create safe conditions for children.

➤ Healing justice must be seen through the lens of seven generations of change. At Hollow Water people are not only concerned with individuals. They are trying to bring an end to generations of harm by initiating generations of health and healing. Following their Anishinabe teaching they work with longer spans of time. Seven generations is the proverbial measure. The teaching of Seven Generations is to understand an action that we contemplate today by its impact on the children seven generations to come (Ross 1996). Also the harms of today should be understood in light of the decisions made in the past seven generations. This broader perspective does not just include the patterns and behaviours of individuals but also of communities, nations, and structures and even of Creation itself.

➤ 'Healing is a life-long journey, not a therapy but a way of life.' These are the words of a CHCH worker which capture themes which came up in most interviews. Healing justice is not like penal justice which is supposed to be completed after you've 'done your time'. Walking a healing journey is a life-time path and involves all areas of your life.

Phase 4: Building momentum and returning to the teachings (1994–1999)

This is the phase outsiders often refer to when speaking of Hollow Water, partly because a number of key reports come out of this period or reflect back on it. Rupert Ross's *Return to the Teachings* (1996) and the National Film Board's film *Hollow Water* (National Film Board of Canada 2000) introduced the story of Hollow Water to many groups around the world. Furthermore, there were government-commissioned reports by Theresa Lajeunesse (1993, 1996) and by Couture (2001b) which reported on the successes of Hollow Water reflecting back on this period. Couture reported a 2 per cent recidivism rate of those who had participated in the CHCH processes. Four Directions, an Aboriginal justice NGO, came out with a report which included a detailed review of the community (Four Directions International 2001). While there were a few criticisms offered, most notably by Lajeunesse, these reports were generally very positive. In fact, they stated there were many signs that the community was flourishing, observing the following:

➤ Healthy vision for how to live life had increased (Four Directions International 2001).

➤ Drunkenness was disappearing; the majority of the community is sober (Four Directions International 2001).[4]

➤ Overall violence had decreased (Couture 2001b).

➤ Education was being completed by more people (Couture 2001b) and more were getting higher education (Four Directions International 2001).

---

4   Couture confirms that alcohol addiction is down but does not quantify this claim.

➤ Unemployment was no longer a major issue (Four Directions International 2001).

➤ Networking relationships outside the community had increased (Four Directions International 2001).

➤ Holistic health of children had improved (Couture 2001b).

➤ Community resources were broadening (Couture 2001b).

➤ Ownership of issues had increased (Couture 2001b; Four Directions International 2001).

➤ Ceremonies had more participants (Couture 2001b; Four Directions International 2001).

➤ Traditional ways were growing in strength (Four Directions International 2001).

➤ 'Dependency mentality' was beginning to dissipate (Four Directions International 2001).

➤ Victims reported being satisfied that they had a stake in outcomes, were feeling understood, and were fostering within themselves community and cultural pride (Lajeunesse 1993).

➤ Taboos had lifted against talk about sexual abuse and dealing with it (Couture 2001b).

➤ Respect for others in both the nuclear and extended family contexts was taught by parents (Couture 2001b).

➤ Relocating back home to Hollow Water by band members was happening (Couture 2001b).

➤ Safeness of the community was now acknowledged by everyone (Couture 2001b).

As the community began to heal, they began to see more clearly the path they needed to follow. First CHCH articulated a position paper on incarceration in which they listed the reasons they rejected incarceration. These included:

➤ Judgment belongs to Creator; when used by humans it works against the healing process.

➤ Incarceration does not deter offenders and does not make the community safer.

➤ Incarceration keeps people from taking responsibility, reinforces the silence and therefore promotes, rather than breaks, the cycle of violence.

➤ A legal system with a lengthy process which presumes innocence until guilt is proven means no accountability, and it sets the conditions for re-offending.

➤ People return from jail having been put out of balance by being told that 'they have paid for their crime'; now, out of balance and believing that they are done, they are more dangerous to the community than before they went in (Community Holistic Circle Healing Hollow Water 1996).

Second, and intimately related to the first, CHCH saw that holistic community healing required them to return to the traditional teachings. This return to tradition has been a slow movement because the community had been so thoroughly traumatized that the traditional teachings have been forgotten, or at least those who remembered did not feel safe in sharing them. Some of the churches in Hollow Water have taught that traditional things are evil while others have encouraged and participated in traditional ceremonies. At the beginning Elders from other communities had to be brought in to help them remember their traditions and create the space where they might practise these traditions (National Film Board of Canada 2000). Even now for many of the victims and victimizers, the first time they hear of the traditional teachings is when they get involved with the CHCH programme. In trying to return to a more traditional path the people at Hollow Water turned to wherever they could to find help. Sometimes this was to the Cree (at times a historic enemy), sometimes people from across the US border and sometimes from other Anishinabe. They pieced together a traditional approach which fits their identity and is similar to the Anishinabe of pre-colonial times. Today many CHCH workers report going to both church and traditional ceremonies. For some this had been a difficult balance in the past but has become more acceptable.

The 13-step process did not change much during this phase, but the supporting ethos became more rooted in traditional ways. Members of the healing movement brought back the sweat lodge, pipe ceremonies and smudging. Just walking through the offices and surrounding grounds, I noticed many signs of traditional practises. A large teepee was set up outside the offices. Behind it was a sweat lodge. Out towards the woods was the traditional ceremony ground with flags on trees, community fire circles and, inside the woods, traditional fasting and vision quest grounds. For many CHCH workers, traditional culture is the source of life to the healing journey. The ceremonies represent the teachings woven into the physical surroundings. As one Elder put it:

> To us ceremonies and everyday life can never be separated. It is a complete package. It's not religion. It can't be separated.

The sweat lodge is used for cleansing for the person and the community. One worker explained to me that the sweat lodge helps them spiritually by giving them the strength to continue the healing path. They do not seem to expect a shortcut on the healing path, to be healed instantly and fully. But they do expect the traditional culture to be a source of much healing.

In Hollow Water CHCH workers also work with Christian community members who are not interested in traditional culture. They find ways of supporting their Christian spiritual journey so that the physical, emotional, spiritual and mental are all in balance, thus applying a traditional insight in 'non-traditional' ways.

Other traditional activities include the Sacred Fire, which is a quarterly community activity which begins and ends with a community feast. This fire is kept alive for four days for prayers for healing. Once a year the community also celebrates Black Island Days. Black Island is an island nearby where most of the community go for a week of the summer. Here they sleep in tents and organize various activities. Alcohol is not allowed. Community members report that 'everything is different there' and that 'people just automatically care for each other's kids, there are kids that come with no food and others just take care of them'. Black Island Days provide a time of being together on their traditional grounds, a community close to creation.

Victims, victimizers and the whole community were encouraged to participate in these activities as part of their healing. Healing includes learning who you are and how you are connected to the rest of the world. For the workers and for those they were working with, this traditional approach bore much fruit. Sentencing Circles in 1993, 1995 and 1998 were large community events and included a number of traditional elements which were offered as options to participants.

Although some see CHCH as an alternative justice programme the workers of CHCH now see their work as returning the community to traditional ways. This return includes doing justice in ways that come out of their traditions. However, it is a problem when victimizers see CHCH just as an alternative to the incarceration programme. They want victimizers to get to the point where they are serious about healing, not just avoiding incarceration. They want victims and victimizers to get to a point where they can be a healing resource to the broader community, rather than seeing the abuse as something dealt with by experts. CHCH works because it is rooted in a holistic spiritual vision.

During this phase community holistic healing became more and more about returning to the traditions, and learning to live in the way of the ancestors, that is, with love, respect, and a strong sense of identity as Anishinabe. In Hollow Water healing is not a programme or project that could be done by a small set of experts. Healing is the work of Creator. It is a spiritual practise where community members can facilitate the coming together of the circle, but it is clear that Creator is the source of healing justice.

During this phase healing justice was well researched and reported to be more effective than anything else in Canada in working with sexual abuse victims. All the studies during this phase showed evidence of some measure of success.

The voice of the critics

Hollow Water's healing movement is not without its critics, both from inside and from outside. In the earliest evaluation Therese Lajeunesse reported that a victim had been forced to disclose her story to a community circle when she would have preferred to go through the courts (1993). In a follow-up study Lajeunesse found that, while the community was generally supportive of the programme, only a relatively small percentage had participated. She also raised a concern that as the CHCH process gives power to networks of families such power could be used to act on larger political and social tensions. She reported that, despite community involvement and support groups, neither victims nor offenders felt much community support (1996).

More recently Dickson-Gilmore and La Prairie outline several other concerns about the model. These include a conspicuous involvement of the 'outside' legal system, concerns that victims are secondary to the CHCH process and concerns that requiring full disclosure of all past abuses in a 'voluntary statement' to the Royal Canadian Mounted Police (RCMP) may represent a dangerous departure from the victimizer's due process rights (2005). They also question Couture's methodology in finding a recidivism rate of just less than 2 per cent. Couture's method measures recidivism as being tracked by the Offender Management System which reports where offenders have been apprehended and convicted of a federal offence.

The criticisms do not seem to be fatal. They point toward potential excesses or dangers without actually questioning the basic direction or conception of healing in Hollow Water. In fact, all of these critics recognize that on balance Hollow Water is a powerful story of healing in Canada and a true community movement.

There are some criticisms from within Hollow Water that move a little deeper. The CHCH staff themselves seem to have grown to a new understanding that their goal is not to work narrowly at reducing sexual abuse offences. Rather their goal is to (re)establish a healthy community rooted in Anishinabe identity. This is a radical goal with implications far beyond what is normally thought of as justice. And yet this is the path that those in Hollow Water are trying to explore. Another internal criticism has to do with how CHCH can draw on traditional wisdom and also relate to a commoditized world. Paying for traditional practises was formerly forbidden. Yet Hollow Water lives in new times and sees holistic community healing as including an economic vision which includes paying their staff. They see this as more sustainable than a volunteer or charity model. How this will be resolved is not clear.

Phase 5: 'The community is not in the driver's seat at this time' – Momentum Sliding (1999–2006)

Over this eight-year period the healing movement at Hollow Water went into a backward slide, even as it continued to broaden its approach to healing.

There were two key indicators of this slide. First was that Sentencing Circles stopped. At the time of my research the last one was in 1998 and they were trying to plan one for 2007. Second, sexual abuse disclosures stopped. From 2002–2006 there were no sexual abuse disclosures, signifying the community no longer felt safe or trusted the CHCH workers. These are devastating marks of problems for a holistic community healing movement, signifying the community's partial withdrawal of participation in the movement.

I asked many questions to try to understand this slide and heard many different ideas. Concerning Sentencing Circles, there were victimizers ready and waiting for circles to happen. But Sentencing Circles didn't happen. As the circles were key times of healing, this seemed to facilitate the community slide. Part of the reason for the lack of circles seems to be a breakdown in the relationship with the Western justice system. Funding from the justice system has continued but is still at 1993 levels as of Fall 2006. Moreover, key figures in the system that worked with the community in earlier phases are no longer there, and CHCH workers feel there is less understanding with new officials.

CHCH also went through a major leadership transition in 1999 when one of the founding leaders left the programme, but not the community, for another job. The new leader had a different style and perhaps different priorities. CHCH started to be restructured more hierarchically. The CHCH morale, which had been quite high, began to slip. Bickering and gossip increased. Use of circles for workers to support each other decreased. New people were hired but without clear roles, orientation, training or mentoring. Some workers got into an 'I'm not paid to do that' mindset. Initially wages had been the same for everyone, but that started to change as some workers completed Bachelor of Social Work programmes in 2000. The disparities created friction with other workers. Some workers went into reproduction mode, trying to reproduce their previous successes without learning new things and inviting people to come and be involved in the growth movement. Some workers seemed no longer to follow a healing journey personally and the boundaries of acceptable behaviour for a CHCH worker were pushed as at least one worker admitted to using drugs and alcohol when off work.

CHCH was a programme within Child and Family Services (CFS) and was housed in the same building. In 2005 the director of CFS felt the pressure for change from staff, so CFS was relocated from CHCH offices to the Band and Council offices. This was a highly visible marker that those who talked about healing and health could not get along themselves. When Burma Bushie was rehired as Coordinator of CHCH her role was different from her previous time in leadership. The Resource

Team, a cross-section of the community supporting the work, was gone. So were other leaders who had shared particular areas of responsibility. Some looked to Burma to be the single spearhead to reengage the community movement. But a single leader could not dictate holistic community healing. Besides, Burma was ill. Reeling from its split, the programme continued to struggle. In a 2006 envisioning workshop which I attended, CHCH admitted that the poor relationship with CFS and Band Council was just fuelling mistrust and confusion in the community. CHCH had lost much integrity and credibility.

Continued marks of healing and growth

However, during this time CHCH continued to expand its ways of doing healing. In 2001 they recovered the traditional summer ceremony which includes a four-day vision quest and fast from all food and water. Those who choose to can fast for their health or for the health of the community. These fasts and vision quests have been held in each of the last six years. People report that the fast helps healing by creating a time to connect with the Creator and to reflect on the interconnections within creation. A number reported having visions, mostly of people who had died and, perhaps, whom they needed to let go, to forgive or to receive encouragement from. It is a time to slow down and connect with spiritual things.

CHCH introduced four new programmes during this time:

➤ *Wilderness Therapy* – This programme takes mostly youths and young adults into the wilderness as part of educating people into healthier ways of living and reconnecting them with traditional activities. They camp together, hunt, listen to Elders and sometimes work with the dog sled teams as a way of healing. In these settings people reconnect with the land, the Elders and ultimately with Creator. Some trips are organized with the school while others are more informal in organization. Some links are made between victimizers and victims, who are encouraged to be part of the wilderness programme and the dog teams. CHCH workers and school staff testify that these times in the wilderness have a profound healing affect.

➤ *Sewing Club* – Sewing Club is an informal time for Elders to get together. The process of doing traditional activities also encourages them to talk about things that happened to them.

➤ *Traditional Dance* – This programme, started in 2005, reintroduces Powwow dancing and singing into the community. This dancing is for exercise, but CHCH sees it as helping people find their traditional identity through practising dance as a sacred bond between a dancer and Creator. Some of those who have been initiated into the Powwow circle have gone on to learn their traditional names, get their colours and learn their clan, all marks of Anishinabe identity. The hope is that such rootedness in identity leads to respectful living.

➤ *Returning to Spirit Trainings (RTS)* – RTS is a training which Hollow Water has borrowed. It is a resource set up to help Aboriginal communities heal from the abuse and fall out of residential schools. Many CHCH workers are taking this training and point towards it as one of the sources of hope and motivation for their work. Through a series of five-day trainings RTS looks at issues of disempowerment and life patterns based in brokenness, and builds toward concrete ways of letting go and building positive identity.

CHCH works in partnership with the local school on a number of projects such as health week, quarterly health symposiums, wilderness therapy programmes and art therapy. It also encourages the school's Anishinabe language-immersion programme.

Expanding vision of holistic healing

As the practises of healing justice have expanded so has the vision. While their vision has always been a holistic community vision, as members of Hollow Water have matured in their healing and deepened their rootedness in traditional ways, they have come to articulate the healing journey to be one of nation-building and self-sufficiency. Sometimes this is communicated as economic or community development, but these concepts are used to point back towards a particular kind of nationhood. They recognize that the community is hugely dependent on the government through the welfare system, which they estimate includes 60 per cent of the community, but also through the Indian Act, which mandates particular kinds of governance, and through CHCH, which is funded by the government. Their desire is to create an economic base where they do not have to rely on the government. They recognize it is insufficient to try to help people heal from the pain of abuse and colonialization and to advocate healthy ways of living when people cannot get a job.

Note that for the Hollow Water healing movement, nationhood is quite distinct from nation state. They are not seeking equality of power with the Western state system. For at least some of them, both the state system and the notion of equality are based a conception of violent power. As explained to me equality seeks to find a balance between two negatives: too much power and not enough. Both too much and too little power result in violence. As one Elder put it:

> What I am talking about is based on a right spirit and the intent of Creation. It doesn't give anyone special rights – it is that power piece that has no place in what I am talking about. It is a birthright, a birth responsibility. Until that is back in place we will always be struggling. That is one of the things that we have to put right.

For the Anishinabe of Hollow Water healing seems to be about rediscovering their birthright and birth responsibility as part of Creator's good Creation.

This phase from 1999–2006 is one of backsliding and building at the same time. The healing movement seems almost critically wounded while at the same time learning to soar. Clearly basic elements in the healing journey were sidelined and the impact was deep and immediate. When the healing path is not regularly tended it starts to slip.

Phase 6: Searching for the healing path again (2006–continuing)

Backsliding, brokenness and darkness might constitute a critical blow for other communities but not so in Hollow Water. At least not yet. Hollow Water knows darkness and brokenness all too well. While some report that it feels like they are back to where they were 15 years ago, Hollow Water has a 20-year record of cultivating holistic community healing. The lessons learned along the way equip them to find the path again.

When even somewhat discouraged CHCH workers are asked how far they have come in the healing journey, they identify many signs of health:

➤ 'Women are stronger. They can stand up and say I don't need to have this kind of a life. I don't need to be beaten.'

➤ 'More than half of the community has been involved in CHCH, but maybe even the whole community, as we are all related here.'

➤ 'We are a small community surrounded by the Métis community. These communities are coming together. This is part of the healing path. I remember when I was growing up there was lots of open fighting between the communities.'

➤ 'You walk around the community and you see traditional things now – sweat lodges – that never used to be the case.'

I asked one Elder if there was anyone who was beyond the possibility of being restored? He paused; then he said, 'I don't know. I haven't seen it yet.' Then he gave a good laugh. Hollow Water has looked into the eyes of the darkest kinds of abuses but has not yet found someone who could not be restored. If this is true for individuals, perhaps it is true for communities.

While I visited CHCH they had two days of re-envisioning. Four Directions International facilitated their efforts to understand where the community stood regarding the healing movement and what steps CHCH could take to build support. They articulated the following ten steps:

1. Enlarge and transform the circle of CHCH management or governance.

2. Reengage the community; it is the support base.

3. Continue culturally based programming.

4. Conduct targeted healing campaigns (for sexual abuse, drugs, alcohol).

5. Work to heal key relationships with political leaders and CFS.

6. Bring healing into the context of nation building.

7. Develop a stable funding base.

8. Create enterprise to pay for social development.

9. Care for yourself; healing begins with the circle of workers.

10. Hold the plan to account.

It is too early to be sure, but perhaps these plans represent a new phase on the healing journey. CHCH workers seemed cautiously optimistic. After an eight-year hiatus they and justice system workers planned a Sentencing Circle in Hollow Water.

Despite the decline described above I was inspired by my time with the CHCH workers and listening to their stories. They have a deep commitment to protecting children and to healing their community. Furthermore, they have touched and tasted what healing justice is like. What is unclear is where the path ahead will lead.

Sustaining dynamics of healing justice

What sustains the Hollow Water experience of healing justice? The people of Hollow Water seem to broadly agree on what the dynamics are. The ups and downs of their own story are good evidence of what helps to sustain healing justice and what acts as a barrier when neglected.

Nine dynamics seem most important. They are listed in the order of frequency in which they were discussed in interviews, ranging from 100 per cent for themes listed first to 60 per cent for those listed last.

Return to Creator and traditional culture – Moving back to stable structures

The source of healing justice is listening to and being in relationship with Creator. This does not mean that those who do not acknowledge Creator cannot experience healing. Nevertheless, a human programme divorced from its roots will struggle to bear good fruit. When the Resource Group began to meet in the 1980s, they did not set out to reestablish traditional culture. However, they discovered along the way that many of the decisions they had made followed traditional understandings (e.g. healing begins with the self). In Hollow Water healing justice is sustained through the traditional ceremonies and protocols. It is also sustained through their traditional language. One Elder explained it to me in these terms:

> It is in the language that you can really see what is happening. It is the language which gives direction to what needs to be done… English language is so critical it is almost overwhelming. In our language it is not as overwhelming and the more you talk the more you see the humour in it… I believe that the Spirit is in the language.

Recovery of the traditional culture means restoring the role of Elders and women and recovering the traditional practises of sweats, feasts and ceremonies. It also means recovering a sense of traditional practises of governance and food production. More and more of the CHCH workers are also wondering if the recovering of the clan system is a necessary part of moving back to stable structures. Recovery of these things does not mean going back to the way it was as if the world had not kept changing. It does mean creating the space where traditions which were interrupted and disturbed have opportunity to speak to the dynamics of today.

Staying close to Creation

One CHCH worker told me 'Change comes in part from being close to Creation.' This theme arose in every interview. Staying close to Creation is closely connected with traditional culture. To find the Good Life, to find a healing path, one must find a path that respects the vast inter-dependencies of Creation. Healing is a way of living in balance with one's self, community and with all Creation. Anything that harms the balance of relationships in Creation leads to suffering, an unbalanced life. Anything that respects those relationships leads to healing and the Good Life. As Hollow Water has matured in healing practises they have found more and more ways to encourage the community to stay close to Creation. Black Island Days, the Wilderness Therapy Programme, the ceremonies, the fasts, the sacred fire are all of this type.

The circle connecting the community

Healing is sustained when the community comes together in a circle to explore healing together. In the early days of CHCH this centred on sharing stories of abuse that happened in the community. Those early circles created a momentum, which was sustained by the consistent circles of the Resource Team. The 13-step process is essentially a process of ever expanding circles where each circle reflects together on what it means to take responsibility, to walk a healing path, to follow the Seven Sacred Teachings, to be Anishinabe. Loss of momentum in healing followed the failure to gather: in the end of the Resource Team, the end of Sentencing Circles and the end of regular staff circles. When the community no longer gathers in these circles, then the healing movement slides.

Preference for the local

The healing path only started to open up when a group recognized that the outside systems were making the community sicker and that they had to find ways to take community healing back into their hands. From time to time they had to decide on what this would look like. CHCH had an uneasy relationship with some of the outside professionals. A psychologist, working from her training and understanding of best practises, strongly cautioned the programme against bringing victim and victimizers into the same circle. CHCH workers followed her advice until some children pushed them to interact with their parents who were their victimizers. By following the local ways of knowing and sometimes breaking the Western best practise rules, Hollow Water discovered a path of healing that is unparalleled in Canada.

Staying close to those who are suffering and treating them like family

Those involved in the healing movement shared their stories and created space for others to do the same. CHCH workers, when at their best, do not work as paid staff but as family members engaging their community. Whereas earlier victims had been blamed and victimizers exported to the criminal justice system, CHCH created space for both to stay to share their stories, to walk a healing path and even to become a healing resource for their community. As one long-term CHCH worker put it:

> I think one of the reasons why we are able to reach offenders is because we treat them like family, like human beings, like you and I. They have feelings. They have pains. We don't shun them or push them away. We treat them like family and talk to them. You have to be tough with them but also to treat them like human beings.

When victims and victimizers are not treated as family, healing deteriorates. However, when a community finds creative ways to stay close to those who are suffering and to treat them like family, it seems that surprising healing paths start to unfold. This dynamic even extends to the CHCH workers themselves. When CHCH workers no longer treat each other as family, healing slides.

Special role of women and children

Most CHCH workers said that what keeps them going in their work is their children and grandchildren. The women of Hollow Water see it as their traditional responsibility to protect children. As the women have stood up to protect children, they have grown stronger. As they have listened to the children, they have also been challenged and shaped to follow more radical healing paths. This double dynamic of the special role of children and women has helped to sustain the healing movement over the last 20 years.

Ongoing training and support of the team to walk a healing path

The healing path is sustained by learning together and healing together. A major breakthrough happened in the healing movement as a consequence of community members committing to a two-year training course. Regular support meetings with the Resource Team also served this function and led to an ethos of CHCH workers supporting each other through circles. At various points in their history trainings were hosted to engage people in learning about abuse and healing. When that support and accountability started to slide so did the healing movement. CHCH workers are clear that when at their best they work not as experts but as people who are also on a healing journey. When they stop working at their own healing, they lose integrity and the trust of the community.

Appropriate and adequate funding

CHCH is funded by provincial funds of $120,000 per year and federal funds of $120,000 per year. Originally this was to cover the salaries of seven sexual abuse workers and one secretary. While CHCH has grown through the years funding levels have never increased. Funding was not even raised after a government-commissioned report on the cost-benefit analysis reported that for every $2 spent in Hollow Water $6–$15 in direct cost was saved (Couture 2001b). In addition there were huge benefits which could not be quantified in dollar amounts. The result is that CHCH worker salaries have not changed since the early 1990s except that those who completed university degrees were given a raise. Today Hollow Water has some additional funding from the Aboriginal Healing Foundation but those funds are a term grant and not stable core funding.

CHCH workers say that the healing path would be better sustained by allowing for normal salary increases.

Hollow Water is also faced with a long-term challenge of what funding should look like in their community. To follow the path of self-sufficiency and nation building might mean funding that is not dependent on Western systems. Within traditional Anishinabe teachings spiritual matters, like healing, should not be commoditized. Working out what this means in today's world of money is one of their challenges.

Healing creates more healing

At Hollow Water people took a step and did something, even when they didn't understand fully what they were doing. As one CHCH worker said, 'Going out and doing it created more healing.' Although there are times when CHCH seems to get stuck in ideas and planning, the healing path seems to flourish when they find a way to take a further step on a healing path. Healing is a resource which seems to multiply when used, like yeast. When the community (and workers) taste it, they find the courage to take more steps.

Barriers to healing justice in Hollow Water

Hollow Water's healing movement has faced many barriers along the way. Besides neglect of the dynamics listed above there have been other impediments. When asked about these respondents spoke of both external and internal barriers. The process of colonialization set up external barriers that still impact the community.

Chief and Council elections

An electoral system was imposed on Aboriginal communities in Canada through the Indian Act. The traditional methods of recognizing leadership within the community were displaced by a system of electing leaders which was more familiar to Western standards. This system was imposed as part of the policy of assimilation or what Couture calls cultural genocide (2001b). In other words the current electoral system in Hollow Water was not designed on healing principles. It is not surprising that this system then mitigates against healing in the community. CHCH relationship with Chief and Council has been better or worse depending on who is in power, but the point about this barrier is not just about who is there. An election every two years leaves the community divided. Furthermore, those community members who rise to the top of such leadership structures often are those that use hierarchical power, further complicating efforts to make healing a community-wide initiative. Notably, while women are the strong majority of CHCH workers, they are very much a minority among elected leaders.

Weak relationship with Western justice system

Although part of what makes the Hollow Water programme innovative is its partnership with the Western justice system, this partnership has been strained at many points. Those in Hollow Water feel neither supported nor understood by the justice system. The low funding rates and the inability to organize a Sentencing Circle for eight years are evidence of this strain and of this barrier for healing. It seems that CHCH either needs a more supportive relationship with the justice system or a more independent one. It is not clear which road they will take or whether these roads are mutually exclusive.

Welfare system that supports poverty

There are many people in Hollow Water who are supported by the welfare system and, some would say, are dependent on it. CHCH workers realize that it is easier to stay on welfare than to go to work. But they believe this dependency affects a person's sense of identity in negative ways which can make them more prone towards abuse and less inclined towards healing. Healing is about learning to value your identity. When that personal identity is devalued by a dependency system like the welfare system, the healing path becomes more difficult.

Church relationships

The relationship of the healing movement with churches has also gone up and down, depending on the church denomination and who is in leadership. From the beginning there have been churches that teach that traditional ways are evil, thus creating a barrier for some to work with CHCH. There are also churches, especially the Roman Catholic, which have supported CHCH from the beginning and have participated in the Resource Group and in ceremonies.

Incarceration

The Hollow Water paper on incarceration clearly names incarceration as a barrier to healing (Community Holistic Circle Hollow Water 1996). Of course incarceration was not designed to promote healing. The Anishinabe perspective is that healing must be the basis for their community structures as well as the healing process. Incarceration interrupts this process. It takes people out of the community and returns them, sometimes, more dangerous than when they left. Furthermore, the rhetoric around incarceration is that once you have 'done your time, you've paid your debt'. This rhetoric runs counter to the need for healing, for taking responsibility, for making things right to the victim, for learning about identity and for offering your gifts to the community.

In addition to the external barriers mentioned above, there are a number of internal barriers.

Keeping the secret

When CHCH first started one of the most significant impediments was the internal dynamic of keeping secrets. Sexual abuse was a taboo subject, but the majority of community members were directly affected in some way. To work at healing on this matter was to reveal secrets which had been carefully hidden. Many people did not want to admit there was a problem. Some even tried harming the CHCH workers. While these dynamics are changing, the absence of sexual abuse disclosures since 2002 is evidence that this is a barrier the community continues to face.

Top-down and diffuse leadership

There have been times when leaders within CHCH imposed top-down leadership and also times when others have looked to single leaders to organize the whole community on a healing path. Then the healing path has suffered. On the other hand there is an Aboriginal culture of not wanting to tell people what to do, but nevertheless expecting everyone to do their work. I have called this 'diffuse leadership'. Hollow Water needs to create a new style of leadership that respects the culture and their understanding of healing. What seems clear is that both strictly top-down and diffuse styles of leadership create barriers for the movement.

Relationship with children and family services

CFS and CHCH were woven together from the beginning. The 2005 split of these two organizations created major barriers to the healing movement. One part of the barrier is the impediment to the flow of information and the need to work together on cases involving children who are under the CFS mandate. Another part is the loss of trust of the community in the workers when the healing movement is threatened with messy public break ups.

Perception that some CHCH workers are not walking a healing path

When CHCH workers are perceived by the community, and sometimes by other workers, as not walking a healing path, then healing seems to slide. Sometimes this happens by workers falling into gossip. Sometimes it is the failure to convene circles to help and support each other. Another example is the breakdown in the relationship between CHCH and CFS. There is at least one CHCH worker who admitted to using alcohol and drugs when not working. In the past, CHCH workers were the ones who became sober. This was seen as a requirement of employment, and some people were dismissed for not following this guideline. CHCH's inability to envision an appropriate response seemed to some a mark of their weakness. That issue may have gone away, as the last reports at time of writing were that the worker was addressing personal health issues and no longer using drugs. However, the larger issue of how to support and encourage CHCH workers to stay on a healing path is an issue that will not go away.

Guilt and shame

Hollow Water has identified guilt and shame as 'emotional blocks, so the person doesn't grow' (Bushie 1997c). Both lead to a paralysis, not to healing. Consequently, at each step in the CHCH process the workers try to remove guilt and shame. The whole community needs to learn that the victims are not to blame, but need release from guilt and shame.

Furthermore, they need healing and maybe the offer of a healing path and a support worker. The same understandings apply to the victimizers.

Being labelled a process or project

CHCH recognizes that one of the biggest obstacles to holistic healing is seeing and treating CHCH as a process or project. CHCH is an alliance of a broad section of the community. It is not narrowly focused as an alterative justice programme but is about holistic community healing. Partly because the programme has paid workers, some see it as a model where a few experts are responsible, not the community. However, taking the community off the hook is a huge barrier to sustaining a community holistic healing movement. When the community has not taken responsibility the healing movement has started to slide.

Losing Creator

What happens when we stop acknowledging? We suffer. We go through that darkness in our community. That's the battle in this community; it is when we forget Creator. It's like going off that path and into a mess. That is when the red flag goes up. That is when a person can do all these crimes. Because he is not connected to Creator and not connected to any kinship, family breakdown starts to happen

I learned from Elders that people are seen as the instruments, but it is Creator who does healing. However there seems to be a tendency to forget Creator, to forget to give thanks for the good things and to just do your own work. The Elders said that when this happens all sort of trouble follows.

Final words

The story of Hollow Water is one of the strongest stories of healing justice in the Canadian context. However, it is also a story full of ups and downs. The fragility in their story suggests to me that healing justice is not a robust process to be adopted but is more like a fragile plant to be carefully tended. Their ups and downs can teach us a lot about what is needed to sustain healing justice. Their story also shines a spotlight on barriers which can hinder a holistic community healing movement.

Chapter 5

The Iona Community

A Touching Place[1]
To the lost Christ shows his face
to the unloved he gives his embrace
to those who cry in pain or disgrace
Christ makes, with his friends, a touching place.

Christ's is the world in which we move
Christ's are the folk we're summoned to love
Christ's is the voice that calls us to care
and Christ is the one who meets us there.

Feel for the people we most avoid
strange or bereaved or never employed
feel for the women and feel for the men
who fear that their living is all in vain.

Feel for the parents who've lost their child
feel for the women whom men have defiled
feel for the baby for whom there's no breast
and feel for the weary who find no rest.

Feel for the lives by life confused
riddled with doubt, in loving abused
feel for the lonely heart, conscious of sin
which longs to be pure but fears to begin.

(Bell and Maule 1986)

---

[1] Taken from *Love from Below* (Wild Goose Publications, 1989). Words John L. Bell and Graham Maule. Copyright © 1989 WGRG Iona Community, Glasgow, G2 3DH, Scotland. www.wgrg.co.uk.

Background to the Iona Community[2]

Not many songs of worship in the Christian lexicon focus on social misfits, the unemployed, rape victims, motherless children and others crying in pain. Somehow the dysfunctions and excesses of social, economic and political structures do not seem to have a significant place in much Christian worship and, perhaps, theology. One of the clear exceptions to this tendency is the music coming out of the Iona Community's Wild Goose Resource Group, such as the song quoted above, which was written by John Bell, a member of the Iona Community, and Graham Maule, a former member and staff person.

These songs of worship are rare and come out of a particular orientation to God, to the world and, indeed, to justice. This particular kind of justice finds its place in the intermingling of healing, politics, spirituality, work, geography, prayer, non-violent action, ecological peacebuilding and worship. The current leader of this community has called this kind of justice, a 'justice that heals' (Galloway 2000).

The Iona Community, founded in Scotland in 1938, is a dispersed network of Christian peace and justice activists. Mostly urban, this community has survived two critical transitions: the transition from a very charismatic founding leader and the transition required when there were no longer any of the founding members among them. Today the Iona Community has about 250 members, dispersed mostly in Britain, and over 1500 Associates and 1400 friends (The Iona Community-n.d.-a).

But what do they mean by a justice that heals? What practises of healing justice are present in this mostly white, urban and dispersed Christian community? What have they learned about what sustains and blocks such a justice?

Because the Iona Community is a community which values diversity, a wide range of views and practises exists within its membership. Their views sometimes conflict. I have tried to capture themes from multiple sources within the Community in the hope that such themes are broadly reflective of the group. However, the reader should understand that 'the Iona Community' does not refer to a uniform community but to a diverse one. I used a different system of citation in this chapter than in the previous one. To respect the diversity of their opinions and their

---

2   The group or community refers to itself as 'the Iona Community'. They do not, by adopting this rather ambiguous name, seek to distinguish themselves from the island community of which they are part. I have followed their practise. About 100 permanent residents on the Isle of Iona are not part of 'the Iona Community'..

different cultural norms I have followed the guidance and permission of the members whom I interviewed and will quote them by name.

To understand how the Iona Community approaches healing justice it is necessary to understand their history. In 1938 the Rev. George MacLeod, founder and first Leader of the Iona Community, set off to the Scottish Isle of Iona on an experiment. MacLeod, a soldier turned pacifist minister in an inner city congregation of the Church of Scotland in Glasgow, was convinced that the church was mostly irrelevant to the life and struggles of the industrialized inner city, a place so often marked by poverty and by the structural failings of the industrialized world. He was also convinced that the way the world tried to solve problems through violent means in fact solved few of the underlying problems. As one member told me, MacLeod was touched by double-edged injustice: the injustice of poverty which made people feel worthless and ashamed on the one hand and, on the other, the injustice of a church that had lost touch with the poor and lost its true vocation (D. Van der Hijden, personal communication, 6 December 2006). This criticism of the structural injustice of church and world has continued in the Iona Community (Harvey 1987). MacLeod believed that the world needed alternative ways of doing politics and economics and of dealing with conflict (G. Brown, personal communication, 19 December 2006). The Iona Community was developed to help build this alternative politics. The first focus was on transforming those who were leading the church. The way to change the church was to change the way it trained ministers. So when MacLeod went to the Scottish Isle of Iona, he took with him a few ministers-in-training and a few unemployed craftsmen. Their task was to rebuild the Abbey buildings while living together in Christian community. Here lay the beginnings of the Iona Community.

In some ways the Abbey on the Isle of Iona is a symbol of the life of the Iona Community. To understand the Community it is necessary to know something of the historical and theological shoulders on which they stand. The Abbey was originally built in 1208 when Reginald, Lord of the Isles, invited the Benedictine order to establish a community on Iona. This order of the Western Church emphasized the role of prayer, community worship, work, scholarship, hospitality and the unity of the church (Ferguson 1998). However, the Benedictines were not the first to establish a Christian community on Iona. The foundations of the Abbey lie on the ruins of St Columba's monastery. Columba came from Ireland to Iona in 563 and established a community of monks which, in its Celtic tradition, emphasized hospitality, healing, love for all creation and regular corporate worship. In those early years Iona was a centre of Celtic spirituality. Today, Celtic spirituality plays an important role in the Iona Community. While it does not see itself strictly as a Celtic community it does present itself as a community with 'Scottish roots and an international membership' (The Iona Community 2006). J. Philip Newell, former Warden at the Abbey and an Associate of the Iona Community, contrasts the key characteristics of Celtic spirituality with the Mediterranean church based in Rome.

> Two major features of the Celtic tradition distinguish it from what in contrast can be called the 'Mediterranean' tradition. Celtic spirituality is marked by the belief that what is deepest in us is the image of God. Sin has distorted and obscured that image but not erased it. The Mediterranean tradition, on the other hand, in its doctrine of original sin has taught that what is deepest in us is our sinfulness. This has given rise to a tendency to define ourselves in terms of the ugliness of our sin instead of the beauty of our origins. The second major characteristic of the Celtic tradition is a belief in the essential goodness of creation. Not only is creation viewed as a blessing, it is regarded as a theophany or a showing of God. Thus the great Celtic teachers refer to it as 'the book of creation' in which we may read the mystery of God. The Mediterranean tradition, on the other hand, has tended towards a separation of spirit and matter, and thus has distanced the mystery of God from the matter of creation (Newell 2002).

As we shall see this view of Christianity is reflected in some interesting ways in the Iona Community.

However, the spiritual history of Iona is not exclusive to the Celts and the Benedictines. Before the Celts the site was sacred to the Druids. After the Celts and Benedictines had come and gone, the island, including the Abbey precincts, came into the ownership of the Duke of Argyll. In 1899 the ruins of the Abbey were placed by him into the hands of the Church of Scotland Trustees with the agreement that 'the Abbey church be restored and all branches of the Christian Church should be able to worship there' (Ferguson 1998). This long history of Iona being sacred ground is also evidenced by the kinds of people who lie in the ancient graveyard: 48 Scottish kings, eight Norwegian kings and a number of Irish and French monarchs (Ferguson 1998).

So the Isle of Iona and its Abbey have a long tradition of being a sacred place that emphasizes hospitality, communal worship, common work, Christian unity and a care for all creation. The history of the Abbey and of Iona itself has immense symbolic significance for the Iona Community.

While the island and the Abbey are symbolic of the life of the Iona Community, they are not the focus. The community has always had three key avenues of action: the two island centres of Iona and Mull, its headquarters in Glasgow and its members dispersed around the world (but mostly in Britain). The 250 Members and 2900 Associates and Friends are considered the core of the Iona Community. These members are the hands and feet of the community around the world. They run their island centres as demonstration plots of life in response to God.

Since the original vision was to train ministers, the Iona Community is not organized as a congregation or primarily as a geographic community. The Iona Community is not a church. Membership was originally open only to Church of Scotland ministers-in-training, and therefore only to men. Over time the craftsmen, who were working and rebuilding the Abbey alongside the minsters-in-training, felt excluded from the organization, and so membership was made open to laypeople and, later still, to women. Slowly opening the doors of the community has been part of the community's journey to healing justice. It has moved from originally excluding women to now fully including women. As evidence, their current leader is a woman. Originally members were expected to spend summers at the island of Iona, working along with the craftsmen at rebuilding, and living in a simple community which worshipped and studied the Bible together. After a few months on the island they were expected to go back to the city, often to housing projects in low-income areas of Glasgow. In fact, they committed themselves to working for two years in an urban parish (The Iona Community 2001b).

Today members are expected to spend a week on the Island and to participate in three plenary sessions (one of which is held regionally). What holds the community together is its five-fold commitment. The Rule that each member commits to includes:

1. Daily prayer and Bible reading.

2. Sharing and accounting for the use of money.

3. Planning and accounting for the use of time.

4. Acting for justice and peace in society.

5. Meeting with and being accountable to each other.

The island centres are built on the small islands of Iona and Mull off the coast of Scotland. Their setting in a beautiful rugged land plays a significant role in the life of the community. Many have described Iona as 'a thin place' where only a tissue separates the material from the spiritual. On the Isle of Iona is the Abbey, which houses the 25 or so resident staff and the over 100 volunteers who come for various periods over the summer. The Warden and as few as two members live on the island year round. The island is very important, but it is not the locus of community. It is a place to host people and to teach them about the vision and practises of the Iona Community. The Abbey hosts up to 48 visitors who come for short courses. They participate in all areas of community life, whether doing the dishes, eating together, sharing in worship planning or in music, crafts, drama, and social events (The Iona Community 1996). The MacLeod Centre, also on Iona, was opened in 1988. This centre accommodates 40 people. This island centre also runs particular courses or programmes. Between the two centres they can host almost 100 people per week through the programme period. In 2007 they scheduled over 60 programmes with themes covering a range of topics, including peacemaking, non-violence, young adults, liturgical celebrations, spirituality of land, Christian spiritual practise, pilgrimage, Black liberation theology, poverty and social justice, non-discrimination and sexuality, faith in politics, money and wealth, music festivals, God and the city, and interfaith and interdenominational dialogues. Camas, a third programme centre on the Isle of Mull, is about three miles from the Isle of Iona and is a centre for young people to come for adventure holidays in a Christian environment. Traditionally youth have come from inner-city Glasgow but also from many other areas. Camas is also the setting where the community hosts young offenders in custody at Polmont Institute. They come to the centre to experience a simple lifestyle in tune with the local environment. While the centres operate on a break-even basis, the Abbey shop, Wild Goose Publications and the contributions of Members, Associates and Friends provide the bulk of the funding for the whole organization (The Iona Community 1996).

In Glasgow the community has a publishing house, Wild Goose Publications, a Wild Goose Resource and Worship Group, a Youth

Department and the administrative base from which they operate a bi-monthly magazine, *Coracle*.

Members work in a variety of jobs, about one-third working as ministers, priests, or chaplains and two-thirds working in other spheres of service such as health, education, justice advocacy and social service (The Iona Community 2007). Members are dispersed around the world. They participate in a wide range of churches and some do not identify with any particular church. They are organized into family groups and regional groups which are geographically based. Family groups are the context of support and accountability in following the Rule of Iona. These groups are arranged as geographic clusters. Individual members follow the annual Iona guide for daily prayer. They also do regular Bible reading and figure out within their context how to live into the commitment for action for peace and justice in society.

During its almost 70 years the focus of the Community has shifted and grown. It currently (The Iona Community n.d.-a) has eight areas of focus:

➤ justice, peace and the integrity of creation (opposing nuclear weapons, campaigning against the arms trade and for ecological justice)

➤ political and cultural action to combat racism

➤ action for economic justice, locally, nationally and globally

➤ issues in human sexuality

➤ discovery of new and relevant approaches to worship

➤ work with young people

➤ deepening of ecumenical dialogue and communion

➤ inter-faith relations.

Many of these areas have dedicated working groups of Iona Community members. They work to develop and promote their themes within the Community through plenary meetings, beyond their own membership through hosting workshops at the island centres or by partnering with groups of like mind.

Within the international church the Iona Community is perhaps best known for its worship resources in the form of songs, liturgies and dramas. The Iona Community is a singing community and has shared the songs and worship resources which they have collected and written through the Wild Goose Resource and Worship Group.

However, this reputation for worship resources is somewhat misleading. Those resources come out of visions and practises of justice, healing, grace and faithfulness. To understand the Iona Community it is therefore very important to understand their historical context and their visions and practises of healing justice.

Healing justice vision in the Iona Community

'Justice as Healing' is a chapter written by the current Leader of the Community, Kathy Galloway (2000), outlining some of the Iona Community's vision and practise of healing justice. She suggests that to be human in Jesus' way is to practise a particular kind of healing justice. A justice that heals is about rediscovering what it is to be human. This rediscovering of our humanity Galloway sometimes calls 'learning our true names'. The language of healing justice is not used by all members of the Iona Community, but many find that it explains the heart of what the Iona Community is about. Tom Gordon, an Iona Member and hospice Chaplain says that the convergence of healing and justice lies at the heart of the Iona Community.

> If communities and the people within them are broken – by hopelessness and alienation and poverty and a lack of opportunity, etc, etc – how can healing be found unless systems change and justice is at the core. So, the two are inseparable, and, as such, gave the Iona Community its *raison d'être*. (Personal communication, 7 December 2006)

While some of the members report that the language of healing justice was new to them, they say that it touched something which was core to the Iona Community, which is the view that justice, peace and healing are inseparable.

The song which is quoted at the beginning of this chapter captures a number of key characteristics of the Community's understanding of healing justice:

> ➤ Healing justice comes out of Christ and faithfulness to Christ.

> ➤ Healing justice is an expansive concept which does not fragment into many different realms.

➤ Healing justice is rediscovering wholeness within the embrace of Christ.

➤ Healing justice recognizes the special place of the broken in encountering God and understanding the world.

➤ Healing justice is about (re)establishing a particular kind of community.

➤ Healing justice is inclusion and acceptance.

Each of the characteristics requires some unpacking to understand the Iona Community's vision of healing justice.

Healing justice comes out of Christ and faithfulness to Christ

Christ's is the world in which we move
Christ's are the folk we're summoned to love
Christ's is the voice that calls us to care
and Christ is the one who meets us here.
(Bell and Maule 1986)

The Iona Community is a Christian community. For them Christ is the beginning, the end, and the way. 'Christ's is the world in which we move.' For the Community this means everything else flows out of and points towards Christ. In their Trinitarian theology Christ, God and the Spirit commingle such that to talk of Christ is to talk of God and Spirit. Drawing on their Celtic and Benedictine roots, they very often speak of God, Spirit and Christ or Jesus.

The Leader of the Community told me that they were a Christocentric community. Then she changed her wording to a Jesus-centred community, suggesting that the Community was focused on the life and humanity of Jesus. She was not denying the divinity of God nor making the divinity of Christ their focus (K. Galloway, personal communication, 22 December 2006). This is significant because the Iona Community is not held together by a common doctrine, orthodoxy, but a common practise, orthopraxy. It is the practise of Jesus. As the song quoted in the opening of the chapter suggests, both the language of 'Christ' and of 'Jesus' is used, but in both cases the focus is on the practise and life that flows out of Jesus and points towards Him.

The Iona Community's focus is not on *bringing Christ to* people or situations and trying to convince them to accept Christ. Rather the focus is on *discovering Christ in* the loving of those who have been marginalized. 'Christ's is the voice that calls us to care, and Christ is the one who meets us there.' All people are Christ's and in each person, particularly in those who are in mourning and those who are without resources, Christ is present. Seeing all people as Christ's or as created in the image of God leads some members of Iona to a non-violent stance, for to do violence to one of Christ's, created in God's image, is to do violence to God (Z. Walker, personal communication, 7 December 2006).

While the founder, George MacLeod, was clearly a pacifist and many in the community share his views, the Community has never adopted this stance of absolute pacifism. The Community understands itself as a Community committed to active non-violence, and that this commitment is spelled out in multiple aspects of the Justice and Peace Commitment which is binding on all the members. The Community also see themselves as nuclear pacifists (K. Galloway, personal communication, 22 December 2006).

Since the face of Jesus is to be discerned in the poor, the hungry, the prisoners and the victims, social and political action could never be divorced from spirituality. Since the whole world is seen as Christ's, and therefore as holy, this view refuses to fragment or to polarize life into dichotomies. Life is always at the intersection of all things because, as the Bible declares, in Christ all things hold together (Colossians 1:17, New Interbnational Version (NIV)). In the Iona Community worship, radical politics and social action flow into and out of each other. Prayer and political action are both equal parts of a Christian discipleship that inspired many of the first people who came to Iona for summer courses. They were trying to 'establish the view that political action for justice and peace was an imperative of the faith' (Ferguson 1998).

One of the early leaders explained the three-fold purpose of Iona in these terms: a call to discipleship which will lead to the peace of the world, finding a way to meet the world's hunger and working for church unity (Morton 1957). The clear expectation is that the Iona Community's mission is not for the conversion of the world (that the world might become Christian) but for the salvation of the world. The root of this word salvation is the same as the root of health and healing. In the Iona Community's context salvation of the world is the healing of the world or the peace of the world.

The focus of the Iona Community is on living a life which flows out of Christ and is a response to Him. Because they see the world as a sacrament of the presence of Christ (G. Brown, personal communication, 19 December 2006), their life together is not based on separation but rather the co-existence of the sacred and the secular, work and worship, prayer and politics. This, too, is partly the basis of the Community's approach to healing. 'The Community's theology of healing was not one of magic intervention, but of the corporate care of the Church in obedience to Jesus' (Ferguson 1998). They see healing justice as something that God does. They are not the healers (R. Burgess, personal communication, 4 December 2006). They bring people to God through prayer and through engaged action, but it is God who heals.

Healing justice as an expansive concept

In the song that opens this chapter, those who are grieved by what we might call crime ('the women whom men have defiled') are grouped together with those who are grieved by the loss of a child, and the hopeless, the lonely, the social misfits, the unemployed, the abused. Mainstream understandings of crime, harm, health and social justice might deal with each of these in separate ways with different sets of experts to aid the process. However the expansive view of healing in the Iona Community does not fragment or break things down in this manner.

Healing in the Iona Community is an expansive concept somewhat similar to what some Aboriginal groups refer to as 'returning to balance'. It includes the healing of body, mind and spirit of persons, and of the memories of communities and nations as well as the healing of the earth. All are part of the ministry of healing, and they are all inextricably linked (Burgess and Galloway 2000).

Concerning these intertwined linkages, Burgess writes,

> I cannot pray for a young person in prison if I do not look for ways to relieve the boredom of unemployment, the pressure of advertising, the board and lodgings legislation that keeps him on the move, and the lure of drugs, that have combined to destroy his liberty. I cannot pray for people who are poor in my community, or for that matter for people who are hungry, oppressed and poor anywhere else in the world, if I do not challenge the way that my country's government spends its resources... If I am blind to the sources of injustice around me, and divorce the needs of an individual from the pain of a whole community, my prayers for healing are non-sense and bear no resemblance to the good news of the gospel. (Burgess 2000b)

Thus, prayer for healing is always connected to the context of the wider world. As Iona Member and Dutch hospice chaplain Desirée Van der Hijden put it: 'Illness may be caused by poverty, which makes praying for healing without working for justice rather useless in the long term' (personal communication, 6 December 2006).

In their resource book for the ministry of healing, *Praying for the Dawn* (Burgess and Galloway 2000), Iona Community Member Burgess and Leader of the Community Galloway reflect this same expansive inter-connectedness through their stories, services and reflections. The stories represent this diversity, ranging from dealing with a young Northern Ireland woman's negative self-image to praying for the wholeness of the earth to the gradual healing of memories of a 63-year-old woman who had been raped three times.

The Community does not try to deal with each of the harms in exactly the same way. They are far too grounded in creation and the life of the housing projects of Glasgow to expect a one-size-fits-all response to healing. By holding this interrelatedness together in the context of a worshipping and learning community, they are trying to live out what one former Leader of the Community calls 'a total gospel which held together worship and work, prayer and politics, personal and corporate healing, peace and justice' (Ferguson 1998).

Kate McIlhagga tries to explain the Iona Community's perspective on the church's healing ministry. 'The healing ministry is first and foremost about justice and peace – about the healing of nations. But intertwined with that divine imperative is the healing of the individual, the healing of memory, of broken relationships' (McIlhagga 2000). Again we see how this 'divine imperative' is intertwined in all of life. The health of the individual is not separate, in cause or effect, from the health of the larger community. The Iona Community focuses on healing prayer, but they refuse 'to hive off prayer and politics into separate compartments' (Ferguson 1998).

An Iona Community publication describes the central theme of their healing ministry:

It has always been a central theme of the healing ministry that we should look at the context in which illness and distress occur: so our ministry is as likely to take us into the realms of local and national politics, in an endeavour to change environments and policies which we believe to be responsible for individual illnesses and adversity of all sorts, as it is to be in direct contact with 'sick' people. (The Iona Community 1996)

One example that often gets repeated in the Iona Community is that it is not enough to pray for someone dying of tuberculosis in the substandard housing in Glasgow. One must also take political action in the matter of the housing project which sets the environment within which one becomes more likely to contract tuberculosis (Ferguson 1998; Macleod 1955). In the context of crime, this means that the issues that lead an offender to offend must also be dealt with as part of a healing justice response (Z. Walker, personal communication, 7 December 2006).

Because 'Christ's is the world in which we move', all things hold together in Christ. If all of life is woven together, then crime, harm, illness, distress and war must be seen within the broad context. This is a vision and strategy of healing justice in the Iona Community.

Rediscovering wholeness within the embrace of Christ

To the lost Christ shows his face
to the unloved he gives his embrace
to those who cry in pain or disgrace
Christ makes, with his friends, a touching place.
(Bell and Maule 1986)

It follows from seeing life and healing within an expansive concept that the object of healing is to return to wholeness. 'Healing is about wholeness of people, "at-one-ment" with themselves, their neighbours, their surroundings, and ultimately with God' (The Iona Community 1996). Returning to this wholeness is not about returning to the state of affairs before the particular harm happened. The wholeness of healing is the wholeness of coming into the embrace of Christ. It is a rediscovering of wholeness from the perspective of the One who created all things and, therefore, the change required of healing justice is not limited to the mainstream boundaries of health, justice and economics, private or public. It also differs from many mainstream understandings of atonement which focus more on righting wrongs than the establishing of wholeness or at-one-ment. In fact, in order to address the brokenness of the world the community saw the need to develop what some have called 'a holistic vision of political and theological justice' (Z. Walker, personal communication, 7 December 2006).

Another way of seeing this wholeness is to practise what Galloway calls 'Jesus' gospel of intrinsic worth'

> in which all living things, including the earth itself, have innate value separate from and beyond their utility; in which the commoditisation, the selling, of all of life is resisted and reversed and in which justice is done. To be human in Jesus' way is to act justly (Galloway 2000).

Thus the Iona Community's sense of healing justice is really as a view of wholeness. A number of Iona members told me that this sense of justice involves responding to wrongs, but it moves beyond a reaction approach. Their holistic view of healing justice includes 'working for change and the renewal of systems so that people are sustained before they become broken by injustice, and, indeed, find their own methodologies to sustain themselves and heal others' (T. Gordon, personal communication, 7 December 2006). Addressing this same issue another member explained how the vision of this justice extends to building compassionate communities:

> The vision certainly encompasses righting wrongs but, like Jesus in his public ministry, we are concerned with building community; healing is about being brought back into community, being cared for and being able to love fully and freely without fear or abuse, treating the earth as the precious resource that we have been entrusted to care for. (Z. Walker, personal communication, 7 December 2006)

So the Iona Community's sense of justice is not merely a reaction against injustice or a repairing-of-harm orientation. It is an orientation toward a deep sacred wholeness which precedes and must inform any healing. Justice is a wholeness found in the embrace of Christ.

The special place of the broken in encountering God and understanding the world

The way into this wholeness is not through escaping from the pain of the world but through entering into the mystery of suffering. In the mystery of suffering one begins to see the face of Christ (McIlhagga 2000). Healing justice in the Iona Community is an entering into the mystery of suffering – the suffering of illness, the suffering of systemic injustice, the suffering of economies of war and the suffering of inflicting harm. They believe that these sufferings and injustices need to be central to the life of the church, but too often the church avoids them or just talks without engaging in meaningful action (T. Gordon, personal communication, 7 December 2006). The purpose of the Iona Community is to support a network of people in ways the church has largely failed to do to help them to engage in encountering suffering and injustice with a vision and practise of a healing kind of justice. Engaging injustice has always been a central part of the witness of the Iona Community.

In the midst of this suffering they expect to discover Christ and to discover a way to wholeness which is healing justice.

Healing justice as inclusion and acceptance

To some people the language of Christianity, which is so central to much of the discourse of the Iona Community, might seem exclusive and alienating. However, from the beginning the Iona Community has tried to create space for those who have been marginalized to be included as friends or brothers and sisters. Because of their view of wholeness and their understandings of Christ, they do not draw sharp boundaries between Christian and non-Christian. All is one. Learning from the Celtic view that God is in all of life and in all of life is God, the Iona Community has developed a theology of inclusiveness. Nick Prance, an Iona Community Member and community mental health practitioner, explains how this vision-of-all prompts engaged action.

> I think if God is, God is one. We don't come into the world. We come out of it. It is this sense that prompts me to work towards a unified vision of humanity, which can hold different perspectives, but see them for what they are, simply perspectives. (Personal communication, 11 December 2006)

They see this vision not just as for their community or for the Christian church. They see it as a vision of healing justice for the whole world, including the land. They believe that by respecting all 'others' and accepting yourself, it is possible to create space for healing justice (Z. Walker, personal communication, 7 December 2006).

Healing justice is about (re)establishing a particular kind of community

The Iona Community was started, in part, to recover some of the communal dimensions of faith. They see Christianity, not as a private faith of individuals, but as a community-faith. The Rule mandates personal pieties such as personal prayer and Bible reading, but the context is within a community vision of faith and life. In each case, whether in their island life, or in the work of their experiments on the mainland, or in the life of their dispersed members, faith is about building a particular kind of community. For them, healing is about being brought back into community (Z. Walker, personal communication, 7 December 2006). To be a community of a particular kind is both a vision and a practise of healing justice.

But what are the characteristics of this particular kind of community? First, as we have already seen, a community is rooted in Christ for the sake of the world. This is a worshipping, praying, learning community. It is also politically engaged, not afraid to speak truth to power.

Second, it is a community willing to enter into the brokenness of the world and there to seek Christ and to struggle together with the meaning of this brokenness in light of a vision of love. Such a community must be willing to risk, to act and to experiment, which is to say, to learn through failing.

Third, 'healing comes through living the questions and not accepting easy answers' (Ferguson 1998). Therefore, communities must be of the type which create space for wrestling with hard questions while, at the same time, coaching people to reject the easy answers.

Fourth, such a community has a strong understanding of both what they stand against and what they stand for. As their booklet, *What is the Iona Community?* explains, 'We hope to be not just a community which stands against injustice, oppression and despair, but also a community which stands for hope, change, and celebration and affirmation of life together' (The Iona Community 1996).

Fifth, such a community must be a sanctuary of love and of rediscovering identity. 'This is the essence of the sanctuary – a place to feel loved, where you are valued for yourself and where your talents are welcome and useful – and if you thought you didn't have any, a place to discover that you have' (The Iona Community 1996).

What healing justice is not

I have tried to briefly summarize the Iona Community's self-understanding of their approach to justice as healing. W. Graham Monteith took on a similar task to outline the Iona Community theology of healing embedded in the practise and liturgy of healing. He highlights several points that overlap with the current survey:

➤ Healing and wholeness concern not only the individual but also the world.

➤ God through Jesus Christ is with us, and the world, in all our experience of life.

➤ Healing is sought through our own volition but granted by the will of God.

➤ An unquestioning faith is not a precondition of healing.

➤ God is always in solidarity with us. (Monteith 2000)

Before we proceed to more of what healing justice looks like in the Iona Community, it is necessary to distinguish within the Iona Community what healing justice is not!

The Iona Community is quick to distinguish healing from magic (Burgess 2000a; Ferguson 1998) and from a substitute for action. Healing prayer provides the motivation and vision for action (Burgess 2000a; Ferguson 1998). Healing is not about quick fixes, but about entering into the complex web of cosmic relationships and trying to find a way back to wholeness. Such a searching requires a long-term commitment to transformation, not an instant quick-fix expectation.

The Iona Community also distinguishes healing from medicine. The relationship between the two is complex. The way of healing is sometimes contrasted with the way of the surgeon, where the surgeon is depicted as adding more harm by cutting the body, and healing is described as gently tending the body so that it has space to heal itself and return to wholeness. Such tending includes 'prayer, deep attentiveness to the suffering of others but also to their giftedness' (Galloway 2000). There is an implied contrast with a medical model, which tends to be more intrusive, focusing exclusively on the material and driven by an expert who has little or no awareness of the giftedness of the one she is treating.

In a similar vein Ferguson, past Leader of the Community, claims the dominant modern scientific approach to life and medicine has also been

> devastating for health. Along with science generally, it has had spectacular successes, but it has led inexorably to 'magic bullet' medicine, where the doctor prescribes a drug to deal with symptoms. The whole person is missing. Everything is cast into the problem/solution mould. (1998)

The Community argue that science is more likely to lead to a magical pill mentality than the kind of prayerful approach they are seeking to cultivate.

However, it would be wrong to assume that the Iona Community is against the medical health discipline. Their Worship Book says both medicine and healing are gifts and work well together (The Iona Community 1991). Former leader Graeme Brown states the relationship this way: 'The Iona Community affirms the Health Service, but is critical of those who assume that medicines alone are required for wholeness' (personal communication, 19 December 2006). Monteith reports that there are many Iona members who are engaged in the healing profession, and that their engaging in both healing and medicine has been mutually beneficial (Monteith 2000).

The Iona Community's approach to healing justice is in contrast with the modern scientific vision, but they do not function in isolation, using only their approach to the exclusion of all others. An example of this is that healing prayer is not offered instead of other action but precisely to spark prayerfully engaged action. Their expansive approach to wholeness and to expecting Christ in the stranger leads them to expect to find giftedness wherever they look, including medicine.

Practises of healing justice in the Iona Community

Behind the Iona Community's practise of healing justice is the Justice and Peace Commitment of the Community. As part of their Rule all members agree to practise this commitment in who they are, what they do and what they don't do (R. Burgess, personal communication, 25 January 2007). It is quoted here at length because of its centrality in the practise of healing justice in the Iona Community.

Justice and Peace Commitment
We believe:

1. that the Gospel commands us to seek peace founded on justice and that costly reconciliation is at the heart of the Gospel;

2. that work for justice, peace and an equitable society is a matter of extreme urgency;

3. that God has given us partnership as stewards of creation and that we have a responsibility to live in a right relationship with the whole of God's creation;

155

4. that, handled with integrity, creation can provide for the needs of all, but not for the greed which leads to injustice and inequality, and endangers life on earth;

5. that everyone should have the quality and dignity of a full life that requires adequate physical, social and political opportunity, without the oppression of poverty, injustice and fear;

6. that social and political action leading to justice for all people and encouraged by prayer and discussion, is a vital work of the Church at all levels;

7. that the use or threatened use of nuclear and other weapons of mass destruction is theologically and morally indefensible and that opposition to their existence is an imperative of the Christian faith.

As Members and Family Groups we will:

8. engage in forms of political witness and action, prayerfully and thoughtfully, to promote just and peaceful social, political and economic structures;

9. work for a British policy of renunciation of all weapons of mass destruction and for the encouragement of other nations, individually or collectively, to do the same;

10. celebrate human diversity and actively work to combat discrimination on grounds of age, colour, disability, mental wellbeing, differing ability, gender, colour, race, ethnic and cultural background, sexual orientation or religion;

11. work for the establishment of the United Nations Organization as the principal organ of international reconciliation and security, in place of military alliances;

12. support and promote research and education into non-violent ways of achieving justice, peace and a sustainable global society;

13. work for reconciliation within and among nations by international sharing and exchange of experience and people, with particular concern for politically and economically oppressed nations. (The Iona Community n.d.-d)

It is the commitment of each member, with support from family groups and the larger Iona Community network, to figure out how to practise these commitments within their own life and location. Just how that is done varies to a considerable degree within the membership. However, there are some practises which seem quite common among the Iona Community.

I will highlight seven aspects of how healing justice is practised by the Iona Community.

Healing justice as creating and living in a particular kind of community

I have already briefly outlined one practise of healing justice in the Iona Community – to live in community together. A whole book could be devoted to describing the significance of this to healing justice. Such a book would no doubt have to consider the role of feasting and celebrating together, sharing in the work of basic survival, struggling together, responding to change, exercises of leadership, decision-making processes, processes of letting go, processes of inspiration and teaching and more. These are not irrelevant to this study, but to focus here might take over this whole study. As I have already indicated their major characteristics in this area I will move on to other practises.

Healing justice as modelling the kind of ecological, political and cultural life hoped for

Most of the members I talked to spoke of trying to model a positive way of justice in their lifestyle. Kathy Galloway calls this the 'practise (of) voluntary self-limitation to model the kind of political and cultural life that is hoped for' (2000). Galloway sees self-limitation needed in areas of consumerism, cultural and spiritual imperialism and in forced or manipulated proselytism. In fact, she says that our inability to live self-limited lives leads to wars, pandemics, structural inequalities and ecological holocaust. Members talked to me of trying to live simply, to decrease dependency on oil by purchasing locally, to grow their own food, and to purchase environmentally friendly products. They spoke of trying to address some of the global inequalities by buying Fair Trade products and eating mostly vegetarian foods. The island centres also model this kind of healing justice. Raising environmental issues to do with sustainable care of the earth is a longstanding tradition in the Iona Community, going back at least into the 1950s and the work of a member named Douglas Trotter (G. Brown, personal communication, 3 January 2007).

It seems that members of the Iona Community model healing justice relationships in the kinds of jobs or careers they work at. Many of them work in some kind of a helping or advocating role. Ronald Ferguson's history of the Iona Community closes with a number of stories of how Iona members have tried, and are trying, to live out this vision of justice as healing in their lives and work. One such story is that of Reverend Walter Fyfe who was concerned that unemployed and poorly paid people needed more power over the direction of their lives. His work was to help train groups to establish credit unions and other money-borrowing schemes. His goal was that they could cut their dependence on loan sharks while at the same time creating local power which could be used to tackle other issues (Ferguson 1998). Other members told me about working at, and advocating for, a host of other issues, a sampling of which includes: anti-discrimination against gay, lesbian and trans-gendered people; the anti-apartheid movement; the anti-nuclear movement; international relief work; life story work with the Alzheimer's Society; political election campaigns and interfaith dialogue.

The Iona Community also seems to value thoughtful reflections. Many members work to advocate the kind of life they hope for by writing books, songs and liturgies around peace and justice issues.

Healing justice as engaging injustice and sometimes breaking the law

A former Iona Community Deputy Leader of 17 years also saw world hunger as a centre of what the Iona Community needs to be about.

> The second great issue (behind the intersection of the peace of the world and Christian discipleship) that we must face is the problem of the world's need. All the questions of international relations come down in the end to bread. And the Gospel, too, in the end comes down to bread. The problem of the world's hunger is the most urgent problem that faces us. The Church cannot meet it by private charity. It is only by political action on the part of the nations of the world that the problem can be solved. (Morton 1957)

The Iona Community encourages their members to stand up to injustices where they are found. Sometimes this even means breaking the law where they perceive the law to be unjust. An example of this would be their work against the nuclear Trident defence plan. Some members used non-violent direct action to try to resist these initiatives and to articulate a more healing and just alternative. For example, some Iona Community members were arrested for lying down in front of traffic outside the location where the Trident nuclear weapons are held. Another member, together with others, destroyed some equipment pertaining to the Trident programme and then turned themselves in and made their arguments through the court system (K. Galloway, personal communication, 22 December 2006).

Healing justice as restoration of harms

The Iona Community believes that restoration of harms can happen through 'respectful dialogue of equals which builds common ground and relationships of friendship while dispelling ignorance and healing the memory of past divisions' (Galloway 2000). When harms arise within the Community they try to follow such a process. However, they were quick to note that the work of responding wisely to harm must begin long before the harm takes place. Building a community of trust, unity, compassion and common vision, prior to harms creates the space for such issues to be worked through (T. Gordon, personal communication, 10 December 2006). However once harm has happened they seem to follow some clear but unwritten procedures.

> ➤ Recognize brokenness. Brokenness happens and if it does not have space to surface in a constructive way it only becomes more destructive.

> ➤ Listen to the story and seek to understand.

> ➤ Find others in the community to help if those in conflict get stuck. Others could help as trainers or as facilitators.

> ➤ Seek forgiveness, if appropriate, and try to make things right as much as people are able. This is done as a direct encounter between the people who have experienced this harm and, sometimes, with the presence of a supporting community.

> ➤ Work for contexts where harming doesn't happen so easily. Trying to address the broader context is one of the hallmarks of the Iona Community's approach to harm, whether it is the harm between persons or the harm of unjust global structures.

Through their youth department the Iona Community has a longstanding relationship with the Polmont Young Offender Institute. Members have been visiting those who are incarcerated and those incarcerated have been coming to the Iona Community Camas centres to experience a simple lifestyle in tune with the local environment. Camas is a centre on the coast of the Isle of Mull which is accessible only by walking a couple of miles. It has little electricity and groups have to work together to feed each other and help each other to survive. Iona Community members have reported seeing huge changes within the young people who had been incarcerated and between them and the adult staff who accompanied them (K. Galloway, personal communication, 22 December 2006).

The youth department is now engaged in a fairly new programme that tries to apply some of these insights of healing justice to youth who have been convicted of crime. This is called Project Jacob (Scotland) and is a partnership between the Iona Community, Project Scotland, the Church of Scotland, Time for God and Project Jacob England. They work with young people aged 16–25 who are completing their sentences at Scotland's Polmont Young Offender Institute. They do have a selection process, but it is not based on the young person's previous charges. The young people are given the opportunity to change their lifestyle as a means of creating the kind of environments that lead to healing justice rather than injustice. By working through the Polmont Institute chaplain, who is an Associate Member of the Iona Community, young people can apply for Project Jacob. In this programme young people are given 'full-time volunteer work, supported accommodation, individual pastoral care and support and befriending' (The Iona Community n.d.-b). Of the first 12 Scottish young people who participated in the pilot project of this programme none has re-offended (The Iona Community n.d.-b). The idea is to help young people to move into a healthy lifestyle, to gain practical experience and confidence and to earn positive references. The Iona Community is working in Glasgow and Edinburgh to partner with housing associations. The Iona Community shares risk by taking out a tenancy agreement with the housing association on behalf of the young person. Through working with the young people for three months to two years and through volunteer mentoring and the support of a care worker, they try to cultivate conditions of friendship and support so that the young people can integrate back into the community in healthy ways.

The longstanding youth work in Camas with young offenders from Polmont Institution and the Jacob Project are two examples of how the Iona Community works within the area of crime. A third is the number of community members who have become chaplains of prisons. A fourth is the Community's work in the 1960s when they were part of the lobbying that helped to abolish the death penalty. The Iona Community works within the criminal justice system but tries to bring aspects of humanization and restorative justice to their relationships with those called offenders.

Healing justice as healing prayer

Macleod, the founding Leader of the Community, called on the community to work at healing by intercession and laying-on of hands (Macleod 1955). Intercessory prayer is part of the healing prayer service which has been part of the Iona Community's witness for over 60 years (Monteith 2000). On Tuesday evening people on the Isle of Iona are invited to gather in the Abbey for a Service of Prayer and Healing.

The service has always given participants the opportunity to place before God people with illnesses, situations with discord and nations broken by strife (Monteith 2000). Prayer requests are received from people who are visitors to the community on Iona and also by letter and telephone from many parts of the world. A list of requests is created to be used during the service and then is left in St Columba's Chapel until the following service. Because the prayer requests are about brokenness in particular people as well as particular situations in the world, the services focus mainly on physical well-being, but also take note of political and social aspects of a situation, and walking with the poor (T. Gordon, personal communication, 10 December 2006).

The Service of Prayer for Healing often opens with this welcome and opening response:

Leader: We gather here in your presence God,
   ALL: IN OUR NEED, AND BRINGING WITH US THE NEEDS OF THE WORLD.

Leader: We come to you, for you come to us in Jesus
   ALL: AND YOU KNOW BY EXPERIENCE WHAT HUMAN LIFE IS LIKE

Leader: We come with our faith and with our doubts;
   ALL: WE COME WITH OUR HOPES AND WITH OUR FEARS.

Leader: We come as we are, because it is God who invites us to come,
   ALL: AND GOD HAS PROMISED NEVER TO TURN US AWAY.
(The Iona Community 2001a)

After a song (like the one quoted at the opening of this chapter) and some scripture reading, the prayers of intercession are offered. Each person or situation is mentioned by name but without much detail. It is as if mentioning them in this context is enough.

The Iona Prayer Circle functions outside of the prayer service but also participates in the work of intercession. This work is regarded as so significant that the Prayer Circle secretary is a permanent appointment within the community. The Prayer List used by them is 'circulated throughout the UK and to the circle of intercessors, living all over the world' (The Iona Community 1996).

Part of the Rule which members of Iona agree to is to pray regularly and frequently for each other. This, too, is part of intercessory prayer. An annual prayer guidebook is created for members which includes prayer for each member by name once a month on a particular day (The Iona Community 2007). Thus, daily intercessory prayer is also part of the Rule of the Iona Community members.

In the Service of Prayer for Healing, immediately following the prayers of intercession is the laying-on of hands. Laying-on of hands is one of the practises of healing in the Iona Community.

Ruth Burgess explains the laying-on of hands.

> What actually happens is that those asking for prayer will come and kneel in a circle on cushions laid out in a space in the middle of the church, and others will stand beside them. When the worship leaders pray for an individual they will place their hands on the individual's head, and at the same time those nearest the person being prayed for will put a hand on the person's shoulder or arm. A prayer is then said for the person, worship leaders and congregation saying the words together, often:
>
> *Spirit of the living God, present with us now,*
> *Enter you, body, mind and spirit, and heal you of all that harms you.*
>
> *In Jesus name, amen.*

Often those not near enough to touch the person being prayed for will put a hand on the shoulder of the person standing nearest to them, as a way of being physically involved in the prayer. When all those kneeling have been prayed for they stand up and let others take their place. They can choose to return to their seats or remain as part of the group sharing the laying-on of hands. (2000a)

Margaret Stewart, medical doctor and minister, spoke in the introduction to a healing service concerning the laying-on of hands:

We come forward with concern for our lack of wholeness, for family and friends, for broken community and by our action in asking and accepting the hands of the people who travel alongside us tonight we open ourselves to the power of the spirit. Such can energise the healing process present in our bodies, our minds and our spirits. (Stewart, quoted in Monteith 2000)

Often this laying-on of hands will happen while a song is sung. The Service of Prayer for Healing then ends with a closing prayer and benediction.

Laying-on of hands is not exercised by one person but by the whole community (Burgess 2000a; Ferguson 1998; Macleod 1955) as they bring a person or situation to the healing attention of God. Typically this laying-on of hands occurs within a healing prayer service. Ruth Burgess wrote part of the liturgy for this service. She explains how she sees the role of community in healing.

My perception of what we do is that we create a space for God to act. This is what worship is…bringing people into an awareness of God's presence and action. It is not us that create energy, we create context, the action comes from God. It can come through us, but does not originate in us, and we cannot 'make' anything happen. We ask God to act. (R. Burgess, personal communication, 10 December 2006)

Another context of prayer is the Daily Office which all members follow. The Daily Office is an annual guide for Iona members. As each day a different member is prayed for, clearly they see healing justice as an ongoing act.

Healing justice as learning from the 'other'

Kathy Galloway explains that justice as healing is a justice that includes learning 'from the justice and peacemakers of other faiths, and from artists, ecologists and community activists among others' (2000). The Iona Community has learned from their interdenominational heritage that they need to be open and attentive to others. They must seek justice, not just within the church, but also by learning from a whole variety of others. Galloway says that these others include both neighbour and enemy. They must seek security through establishing friendships and through seeking the security of others rather than their insecurity. The Iona Community and its members are quite active in interfaith relations as they take the opportunity to participate in and to host forums to explore these themes.

Healing justice as accountability

Members reported that their practise of healing justice included being accountable for their finances and their time. Such accountability is indicated in the second and third items of the Community's Rule. Members meet together in Family Groups for support, encouragement and accountability. These Family Groups are one of the places members are challenged and supported to live out the Justice and Peace Commitment. Members are encouraged to account for 90 per cent of their disposable income. It is expected that they tithe, some of their donation going to the Iona Community, some to the church and some to charities that the member supports. A former Leader of the Community summarized how this practise is experienced in the community:

> This kind of transparency is quite a demanding and, at times, painful thing. We tend not to be very hard on one another, but we do believe that this kind of exercise is intrinsic to our personal and corporate search for justice. (G. Brown, personal communication, 1 January 2007)

By being accountable for their time and money, they create an environment that supports innovative experiments in living and modelling their lives, based on their best insights so far into what healing justice looks like in practise.

The goal is to be purposeful in every aspect of how life is lived. How we spend our money and time marks how we move through the world. The Iona Community seems to believe that we can move through the world in violent and destructive ways or in just and peaceful ways. By calling people to follow the rules of accountability for time and money, the Community is trying to offer its members support and encouragement to move through the world in more just, peaceful and healing ways.

In some ways the practises of healing justice in the Iona Community are as diverse as its members, each one embodying the vision in different ways and in different places. In the preceding section I have tried to highlight some of the common features of that practise. But what inspires or sustains such a vision of justice? That is the subject of the next section.

Sustaining healing justice in the Iona Community

How does the Iona Community identify the various conditions and factors, the cultural dynamics, which sustain their vision of justice as healing? As with each of the communities examined here, none of these factors independently stand on their own. Each dynamic is connected to and informed by the others. It is better to imagine these as a web of dynamics than a list of ingredients.

Cultivating common directions and tasks

Healing justice is sustained by a sense of a community holding common directions, principles and tasks. For the Iona Community that common direction is largely summed up in the Peace and Justice Commitment. One member called the common direction the Kingdom of God (D. Van der Hijden, personal communication, 23 December 2006). Another called it a commitment to a radical understanding of the gospel (T. Gordon, personal communication, 04 January 2007). Their five-fold Rule offers a practise that all community members agree to pursue. These common practises, over time, create both the cohesions and tensions of belonging to a diverse group. When it is working, the practise of the Rule creates the trust and openness required to pursue justice as healing (T. Gordon, personal communication, 04 January 2007). Healing justice is sustained by common vision.

The Iona Community believes that ideas are not enough. They believe that ideas must be embodied in a living community before they can be of service. This view is sometimes called incarnation in reference to how God became flesh in the person Jesus or in the world. Jesus is not seen as some distant ideal but as a way of embodying the love of God in the midst of the varying social, political and material dynamics of the day. This embodying of love at every stage is the vision, the means and end of ministry of the Iona Community.

The founding Leader of the Iona Community, George MacLeod, stressed this focus on engaged love by focusing on common tasks. In his words, 'A compelling common task alone creates community.' This initial task was the rebuilding of the Abbey and the engaging of the political-theological imagination of the workers. The second Leader of the Community, Ian Reid, also affirmed that their task was the rebuilding of people and relationships (G. Brown, personal communication, 3 January 2007). A ministry of friendship has been a defining characteristic of the Iona Community since the very early days (Ferguson 1998). The current Leader claims that the Iona Community is not sustained through theories or commandments but through something like the urge to friendship.

> The impetus to do this hard and often unpopular work [of justice as healing] does not come from theories, or 'thou shalts.' It comes, like the urge to friendship, from our desire for what is lively, vivid, life-enhancing, for freedom and laughter, for all the things we give and receive in friendship. (Galloway 2000)

Healing justice is sustained by a common direction and task that is at one and the same time relational, spiritual and political. The Rule calls on members to be engaged outside of their own Community in the task of building and rebuilding a politics of love in the world.

Bible reading, prayer and worship

The Iona Community members were very clear that their orientation to a justice that heals is sustained by practises of Bible reading, prayer, liturgy and worship. Their first Rule has to do with daily prayer and regular and frequent Bible reading. The knowledge that someone is praying for you and that you need to pray for others helps to sustain them in their work for peace and justice.

They believe there is a link between these practises of Christian faith and healing justice in the world. The Iona Deputy Leader of 17 years, Ralph Morton, claims that there is a direct link between Christian discipleship and the peace of the world. Moreover, he claims that finding 'anew the way of discipleship' is the beginning place of all other action.

> The first thing that is demanded of the followers of Jesus Christ is that they find anew the way of discipleship for men in the world to-day. This is the first demand, because without it we can never begin and therefore never do anything else… It may seem ridiculous to link such

a seemingly ineffective thing as this with so terrifying a problem as the peace of the world. But it is the only thing we have to offer. It is the only way by which the peace of the world will be assured. (1957)

In Morton's perspective the Iona Community cannot begin to contribute towards the peace of the world directly. It can do so only by looking again at what it means to be a follower of Jesus Christ. This Christ that the Iona Community must follow cannot be reduced to principles, values or universal cultural dynamics. The Community will need to find its direction by seeking out ways of following Jesus, ways that perhaps have been forgotten and need to be revived or perhaps new ways that are responsive to the world today.

The Iona Community is quick to recognize how Christians have been embroiled in colonialization, genocide and capitalistic empire building. While the Christian Right is perhaps the most well-known current movement trying to bring Christian piety and politics together, the Iona Community is articulating a very different alternative. For them, the solution is in taking Jesus more seriously. It is their prayer, Bible reading and worship that lead them to engage in healing kinds of justice. This radical particularity, they believe, equips them to be a gift for the world and to respectfully connect and participate with those who have different religious beliefs.

Facing the suffering of the world

One of the most significant factors in sustaining healing justice in the Iona Community is that they choose to stand near the disadvantaged. The Iona Community believes that it is 'where it stands that will enlighten what it thinks' (Ferguson 1998). The Community stands with one foot on an island of great beauty and the other in the heart of the inner city. In both places they encounter the beauty and the suffering of the world. It is what Iona Member Tom Gordon calls a focus on reality.

What, I believe, has sustained the Iona Community, through changing generations and membership, is its focus on reality. It seeks not to stand apart but to engage with real issues and real people. This is not to say that it has now, or ever has had, all the answers. But it faces real and painful issues honestly, and is prepared to take a stand on what is important. (T. Gordon, personal communication, 04 January 2007)

Another member of the Iona Community explains how facing the suffering of the world sparks the practise of healing justice.

> Actually, the greatest impetus to sustained commitment to healing justice is the state of the world in which we live. It was the needs of the developing world which drew me into Christian education in Africa. It was the starvation of the people of Biafra which drew me into relief work. It was the oppression of black people in South Africa which drew me to share in theological education there and then into the anti-apartheid struggle. In all of these areas there were members of the Iona Community there before me. (G. Brown, personal communication, 3 January 2007)

Facing into the suffering of the world with the eyes of Christ leads members of the Iona Community to engage more deeply with the world.

Standing near Creation

Drawing on the Celtic insistence that all of life is sacred, the Iona Community is sustained by standing near Creation. One member said the Creation is an incarnation and emanation of God (D. Van der Hijden, personal communication, 23 December 2006). Creation flows out of God and gives body to the character of God. By standing near and recognizing the sacredness of Creation you touch God, and this transforms your way of living. This view of the sacredness of all life creates what Kathy Galloway calls a 'self-disciplined ethos of reverence and respect for cultural, spiritual and bio-diversity alike' (2000).

Ferguson argues that the survival of the planet is dependent on the notion of sacramental reverence replacing notions of dominance and exploitation.

> The whole earth is sacramental... Reverence for the earth, God's sacrament, is not only right and fitting, it is essential for the survival of the planet. So it is too with reverence for people, bearers also of the life of God. The image of man as dominant exploiter of the earth must be replaced by man[3] as steward of God's creation, holding all things in trust. (1998)

Healing justice is sustained by seeing the sacredness of all of life, all of creation.

---

3   The Iona Community today tends not to use exclusive male language to refer to all of humanity. Because including those who have been marginalized is a key theme of the community, it is important to them to avoid exclusive male language.

Engaging your own brokenness and complicity

In the Iona Community healing justice is sustained by engaging your own brokenness and your complicity in the brokenness of the world.

> But for many of us, healing only begins when we recognise our own complicity, not only as victims, but also as perpetrators, and we go at last to all those who suffered for us and ask to be received back. In some deep sense, those who died were the random victims of all of us who survived. And those who mourn, mourn for all of us. (Morrow 2000)

Duncan Morrow was speaking about how their lens of healing justice interprets the situation in Northern Ireland. He captures a number of factors which seem to sustain healing justice in the Iona Community. Healing justice does not come from distant experts. It comes from those who are complicit in the wrongs of the world but nevertheless are trying to find a path of healing. It comes not from those who have the perfect plan for restoration, but from those who are willing to confess their own brokenness. The Iona Community has traditionally seen itself as a servant of the church at large. They are quick to remember that 'Christianity itself needs to be healed' (Ferguson 1998). One example of this is the daily morning prayer which includes a section on confession (The Iona Community 2007). Such a focus could nurture a paralysis of guilt, but here it seems to sustain a way of being engaged in healing of others as you are in the process of healing. It is the willingness to engage your own brokenness that helps to sustain healing justice (R. Burgess, personal communication, 18 December 2006).

Living as an engaged collective

The Iona Community was established, in part, to experiment with how living in community might sustain a different vision of being church in the world. Through sixty plus years of experiment they are convinced that a supportive community is needed to sustain their life and vision, but that such a community is not an end in itself (Ferguson 1998). As one member told me (T. Gordon, personal communication, 4 January 2007), they try to offer an alternative to two flawed models of church: the church as one-to-one relationship with God (the liberal individualist model) and the church as self-serving and self-perpetuating institution (the conservative model). Each model has difficulty sustaining healing justice, the individualist model because it cannot see beyond the individual; the conservative model as it cannot see beyond itself. Being engaged as a community is about discovering and responding to Christ in the world. When healthy, this community sees beyond itself, even to the point of letting itself die. This community, in the Iona Community's understanding, is there for the good of the world, to bring healing, justice and peace.

Supporting each other

The Iona Community continues today as a support network for Christians engaged in peace and justice activities that cannot find support within the traditional church structure. One aspect of this support is accountability, the fifth and last rule of the community. Numerous members told me that what sustained their practise of healing justice was the support and loving challenges that they received from the community through monthly Family Groups, Community Week, plenary meetings and through prayers.

Being a movement rather than an institution

The Iona Community believes that to sustain their practises of healing justice they must organize as a movement or an organism rather than an institution. To live as a movement means a wide range of things: to maintain light structures (G. Brown, personal communication, 3 January 2007); to be attentive to the vision, stimulus and change which young people bring; to let some things die (Ferguson 1998); to see the community as scaffolding rather than as building; to listen to and be surprised by other people's ideas and stories; to accept change, and to take risks.

The Iona Community does not see healing justice as something that can be institutionalized. They believe that the less institutionalized and geared towards permanence they are, the more space they have to risk and explore the kinds of relationships which come out of a justice that heals.

Listening to the stories of those who have gone before

One feature that surfaced in several interviews as a sustaining factor was listening to the stories of other members of the Iona Community. Just hearing the stories of what others have done and are doing inspires them to action. This seems to be the main purpose of the community's bi-monthly magazine, *The Coracle*, and many of the books published by the Iona Community's publishing house, Wild Goose Publications (Macdonald 1999; Meaden 1999; Steven 1990). Listening to the stories of others doing the work of healing justice seems to spark the courage and imagination necessary to engage injustice in your own context.

Nurturing deep roots and indigenous expressions of faith

The Iona Community believes that a charity model of aid is insufficient to sustain a justice that heals. The focus of international peace needs to shift from 'focusing on quick fixes, and emergency aid, [to focusing on the] issue of war on want' (Ferguson 1998). It is the greed of the world which must be addressed through forms of decreasing want and increasing sharing. What sustains their view of justice is a desire to move beneath the symptoms and crisis and to find paths of healing that are grounded in the life of the world and therefore also in the reverent respect for all of life. The grounding in life is what they see as having sustained their commitment to healing (Monteith 2000).

In the various experiments of faith in inner city Glasgow and also around the world, the Iona Community has tried to nurture indigenous expressions of faith.

> The goal of the small and vulnerable churches in the housing schemes and inner-city areas is to struggle to form indigenous expressions of faith over against a paternalistic, dominant Church…(Ferguson 1998)

The refusal to impose a system on everyone helps to create space for the rise of indigenous or locally rooted expressions of healing justice. This desire for local expressions of faith and life came out as a strong theme in my interviews.

A tension or inconsistency emerges here. Within the Iona Community's project to nurture meaningful worship they have collected songs from around the world and written many of their own, sometimes following local folk songs. They have also written a number of dramas and liturgies. As these materials are made available through the worship resource group and publishing arm, they have become an export commodity and are used around the world. Some churches depend more on importing the resources of the Iona Community than on creating their own. However, the goal of the Iona Community is not for other groups to become like them but rather that peace, justice and healing are nurtured and supported in local ways by local people.

Critical solidarity with the state

The Iona Community engages in political debate with the leaders of the day. In the last election in Scotland, Iona Members or Associates ran for five different parties (K. Galloway, personal communication, 22 December 2006). However they do so from the standpoint of critical solidarity (G. Brown, personal communication, 3 January 2007). In the Iona context the frame is not the usual separation of church and state, nor is it an agenda for a neo-Christendom. They seem to believe that the church is at its best when it is 'radical, freewheeling, prophetic, refusing to bend the knee. When it degenerates into a prudential buttress for the powers-that-be, it sells Jesus down the river' (Monteith 2000). Christians need to have the ability both to challenge and to support the state to act in just ways.

In the view of the Iona Community, Christians must have the capacity to break the laws of the state if they are seen as unjust. A number of Iona members have spent time in jail because of what they see as witnessing against the unjust ways of the state. There is an important distinction being made here. The church ceases to be a sustaining force for healing justice when it becomes an unconditional buttress to the powers-that-be.

The dynamics that sustain healing justice approaches in the Iona Community do not function in isolation. Each dynamic is interconnected with the others, all functioning together to help support a justice that heals. To better understand their approach it is also necessary to understand what they believe acts as a barrier to healing justice.

Barriers to healing justice

In my dialogues with members of the Iona Community I got a wide range of responses concerning what functions as a barrier to healing justice. Again, I have only listed here ideas that surfaced from more than one source. If members of the Iona Community were brought together to dialogue on this topic they would probably have a much longer and more in-depth list.

Prejudices, beliefs and mistrusts of the advocates of healing justice

The Iona Community believes that barriers to healing justice arise internally, sometimes even within those individuals seeking after such a justice. Members told me stories of when thinking you owned the truth

(D. Van der Hijden, personal communication, 23 December 2006) or mistrusting difference in others (R. Burgess, personal communication, 18 December 2006) created huge barriers between people. One member (G. Brown, personal communication, 3 January 2007) told of how the prejudices of a member damaged the relationships with a group the community was trying to reach out to and thereby set back relationships and opportunities to enhance healing justice. A barrier to healing justice may come from within or among its advocates.

Church as part of injustice

Although many members of the Iona Community work within the church, the church is also seen as potentially one of the barriers to healing justice. They listed a number of ways the church has been and continues to be involved with injustice rather than healing justice. Some of the particular issues were excluding gay and lesbian couples from leadership roles in the Church (G. Brown, personal communication, 3 January 2007), excluding women from the church (D. Van der Hijden, personal communication, 6 December 2006) and teaching people that sickness is a result of lack of faith (R. Burgess, personal communication, 18 December 2006). Christian theology and teaching that focuses on 'personally being right with God' (T. Gordon, personal communication, 4 January 2007) as the only item of concern was also used to illustrate how sometimes the theology of churches blinds them to seeing their own systems and structures which also need transforming and reconciling.

Power struggles and the desire to impose

It seems that hierarchical power structures act as barriers to healing justice. The desire to win, or to impose one system, idea or ethos on everyone was identified as a barrier to the creation of communities of healing justice. Similarly, patriarchal power structures were identified as a barrier. Both patriarchal and hierarchical power were seen to limit risk-taking, creativity and the ability to let go, factors which were seen as necessary components of a community committed to healing justice.

Mainstream political systems

Many features of mainstream political systems were highlighted as creating barriers to healing justice. I think the focus here on mainstream systems came in part from their relative influence but also from the desire to be accountable for one's own system. The significant apathy and disillusionment with politics among the general population was highlighted as a symptom of a system not working. Healing justice tends to be grassroots by nature and in mainstream political systems it is inhibited by the distance between those in power and those in real life (T. Gordon, personal communication, 4 January 2007). The tradition of separating government and religion was also identified as a barrier (D. Van der Hijden, personal communication, 6 December 2006; R. Burgess, personal communication, 18 December 2006). Because the Iona Community comes at healing justice through a politics modelled after the life and teachings of Jesus, separation of church and state makes little sense to them. When church is ruled out of the public sphere and is regarded as a private spiritual matter a barrier to healing justice arises. A justice that heals is interested in spiritual and physical, the political and the personal, the wound and the structures and systems which surround it. Mainstream politics sometimes leave little room for this kind of expansive view of justice and therefore can act as a barrier to it.

Capitalism, the division between rich and poor and the fear of loss

Economic and political theories like capitalism were identified as key barriers to healing justice (D. Van der Hijden, personal communication, 23 December 2006). In part, this is because Community members believe that such structures are designed to keep people poor and uneducated (R. Burgess, personal communication, 18 December 2006). Those in the West tend to live at ecologically and culturally unsustainable levels. Even within the West the gap between rich and poor continues to grow. Members of the Iona Community by and large self-identify themselves as the rich, relative to the majority of the world. They recognize that the healing of injustices around the world would require different economic systems and ways of living, especially from the rich. A barrier to such change is the fear of loss of wealth, power and control. The rich would have to move out of their comfort zones, and this is one of the major barriers to healing justice (T. Gordon, personal communication, 4 January 2007).

Desire for permanence

The desire to keep organizations and structures alive forever is another part of what keeps healing justice from flourishing (R. Burgess, personal communication, 18 December 2006; T. Gordon, personal communication, 4 January 2007). When corporate identities outlive their purpose they tend to institutionalize, bureaucratize and move into a replication mode. Under these conditions healing justice struggles. Communities that support healing justice need space for change, transformation, the dying of outmoded ways and birthing of new ideas. The institutional desire for permanence acts as a barrier to healing justice.

Final words

In this case study I have tried to outline the story of the Iona Community from the perspective of healing justice. It is an attempt to tell the story of how they understand and approach healing justice. For the Iona Community healing justice clearly comes out of their faith orientation but pushes them to work in solidarity with many people who do not share that faith orientation. For them healing justice is a theo-political way of engaging the world. A defining feature of their approach is to focus on the personal, the structural and the spiritual as if they are one. This orientation has taken them from the inner city to global politics, from disease to the problems of capitalism, from crime to issues of poverty and greed. Here healing justice moves freely between personal episodes and structural change. At each step along the path of healing justice, the Iona Community has tried to recognize the sacredness of all creation such that healing justice becomes finding your humanity, recognizing the image of God in others, listening to and caring for creation and finding ways to embrace those on the fringes.

Chapter 6

Plum Village

Please Call Me by My True Names[1]
Don't say that I will depart tomorrow
even today I am still arriving.

Look deeply: every second I am arriving
to be a bud on a Spring branch
to be a tiny bird, with still-fragile wings
learning to sing in my new nest
to be a caterpillar in the heart of a flower
to be a jewel hiding itself in a stone.

I still arrive, in order to laugh and to cry
to fear and to hope.

The rhythm of my heart is the birth and death
of all that is alive.

I am the mayfly metamorphosing
on the surface of the river.
And I am the bird
that swoops down to swallow the mayfly.

I am the frog swimming happily
in the clear water of a pond.
And I am the grass-snake
that silently feeds itself on the frog.

---

1   Reprinted from *Call Me By My True Names* (1999) by Thich Nhat Hanh with permission of Parallax Press, Berceley, California, www.parallax.org.

I am the child in Uganda, all skin and bones
my legs as thin as bamboo sticks.
And I am the arms merchant
selling deadly weapons to Uganda.

I am the twelve-year-old girl
refugee on a small boat
who throws herself into the ocean
after being raped by a sea pirate.
And I am the pirate
my heart not yet capable
of seeing and loving.

I am a member of the politburo
with plenty of power in my hands.
And I am the man who has to pay
his 'debt of blood' to my people
dying slowly in a forced-labor camp.

My joy is like Spring, so warm
it makes flowers bloom all over the Earth.
My pain is like a river of tears
so vast it fills the four oceans.

Please call me by my true names
so I can hear all my cries and my laughter at once
so I can see that my joy and pain are one.

Please call me by my true names
so I can wake up
and so the door of my heart
can be left open
the door of compassion.

(Hanh 1993)

In response to the rape by a sea pirate and the subsequent suicide of a 12-year-old girl, Thich Nhat Hanh,[2] the founder and leader of the Buddhist monastery Plum Village, became very angry and went home to meditate on what would be a just or right response. He had cultivated practises of looking deeply at the true nature of things, of using his breath

---

2   Thich Nhat Hanh is his Buddhist Dharma name and the name he uses in publication. His name at birth was Nguyên Xuân Bảo. In this chapter I will use the Dharma names of the monks and nuns rather than their birth names. Where a person is known more broadly by both names, I will also indicate the birth name.

to build the energy of mindfulness, of structuring life so that every step, every look, taste and action would call him back to his true self, a self capable of deep suffering and deep joy. And so with all these practises behind him, his anger transformed into compassion and he wrote this poem. One could read it as an Engaged Buddhist response to 'serious crime'.

The poem does not use the language of crime, nor even of justice. In fact the language of justice is almost entirely missing from the discourse of Thich Nhat Hanh and Plum Village. Some Buddhist scholars have called this approach healing justice. Here we can begin to see that healing justice has a different place and focus in the life of the community than most Western forms of justice (Loy 2001). Healing justice is about learning our true names, about seeing ourselves in the web of interconnection and change, about cultivating compassion for and in all beings and even with non-beings. Healing justice is about arriving home. For some people this language may seem too airy, romantic or even naive. But this way of healing justice was born out of the suffering of the Vietnam War as part of a renewal movement within Buddhism. In 1959, when the Vietnam War started, Thich Nhat Hanh was 33 years old and his future assistant Sister Chân Không[3] was 21. Through this brutal war which killed an estimated 5.1 million Vietnamese and an additional 63,484 foreign troops (Smith 2000), these two Buddhists worked in the war zones and the slums of Vietnam, searching for how to cultivate and manifest compassion, peace and what would later be called healing justice. They saw themselves as working for the renewal of Buddhism, what they called 'Engaged Buddhism' (Hanh 1967).

Thich Nhat Hanh was later to be exiled from Vietnam because of his stand for peace and for compassion for all Vietnamese people, more specifically for his refusal to take sides. In exile, together with Sister Chân Không, he established Plum Village as a community based in the visions and practises which were formed in the fire of suffering and war. Plum Village always had three goals: to model a community based on the practises of compassion and loving-kindness; to be a support and advocate base for the plight of people in Vietnam; to be a teaching and practise centre for those who want to learn about Engaged Buddhism. Today, both Sister Chân Không and Thich Nhat Hanh live at Plum Village and

---

3   Sister Chân Không has the birth name of Cao Ngoc Phuong under which she has published some writing.

are known in the West as key figures that helped to bring Buddhism to the West.

My hope was that if I could convince Plum Village to participate in this study, they would offer a profound example of what healing justice tastes like, looks like and sounds like. I offer four reasons for their inclusion here. First, Buddhists are one of 'the longest-enduring groups in human history – over 2,500 years' (Hanh and Lawlor 2002). By comparison the experiments of the Western criminal justice and penal justice are relatively recent. Healing justice is used by communities who draw on long wisdom traditions. Perhaps there is something to learn about how to live together from a community which has lasted so long. Second, Engaged Buddhism featured strongly among the groups that use the language of healing justice surveyed in Chapter 1 and also played an important role in the United Nations-initiated 'cultures of peace' movement (Chappell 1999). Being the home of one of the leaders of the Engaged Buddhism movement, Plum Village is potentially a strong example of an embodiment of that movement. Third, the leader of Plum Village is an internationally respected and renowned Buddhist peacebuilder worthy of our attention. When Martin Luther King, Jr, nominated him for a Nobel Peace Prize, King argued that conferring the prize on him would 'remind all nations that men of good will stand ready to lead warring elements out of an abyss of hatred and destruction. It would re-awaken men to the teaching of beauty and love found in peace. It would help to revive hopes for a new order of justice and harmony' (King Jr 1967). King believed that listening to the wisdom of Thich Nhat Hanh could reawaken people to a different kind of justice. If the exploration into healing justice is to be compelling we would do well to explore what King saw as so pregnant with possibilities. Fourth, in my experience the teaching and practises of Thich Nhat Hanh and Plum Village have the ability to transform the nature of one's imagination.[4] As healing justice is being explored as an alternative imagination, it is natural to turn to such a community.

At the outset it is important to make a clarification on language. I have already noted that the language of justice is almost absent from the vocabulary of Thich Nhat Hanh and Plum Village. Neither do they use

4   Previous to this research I had not been to Plum Village. I had read several books by Thich Nhat Hanh and had used one of them as a text in an undergraduate course I taught at the Canadian Mennonite University in Winnipeg.

the language of healing justice. In the opening chapter we saw David Loy speak of a Buddhist perspective on restorative justice as one of 'healing justice' (2001). Loy points not to Plum Village but to Tibet as a recent example of Buddhist healing justice worked out in lay society. However, David Loy is part of the movement of Engaged Buddhism, a movement championed, and some people say started, by Thich Nhat Hanh. Engaged Buddhism brings together traditional meditative practises with active non-violence. It is a way of being Buddhist that engages the large issues of the contemporary world. So if David Loy's perspective is correct, that an Engaged Buddhist perspective on justice is a kind of healing justice, then by reasonable extension we could name the kind of justice practised at Plum Village as healing justice. But this is an extension rather than the community's own language. When I asked them about this absence of the language of justice, I was told that the language of justice was perhaps seen as too abstract and too loaded with connotations of judgement and punishment, neither of which they believe has a place in a more healing orientation. I was told that justice often misses the point of 'healing, healing not just of the individual but the society which allows the conditions to exist where people become criminals' (anonymous novice monk, personal communication, 16 January 2007). They used the language of healing, understanding, compassion, transformation and being peace. They have no additional concept of justice which is held in tension with their kind of healing and peace. Transformation and healing is the response. In fact, one nun told me that all their practise is healing (Nhu' Nghiêm, personal communication, 17 January 2007). A monk, who was also a medical doctor, explained that this broad approach to healing at Plum Village was different from what he had learned in conventional medicine. Medicine tended to focus on fighting disease whereas Plum Village is more focused on cultivating conditions for health (Pháp Liêu, personal communication, 18 January 2007). This pointing away from a punitive model of justice toward a more compassionate one based on traditional teaching, is a key feature mentioned in Chapter 1 among those who use the language of justice. While Plum Villagers do not use the language of healing justice they do use the language of healing to express a similar sentiment and others close to them describe their kind of practise as healing justice. As all their practises together are healing, this case study must look broadly at their practises and visions to understand their approach to healing justice.

After giving an introduction and historic overview of Plum Village and its leader, Thich Nhat Hanh, this chapter will outline their praxis of healing justice. To do this adequately it is necessary to tell the story of Plum Village without separating their vision from their practises and from the dynamics which sustain that vision and practise. For them the teaching is the practise, the practise is the teaching. The life of the community, called Sangha, is the teaching, called Dharma. Thich Nhat Hanh calls this intersecting point 'the living Dharma' (Hanh 2002b).

Rather than separating what belongs together, we will examine the praxis of healing justice at Plum Village through the themes that emerged from my looking at, and listening deeply to, their life together.

History and overview

Plum Village is a Buddhist monastery started by the Unified Buddhist Church in 1982 to replace its predecessor of Sweet Potatoes Community, started in 1975. The Unified Buddhist Church[5] was founded by Plum Village's spiritual leader, The Most Venerable Zen Master Thich Nhat Hanh, affectionately known as Thây, meaning teacher. Because this research approaches Plum Village to respectfully learn from them, I will frequently use this term to refer to their leader.

Thich Nhat Hanh was born in central Vietnam in 1926. He joined the monastery at the age of 16. During the Vietnam War he became known within the international community for his peace work. He believed that Buddhist monks could not hide or meditate in the temples when their people who were suffering the devastation of war needed them. He initiated what he later called 'Engaged Buddhism' which developed the capacity for a socially engaged spirituality. One of Thây's disciples in the West describes engaged practise as having 'the potential to influence and transform certain habit energies in our society (such as materialism, militarism, and intolerance) with insight, equanimity, and compassion that are the fruits of sustained and wholehearted practise' (Hanh and Laulor 2002). Thây saw himself as working for the renewal of Buddhism in Vietnam. He struggled against the conservative hierarchy (Cao 1993) and tried to refocus the Pure Land Buddhism tradition which had been popular in Vietnam for 300 years. Thây is from the Zen tradition,

---

5   The UBC is an official body in France but is not directly connected to The Unified
     Buddhist Church of Vietnam which sometimes worked with and sometimes against the
     projects and teaching of Thich Nhat Hanh.

which predates the Pure Land tradition in Vietnam (Nguyen 1997). He does not see a contradiction between these traditions. However, when the Pure Land tradition is taken to extremes it treats the Buddha like a god and focuses on the future where this world can be escaped by entering the Pure Land (Pháp Liêu, personal communication, 18 January 2007). Thây's teaching is that the Pure Land can be touched in the present moment, right where you are. Quite often he says that he 'walks everyday in the Pure Land.' He teaches that the key to well-being is found right in the midst of ill-being, that happiness is not something that you need to wait for until the next life, or until through many years of suffering you have perfected the art of meditation. For him happiness, meditation and healing can happen in the present moment, with each breath and each step. Moreover, he returned to the origins of the Buddha, examining what the Buddha actually said and did. From this he is clear that the Buddha is not a god and that within every person, even the criminal and the enemy, there is a Buddha nature which can be awakened and can bloom when watered with compassion and understanding. All these views lead him to an ethic of engaged nonviolent action.

In the 1960s Thich Nhat Hanh started a relief organization, the School of Youth Social Service, to train social workers in this ethic of social change based on love, commitment and responsibility (Cao 1993). Upon graduation these workers were sent to remote areas to serve the poor (Cao 1993). While the war raged around them, these workers took on many tasks: cleaning up corpses, developing pioneer villages as models for social change, establishing resettlement centres and creating educational programmes for children and adults. Thich Nhat Hanh and a number of other monastics provided the imagination and inspiration. Others like Sister Chân Không provided the practical creativity of how to be present in respectful ways to those who were suffering while at the same time cultivating the conditions of more healthy living.

Thich Nhat Hanh also founded the Van Hanh Buddhist University in Saigon and started a publishing house and a peace activist magazine. During the war, Thây refused to take sides, instead calling for peace from all parties. This was too much for the government, and in 1966 he was banned from Vietnam by both the communist and non-communist governments. He began an exile which lasted 39 years. He went to France as part of a Buddhist delegation to the Paris Peace Talks, talks which eventually resulted in accords between North Vietnam and the United States (Hanh 1998).

While in exile Thich Nhat Hanh and Sister Chân Không decided to make France their home base as they continued to develop their practise of Engaged Buddhism. After the war, when people were fleeing Vietnam by going out to sea in inadequate boats, Thây and Sister Chân Không hired boats to rescue the boat people and advocated for them. Today they continue to help to raise awareness of wrongful arrests in Vietnam. They try to give voice in the West to human rights abuses in Vietnam. Sister Chân Không developed a network of families from Vietnam and Europe which would give monthly to the support of poor people in Vietnam. Both Thây and Sister Chân Không visited many high-ranking politicians to ask for their support in encouraging the Vietnamese government to act with compassion. During the war they tried to confront and challenge the US peace movement. That movement was so focused on how destructive the US presence was in Vietnam that they incorrectly assumed a victory of the North would help bring peace.

This history is important to show that practises of Plum Village were developed in the fire of war, grassroots community development and international politics. It comes from those who picked up the bodies of corpses and buried them while soldiers from both sides were firing overhead. It comes from those who have seen the suffering of war and of crimes of all kinds and believe that the most fruitful social change comes through compassion and love for all living beings. One of the nuns at Plum Village, who used to be a lawyer in the US, summed up the core of Plum Village's practise in this way: 'We do these practises so that we can see what brings us health and happiness and what doesn't. We try to train ourselves to do the things that bring health and happiness and to avoid the things that do not' (Tùng Nghiêm, personal communication, 15 January 2007). Knowing this history and their teaching, it is clear that the happiness of which they speak is not the superficial happiness so often sold as a commodity in the West. Rather it is a deep joy of facing the depth of suffering and still being able to recognize the beauty of life, even in the eyes of an enemy.

While in France Thây and Sister Chân Không started a community to support their work. They called it Sweet Potato Community. When the community put on their first summer retreat in 1981, more people came than could be accommodated and so the community started to look for a new home. Plum Village was begun in 1982.

Plum Village started as a Vietnamese community of the followers of Thich Nhat Hanh. Over the last 30 years the community has grown and changed in many ways. Today the community welcomes thousands of visitors on retreat every year from all over the world. As of January 2007 the community is comprised of four hamlets: Upper Hamlet housing 48 monks, Sol Ha Temple housing 14 monks, Lower Hamlet housing 31 nuns, New Hamlet housing 35 nuns. These hamlets also house the retreatants and resident lay-practitioners which number as high as 650 people at a time during the summer. Each hamlet is autonomous spiritually, financially and organizationally although they all share the same purpose and teachings. The community has roots in Vietnam, but has had to grow to be appropriate for the environment where it has been planted (Hanh 2003c). The monks and nuns come from a large variety of backgrounds: French, English, Dutch, German, American, Russian, Italian, Spanish, Vietnamese, Cambodian, Thai and Canadian.

Within Buddhist traditions the community blends several traditions. Key sutras are drawn from original Buddhism along with key principles of the Mahayana tradition, and these are implemented through the Zen tradition (Plum Village delegation 2006). Ordained practitioners at Plum Village belong to the 44th generation of the Lin Chi School and the 10th generation of the Liễu Quán Dharma Line.

Thich Nhat Hanh has written over 100 books covering a range of topics: guides of engaged mindful practise, renewing the teaching of Buddhism, concerning anger and on Christian Buddhist dialogue. Those interested in Thich Nhat Hanh should read his autobiography *Fragrant Palm Leaves: Journals 1962–1966* (1998) and biography *A Lifetime of Peace* (Willis 2003). Sister Chân Không has written about her own story in *Learning to Love: How I Learned and Practised Social Change in Vietnam* (Cao 1993).

To locate the community within history and geography does not yet give an indication of what it is like to walk into Plum Village Community. One arrives at any of their hamlets by driving through the French hills and vineyards found between Bordeaux and Bergerac. The hamlets are old farms which have been renovated for their purposes, but driving up one is not at first aware that one is on a farm. My first impression was the absolute beauty and quiet of the place. Each of the hamlets has been chosen and cultivated to be a place of beauty. This natural beauty of the views, the trees and the hills is the first impression. But it doesn't take long to realize that there is something different about this place. Some monks and nuns appear with their shaved heads bare and some with Vietnamese conical hats made of hand-woven leaves which have the round rim and pointed top. They wear brown or grey robes. Watching them, it does not take long before they bow to someone. The bow comes with hands pressed together almost as in prayer. They explain that when you bow you offer the lotus flower (your hands in this position look like a lotus flower bud) to the other person and recognize them as a Buddha-to-be. They bow to say thank you, goodbye and hello. Most of the people at Plum Village walk slowly, some very slowly, trying to enjoy each step and each breath.

In fact, the slow pace of this life is a theme of the place. Some of them believe that the pace of modern life is one of the key barriers to cultivating compassion (Đào Nghiêm, personal communication, 17 January 2007). Some of the people look very serious, which I later learn is more concentration than seriousness, but you can tell they are trying hard to slow down and take each step with intentionality. But it is never long between smiles and laughter. The guests seem more serious than the monastics, or at least some of the monastics. Going into buildings it is clear that things are designed simply, not extravagantly. Each hamlet has a large kitchen and dining hall, an office, a few meditation halls, at least two lotus ponds, a bookstore, a large Vietnamese bell tower and, of course, accommodations for the monastics and the visitors. While the buildings are modest it is clear great care and attention has gone into creating each place as a home. It is also clear that Thây has a very important role in this community. People speak of Thây and the 'spirit of Thây'. If he walks by, people may bow out of respect. People seem to enjoy and slow down just being in his presence. I'm not used to seeing a person held in such regard and it creates a mixed response within me. Plum Village is a monastery and retreat centre. It does not fit some of my associations with monasteries as being more rigid, cold or stiff. This is a place of space, flexibility, suffering and joy, but the emphasis is much more on joy.

Plum Village is not just limited to France. Since 1994 in addition to life at Plum Village in France, the community has established a presence in the United States. The Maple Forest Monastery was founded in 1997 in Vermont, Green Mountain Dharma Center in 1998, also in Vermont, Deer Park Monastery in 2000 in California and Blue Cliff Monastery in

New York in 2007. Members of Plum Village Community go every other summer with Thich Nhat Hanh to the United States to lead retreats and to build up these communities. In addition to these communities Plum Village claims 'more than eight hundred local Sanghas have developed in this tradition' (Hanh 2003c). The community is also still very engaged in Vietnam where they have two temples, 385 monastics, plus hundreds of social workers and teachers who are paid a modest salary from Plum Village. With the assistance of the social workers and teachers in Vietnam, Plum Village support many projects like building schools, wells and bridges as well as supporting flood victims with the poor of Vietnam. All these are funded, in part, by the profits from retreats, the bookstores and other donations which are given to Plum Village.

Visions, practises and sustaining dynamics of healing justice

Why does this all exist? The members of Plum Village see their community 'as a Buddhist "laboratory" where they experiment with new "medicines". When a medicine is proven effective in our laboratory, we offer it to the world' (Plum Village delegation 2006). They see their life as a microcosm of what the world could be, so we turn now to their praxis of healing justice.

Healing justice as coming home to the present

> Everyone walks on the earth, but there are those who walk like slaves, with no freedom at all. They are sucked in by the future or by the past, and they are not capable of dwelling in the here and now, where life is available. If we get caught up in our worries, our despair, our regrets about the past, and our fears of the future in our everyday lives, we are not free people. We are not capable of establishing ourselves in the here and now. (Hanh 2002a)

These encouragements to walk as free people rather than slaves were given to inmates in the Maryland Correctional Institution at Hagerstown USA on 16 October 1999. Thây suggested that you could be free even in prison because freedom doesn't depend on your external situation but rather on the ability to dwell mindfully in the present moment. The first challenge of healing and transformation then is to come home to the present.

All of life at Plum Village is designed to remind the practitioner to dwell mindfully in the present moment. The practise of mindful breathing (Hanh 1992a) is the practise of following your breath in such a way that mindful awareness is developed. When Plum Village people practise mindful breathing, they focus their attention away from the thinking mind, into the belly. The busy thinking mind is often racing, dispersed and caught in wrong perception. They don't fight the mind on this, for it is part of them. And as they keep reminding me, in this practise there is no violence. The mind is acknowledged and their focus moves to watching and enjoying their breathing. They simply recognize that attention is like a watering can – whatever you focus on will grow. So they focus their attention on dwelling happily in the present moment (Đinh Nghiêm, personal communication, 15 January 2007). It is the practise of touching nirvana, the Pure Land or the Kingdom of God, in the present moment (Pháp Liêu, personal communication, 18 January 2007). As breathing is the primary rhythm of life, it is here that they start cultivating mindfulness. As they breathe in they may say, 'I know I am breathing in'; as they breathe out they say, 'I know I am breathing out.' Being aware of what you are doing as you are doing it is a very simple practise but it is not easy. Whenever they feel emotions or thoughts which carry them away from the present, they come back to the breath. The monks and nuns I spoke with reported that this is very healing. They claim breathing in and out like this just three times can be calming and relaxing.

Thây teaches his disciples that the present moment is the only moment. Within Plum Village this does not mean some kind of existential, ahistorical, or apolitical way of being in the world. Rather, it is an insight that the way to be fully engaged in life is to be fully aware of the present moment. The practise of mindfulness is not an escape into the self, the spirit world or some form of emptiness. It is the practise of being here for the benefit of the whole world (Hanh 2002b). So at Plum Village they practise mindful breathing, mindful walking and mindful sitting. In fact they try to be mindful in everything they do. In this way, Plum Village is full of the everyday habits practised elsewhere: waking up, getting dressed, going to the bathroom, eating, drinking, greeting others, responding to suffering, enjoying life. However, in Plum Village every act is like a holy, sacred act where the fullness of life can be experienced in every step of every day as one lives in the present moment.

Children are looked upon as persons who already know something about being truly mindful. Children of retreatants report that they enjoy coming to Plum Village because it changes the way their parents act; they are more understanding, more happy, more patient (Hanh 2003c). In fact children seem to have a special place in the life of the community. When Thây gives a dharma talk, he first addresses the children. Children are part of the practise of the community. The schedule of the summer retreat seems to work against children as it is modelled on a monastic life. The schedule demands an early start: Wake up is at 5:30 am, sitting meditation at 6:00 am and breakfast at 6:30 am. With activities that go well into the evening and long periods of Noble Silence when the community is encouraged to be silent, children, especially young ones, sometimes have a difficult time. However, community and friendship is cultivated among the children. The community understands that children cannot be quiet for long periods because they are connected with the present moment. If they see a frog they will yell, 'Frog!' Children are not constantly hushed or pushed away. The noise of children calls others to mindfulness.

For Thây, the opposite of being truly mindful in the present moment is forgetfulness (Hanh 2002a). Forgetfulness is not being aware of, or present to, what it is that you are doing. Forgetfulness both causes great suffering and prevents you from being able to truly enjoy life. Mindfulness, which is the basis of healing justice at Plum Village, is about enjoying the present moment.

Healing justice at Plum Village is not focused on righting a dispute in the past but is rather about learning to enjoy life in the present. It is about freeing people from being a slave to the preoccupation with past or future, and about cultivating the ability to be fully present such that they can see things as they really are. Healing justice, then, is a path to joy which comes through suffering. Healing justice as arriving home in the present means that it is about learning to stop running, striving or accomplishing. Perhaps Plum Village offers a glimpse of how a 'justice system' that is focused on a coming home to the present might look.

Healing justice as coming home to the Earth

We should give up our personal and national interests, and think of the Earth as our true home, a home for all of us. To bring the spiritual dimension to your daily life, to your social, political and economic life – that is your practise. (Hanh 2002c)

The Earth plays a special role in the community of Plum Village. The opening poem illustrates how careful listening to the Earth, in its living and dying, reveals something of the wisdom of compassion. In fact at Plum Village they believe that 'if you are mindful, then when the wind blows through the trees, you will hear the teachings' (Hanh 2002b). Buddhist scriptures typically speak of four communities: monks, nuns, laymen and laywomen. But at Plum Village they include non-humans – the trees, the water, air, birds – as members of the community (Hanh 2002b).

The teachings and life of Plum Village are full of awe and respect for all of life, human and non-human. Thây often quotes a ninth-century meditation teacher and founder of the Rinzai Zen School, Master Lin Chi (also known as Master Linji), who said, 'The miracle is not walking on water but walking on the Earth' (Hanh 2002a). Walking meditation is a way of walking gently on the Earth to remember and experience this respect. Walking meditation is a way of not doing anything, except touching the Earth and touching the wonders of life. It is a way of walking mindfully so that one is aware of the miracle of life as one is taking each step. Many of the people I spoke to claim it is refreshing, transforming and very healing. In walking meditation when the disciples take a step they are taught to say, 'I have arrived', and then in the next step they say, 'I am home', 'in the here', 'in the now'. The goal is to bring them back home to the present moment. As Thây puts it, 'If you miss the present moment you miss your appointment with life' (Hanh 2003d). I was told time and again that this sort of thing was their 'main concrete practise' (Định Nghiêm, personal communication, 15 January 2007). Sister Chân Không reports that throughout her time as a social worker and peace activist it is this practise of walking meditation which nourished her and continually helped to transform her anger (Cao 1993). One nun told me that someone had asked Thich Nhat Hanh what single practise one should do to change one's life. He said walking meditation (Tùng Nghiêm, personal communication, 15 January 2007). This is the practise of slowing down and experiencing life. They say if you are not able to do that with your walking you will not be able to do it in other ways. The practise of walking meditation is to calm the busyness of your thought and emotions and to replace that energy with the nourishment of enjoying the miracle of walking on the earth.

There seems to be something of an economic theory behind this practise. At Plum Village they claim that we in the West have been trained to nourish ourselves on consumerism (Định Nghiêm, personal communication, 15 January 2007). The consumerist culture feeds our greed and craving without ever satisfying it. Moreover much violence is created by building a consumerist culture – the violence of wars for oil, the violence of animal slaughter, the violence of child and slave labour, the violence of structural readjustment for debt. Thây teaches that the American Dream of owning your own car, house and other such symbols, is ecologically unsustainable. There are simply not enough resources in the earth for the whole world to use as much oil as the average American does. So non-violence as coming home to the Earth has to be about letting go of the American Dream and replacing it with a different kind of dream. Walking meditation is one way of nourishing your spirit that is not based on a violent economy but on listening to and enjoying the earth.

At Plum Village they have a practise called Touching the Earth. They describe it in the following terms:

> The practise of Touching the Earth is to return to the Earth, to our roots, to our ancestors, and to recognize that we are not alone but connected to a whole stream of spiritual and blood ancestors. We are their continuation and with them, will continue into the future generations. We touch the earth to let go of the idea that we are separate and to remind us that we are the Earth and part of Life. (Monks and Nuns at Plum Village 2003)

The Earth serves as teacher, memory, connector, source of hope and healer. But the Earth is also us. They do not make a distinction between humanity and nature. One monk explained it to me like this:

> There is not a boundary between me and the world I am living in. If I don't respect what is inside, or what could be called inside, I will suffer. But if I don't respect that which could be called outside, I will suffer just as much. We are completely dependent. I need my lungs as much as I need the trees... My body is composed of 70 per cent of water. If I don't respect the water, if I poison it or contaminate the land... I poison myself. There is no difference between the blood in my veins and the water in the river. Today the water is in the river; tomorrow it is in my blood... You see when you have this understanding you can bring more justice

because when we see in the correct way we will act in the right way with more compassion and understanding. (Anonymous novice monk, personal communication, 16 January 2007)

The 'more justice' he refers to is about finding a lifestyle which is not based on killing but on sustainability, on understanding of, and compassion for, all beings. The Earth plays a key role in this understanding. Healing justice, then, is about coming home to the Earth.

Healing justice as returning to true self

Dear friends, you are nothing less than a miracle. There may be times when you feel that you are worthless. But you are nothing less than a miracle. (Hanh 2002a)

Again, speaking to the inmates at Maryland Correctional Institute, Thây tells them how beautiful they are. Transformation for them requires the journey from seeing the self as isolated and worthless to seeing the true self as beautiful, miraculous and part of the ever-changing cosmos. In an essay on building Sanghas, Thich Nhat Hanh expresses the wisdom of Plum Village.

Your heart can grow as big as the cosmos; the growth of your heart is infinite. If your heart is like a big river, you can receive any amount of dirt. It will not affect you, and you can transform the dirt very easily... you don't practise to suppress your suffering; you practise in order for your heart to expand as big as a river. (2002b)

The role of the community, even the role of the penitentiary, should be to remind people of their true self. Imagine a justice not focused on punishment or vengeance but on revealing to all parties that they are beautiful, miraculous and fragile beings. As the opening poem illustrates, it is when we learn our true names that the door to the heart can be left open.

In Plum Village, as in Buddhism more generally, the true self is not an individual or a private matter. In fact they don't believe the self really exists in any independent state. One of the basic teachings of the Buddha is the teaching of non-self. The self is always dependent on many other relationships. If life is more like a web of connection, then rediscovering one's true self is rediscovering that we are part of everything and everything is part of us. They use this lens of the non-self to examine any phenomenon, including suffering. For example, a younger nun told me when she first came to Plum Village she didn't really like herself and suffered from much anger and confusion. At Plum Village she learned that both her sufferings and her joys come, in part, from those she is connected to. She expressed this wisdom of non-self: 'Learning I am the continuation of my parents, of this community, it is very beautiful. But it is a daily practise; if I don't look at myself this way, I forget and go back to the old way of seeing myself' (Tôn Nghiêm, personal communication, 18 January 2007). She reported that Thich Nhat Hanh says that the shortest teaching is 'This is because that is.' This is the wisdom of non-self which is sometimes called inter-being. I was told that when we look closely at our own suffering, we see that some of it comes from our ancestors and some of it comes from the kinds of toxins we ingest from our environments, like cravings from mass media or violence from television. When you see through the lens of this wisdom of non-self, you must act with great responsibility because what you do will be passed on to those to whom you are connected.

The wisdom of non-self connects with the Buddhist wisdom of non-discrimination. It is the wisdom of non-discrimination that makes peace possible (Hanh 2005). This non-discrimination is about seeing the connection between and within all things. Notions of low self-esteem, high self-esteem, inferiority, superiority or even of equality are all seen as sickness or wrong-thinking since they are based on the belief of an independent self. It was the wisdoms of non-self and non-discrimination that lay beneath Thây's ability to see himself as the 12-year-old girl who had been raped as well as the sea pirate who had raped her. In this frame all suffering and all joy are deeply personal, but not individual.

The true self is not the creation of some ideal type that is free of suffering. As the opening poem illustrates, the true self can see that the pain and the joy are one. This means, then, that weaknesses in you and in others are not excluded or hidden away; rather, such conflicts become very important opportunities to learn and to be transformed. The first teaching or noble truth according to the Buddha is that there is suffering. One monk explained it to me this way:

> The first act of justice is to acknowledge your own suffering. It's an act of justice because this suffering has been denied and ignored. We can call this an act of justice that heals. It does not blame; it just acknowledges what is true. (Anonymous novice monk, personal communication, 16 January 2007)

In the true self you cannot do violence to yourself by trying to fight or exclude negative feelings. There is no violence in the practise of mindfulness. Similarly, the true self cannot act violently toward the 'other' for the other is also part of self. However, neither can the true self simply be a passive bystander. As one nun put it, 'When I really accept who I am, it is more easy to love people I find difficult to love' (Mai Nghiêm, personal communication, 18 January 2007). Returning to the true self is about learning to gently transform and engage the world of which one is a part.

At Plum Village, every so often a bell will ring and everyone will stop. The function of the bell is to remind everyone to be still and know who he or she is.

> When we hear the bell we come back to ourselves and breathe, and at that point we improve the quality of the Sangha energy. We know that our brother and sister, wherever they are, will be stopping, breathing, and coming back to themselves. They will be generating the energy of right mindfulness, the Sangha energy. (Hanh 2002b)

Buddhist approaches to peace are often characterized as starting with inner peace. In the West it is difficult to understand this because inner peace is often equated with notions of self and the individual. Indeed, Plum Village works with the inner self to engage peace in the world. Thây challenges correctional officers, saying that they should have a role in reducing violence in the community, but can not do so unless they learn to handle the violence within themselves (Hanh 2003f). When Plum Village people work with exchanges between cultures and religions they do so from the premise that 'the basic condition to have a successful exchange between different cultures is for each person to have his or her roots firmly established' (Hanh 2003c). Having roots, or knowing who you are, is what makes exchange possible. The community at Plum Village are encouraged to talk every day to the five-year-old child within them. They find this is a very healing experience (Hanh 2003f). So we can see the focus on inner peace. However, it is not correct that inner peace 'leads to' outer peace. Within the true self exists both the inner and the outer. Inner peace is outer peace and outer peace is inner peace.

Plum Village is organized around the belief that to understand the true self you need to be involved in a healthy teacher–disciple relationship. Thây says that it was only later in his practise that he understood how important this relationship was to doing the type of mindful trans-formation lived out in Plum Village (Hanh 2003c). Many of the monks and nuns said that Thây was an inspirational and sustaining force at Plum Village, although some were quick to point out that they have worked hard to make Plum Village not dependent on his physical presence.

Healing justice at Plum Village is about learning who you are, how you are connected to the world. It is learning to see the world through the lens of compassionate mindfulness rather than through the usual lenses of blame/guilt, victim/offender, justice/injustice, them/us. Such dualisms, according to Plum Village, separate what cannot be separated. They create barriers to finding the true self and nurturing compassion.

Healing justice as being peace

Doing peace is not possible without being peace. Recognizing the pow-ers of anger within you and transforming them; getting in touch with the nourishing things in you – that should be your daily practise. (Hanh 2003f)

Peace is a fundamental part of healing justice at Plum Village. For them, peace is not some distant shore in the future. It is not a static end for which we strive with imperfect steps. Peace is not something that can be used to rally the troops of war. There is no path to peace. There can be no violent means to achieve this peaceful way of being. Peace is a way of being. Two of Thich Nhat Hanh's more popular books, *Peace is Every Step* (Hanh 1991) and *Being Peace* (Hanh 1987a), express these wisdoms which lie at the heart of the life of Plum Village.

The goal of their practise is 'to transform the suffering within our-selves and to find ways to help others to do the same' (Lawlor 2002). In Plum Village life is structured by the Five Mindfulness Trainings. These are essentially guides on being peace. The trainings describe the mindful-ness of transformation where each step is peace. As this is a foundational document to their way of being peace, I have quoted it here in full.

The First Mindfulness Training
Aware of the suffering caused by the destruction of life, I am commit-ted to cultivating compassion and learning ways to protect the lives of people, animals, plants and minerals. I am determined not to kill, not to let others kill, and not to support any act of killing in the world, in my thinking, and in my way of life.

The Second Mindfulness Training

Aware of suffering caused by exploitation, social injustice, stealing and oppression, I am committed to cultivating loving kindness and learning ways to work for the well-being of people, animals, plants and minerals. I will practise generosity by sharing my time, energy and material resources with those who are in real need. I am determined not to steal and not to possess anything that should belong to others. I will respect the property of others, but I will prevent others from profiting from human suffering or the suffering of other species on Earth.

The Third Mindfulness Training

Aware of the suffering caused by sexual misconduct, I am committed to cultivating responsibility and learning ways to protect the safety and integrity of individuals, couples, families and society. I am determined not to engage in sexual relations without love and a long-term commitment. To preserve the happiness of myself and others, I am determined to respect my commitments and the commitments of others. I will do everything in my power to protect children from sexual abuse and to prevent couples and families from being broken by sexual misconduct.

The Fourth Mindfulness Training

Aware of the suffering caused by unmindful speech and the inability to listen to others, I am committed to cultivating loving speech and deep listening in order to bring joy and happiness to others and relieve others of their suffering. Knowing that words can create happiness or suffering, I am determined to speak truthfully, with words that inspire self-confidence, joy and hope. I will not spread news that I do not know to be certain and will not criticise or condemn things of which I am not sure. I will refrain from uttering words that can cause division or discord, or that can cause the family or the community to break. I am determined to make all efforts to reconcile and resolve all conflicts, however small.

The Fifth Mindfulness Training

Aware of the suffering caused by unmindful consumption, I am committed to cultivating good health, both physical and mental, for myself, my family and my society by practising mindful eating, drinking and consuming. I will ingest only items that preserve peace, well-being and joy in my body, in my consciousness and in the collective body and consciousness of my family and society. I am determined not to use alcohol or any other intoxicant or to ingest foods or other items that contain toxins, such as certain TV programmes, magazines, books, films and conversations. I am aware that to damage my body or my consciousness with these poisons is to betray my ancestors, my parents, my society and future generations. I will work to transform violence, fear, anger and confusion in myself and in society by practising a diet for myself and for society. I understand that a proper diet is crucial for self-transformation and for the transformation of society. (Hanh 2007)

As will become evident in a later section on responding to harm, Plum Village strives to use these practises of being peace at every stage of responding to harms and sufferings.

Part of being peace is cultivating 'right thinking'. 'Without right thinking we will cultivate suffering. Right thinking is reflecting the situation as it is without misperception, to be loving, to be compassionate, to be free' (Hanh 2003g). Right thinking is a way of seeing the world – through the lens of the non-self, of non-discrimination and through the wisdom of impermanence. Impermanence is the wisdom that nothing is static and that everything is flowing and changing. Wrong thinking is all the thinking that goes against this wisdom. For example, 'wrong thinking' urges you to blame the other for all difficulties (Hanh 2003g). Wrong thinking is seeing conflict though the lens of the static labels of victim and offender (Hanh 2003f). Such labels strip people of their ability to be peace with each step.

Justice in this context is not separate from healing or transformation. Healing justice, or being peace, is the normative ethical practise which cannot be suspended. Healing justice here is a way of being that is characterized by compassion, understanding and joy. If one were to evaluate this justice, rather than measuring satisfaction or mere compliance with agreements, one would need to see if the justice experience helped all parties to be peace. Justice as being peace is different from both justice as punishment and justice as repairing harm.

Healing justice as cultivating the environments which lead to beauty, solidity, true reflection and freedom

The quality of happiness of a human being depends on the quality of the seeds they have stored in their consciousness. We should arrange our life in such a way that the wholesome seeds can be watered every day and prevent the negative seeds from being watered. This is a very crucial practise. I don't think our society can get out of the situation of despair without this kind of practise. (Hanh 2003f)

One of the central insights of Plum Village is that the environments we live in have the potential to strengthen within us both the seeds of violence and anger and the seeds of mindfulness and compassion. Only superficial and temporary healing happens when we treat the symptoms but leave the underlying roots of the problem untouched. Thây offers the following example:

Suppose a person drinks something that gives them diarrhea, the first thing is to get them to stop drinking the things that will worsen the situation. It is the same with the seed. If you want to help heal a person, you have to help bring them out of the environment where they ingest the toxins of violence and fear. (Hanh 2003f)

To tell someone to stop acting violently but to do nothing to stop that anger from being fed is neither wise nor does it lead to healing. The environments we live in often hold the roots where we feed the seeds of anger and violence many times a day. You cannot meaningfully work at healing without changing the environment. Thây teaches that if a child gets into trouble at school for fighting, rather than blaming the child, the parent should recognize that the child's actions are a result of the environment which the parent has helped to create. The parent, even at great cost, should change the environment for the sake of the child. In the same way, Plum Village is very critical of some of the Western ways of organizing life such that the seeds of violence and craving are fed every day through media, capitalism, globalism, and some religious views.

The organizing principles behind the structure of Plum Village life reflect this need for cultivating, or arranging, an environment where the seeds of compassion are watered and the seeds of violence are not watered (Mai Nghiêm, personal communication, 18 January 2007). As Thây puts it: 'If you put yourself in such an environment, then transformation will happen without much effort' (Hanh 2002b). In fact, many of his teachings focus on choosing the right environments (Định Nghiêm, personal communication, 15 January 2007). He often begins with the call 'organize your life in such a way that...' The idea is that we should organize life in ways that feed compassion but not violence. At Plum Village a number of the monastics said the schedule of life at Plum Village helped them to feed and sustain their compassion.

The schedule changes slightly according to hamlet but follows this basic pattern:

05:30	Wake-up bell	18:15	Dinner
06:00	Sitting meditation	20:00	Orientation or Dharma practise
07:30	Breakfast		dis-scussions or festival celebra-
08:30	Dharma talk		tions or Beginning Anew
11:30	Outdoor walking meditation	21:30	Sitting meditation
13:00	Lunch	22:15	Bedtime
14:00	Personal time		
15:00	Work meditation		
16:30	Mindfulness Trainings Presentations or Q & A or Tea meditation or Touchings of the Earth		

The schedule is an attempt to support the cultivation of mindfulness, awareness, healing and transformation.

Cultivating such an environment requires creating space for getting in touch with the positive elements (Đào Nghiêm, personal communication, 17 January 2007). Mindful breathing, smiling, resting, walking and working are ways Plum Village try to nurture such an environment. Such work requires a community, for it is in seeing a community dealing compassionately with the world that we also learn to be compassionate and to let go of individualism, wrong perceptions and past harms. Cultivating healing environments then is about transforming the social, political and economic structures of life.

Pebble meditation is a way that Plum Village has tried to remind themselves and to teach others of the kind of environment they are cultivating. Thây, a monk who owns nothing, keeps four pebbles in his pocket. The pebbles are for pebble meditation, originally designed for children. In pebble meditation each pebble symbolizes some aspect of life and identity. A pebble is picked up and held. One pebble symbolizes the flower. When the meditator holds it she remembers the many ways that she is like a flower. She breathes in and thinks, 'I see myself as a flower', and then breathes out and thinks, 'I feel fresh.' After several breaths she takes the next stone. This one symbolizes a mountain. She breathes in, 'I see myself as a mountain', breathes out, 'I feel solid.' The next pebble symbolizes still water. Breathing in, she thinks, 'I feel like still water', breathing out, 'I reflect things as they truly are.' After several breaths she takes the last pebble, which symbolizes space, breathes in, 'I see myself as space', breathes out, 'I feel free' (Hanh 2003g). In this way children and adults are taught about their true identity and about the conditions needed in a healthy environment: beauty-freshness, solidity, true reflection and freedom.

At Plum Village they believe that the seeds of anger and the seeds of compassion are in everyone. But they believe that the seeds cannot turn on and off by themselves. The seeds respond to the environment (Hanh 2005). So the healing justice which goes to the roots of understanding seeks to avoid environments which turn on the seeds of anger while cultivating environments which feed the seeds of compassion.

In their experience, what works in one environment is not necessarily what works in another environment.

> When we bring plants from Vietnam and plant them in the West, they do not grow the way they would in Vietnam. When we grow mustard greens in France, they grow thorns. That would never happen in Vietnam. We have to know how to adapt to our surroundings, and we have to know how to absorb the beautiful things for culture. (Hanh 2003c)

Plum Village has tried to bring Buddhism to the West but has insisted that it should not look like the Vietnamese Buddhism. It should be authentically rooted in its own environment. In this way they argue that the ways of doing 'being peace' or healing justice cannot be based on exporting Vietnamese practises into foreign environments.

However, healing justice in this context should be less focused on episodes of harm and more focused on cultivating the environments that lead to beauty, solidity, true reflection and freedom.

Healing justice as mindful consumption – eating loving-kindness

> The Buddha said that nothing can survive without food. Our joy cannot survive without food; neither can our sorrow and despair. (Hanh 2002a)

Mindful consumption is directly related to healing justice as cultivating right environments. In Plum Village Community believes that it is our consuming that feeds the various seeds within us. Buddhist psychology teaches there are many seeds within us, such as the seeds of violence, fear, hatred and despair, also the seeds of compassion, forgiveness and understanding (Hanh 2003g). The ones that grow are the ones that are fed. We feed these seeds by what we consume. As one nun put it, 'We are what we consume' (Định Nghiêm, personal communication, 15 January 2007). We consume by the way we eat, by what we see, touch, feel and think about.

Take eating. Thây's book on anger begins by saying that if you want to understand your anger you need to think about what you are eating, in this case, literally eating (Hanh 2001). He argues that our methods of food production are very violent to animals, to the forests and to the water. By the time these elements come to our plate they are full of the toxins of anger and violence. That is what we are eating (Hanh 2003f). By such eating we bring a lot of toxins into our body, and we feed the seeds of violence and anger within. By such eating we have caused a lot of suffering both around us and within us.

At Plum Village eating is a daily act of communal celebration and meditation. Following the mindfulness training of non-killing, the food is vegetarian and is prepared slowly and happily, most of the time. At the beginning of each meal they say the Five Contemplations.

➤ This food is the gift of the Earth, the sky, numerous living beings and much hard work.

➤ May we eat with mindfulness and gratitude so as to be worthy to receive this food.

➤ May we recognize and transform unwholesome mental formations, especially our greed.

➤ May we take only food that nourishes us and keeps us healthy.

➤ We accept this food so that we may nurture our sisterhood and brotherhood, build our Sangha, and nourish our ideal of serving living beings. (Hanh and Monks and Nuns at Plum Village 2007)

They consume in such a way that they feed the seeds of compassion and not the seeds of violence. For them this means eating slowly and enjoying each bite. Most meals happen in silence or at least the first half of the meal is in silence so as to encourage mindful eating. Consuming is part of the practise of healing justice.

However, consuming is much more than eating. It includes everything we look at, feel, think about, smell, or touch. One example of a way of consuming is watching television. At Plum Village they believe that much of the consumption of television feeds the seeds of violence.

In this understanding healing justice is about understanding the habits of consumptions that lead to violence, hatred, despair and fear, and replacing them with habits of consumptions that lead to joy, compassion and deeper understanding. This kind of healing justice can be practised by anyone because it is not outside the habits of daily life (Như· Nghiêm, personal communication 17 January 2007).

Healing justice as growing roots: Taking refuge in the Sangha

> Alone we are vulnerable, but with brothers and sisters to work with, we can support each other. We cannot go to the ocean as a drop of water – we would evaporate before reaching our destination. But if we become a river, if we go as a Sangha, we are sure to arrive at the ocean. Taking refuge in a Sangha will allow the Sangha to carry us, to transport us, and we will suffer less. (Hanh 2002c)

Thây is very clear that it is community – the Sangha – that sustains Plum Village, but also the rest of the world (Hanh 2003g). Thây goes so far as to say that Sangha-building is the most important practise of our century (2002c). He sees it as the basic need of all people (1992b). Sometimes he likens the Sangha to the soil and the person to the seed. The seed needs the soil to grow into a beautiful flower. (2002b)

The Sangha is the place that develops the collective energy of mindfulness. This collective energy has the capacity to embrace fears and sorrow, to offer healing, transformation and nourishment (Hanh 2003d). It is the task of the Sangha to create the kind of space and embrace that gives its members the opportunity to transform. A Sangha should be a community of such mindfulness that just being in their presence is healing. All of my interviewees highlighted this as an important sustaining theme in their practise. They spoke of being nourished (Pháp Xả, personal communication, 17 January 2007) and inspired (Như· Nghiêm, personal communication, 17 January 2007) by the Sangha. Some of them said the other members of the community were like mirrors, reflecting back to them their true nature, helping them to see more deeply their paths of transformation (Tùng Nghiêm, personal communication, 15 January 2007; Mai Nghiêm, personal communication, 18 January 2007).

The Sangha is that community which reflects 'the elements of the Buddha: the elements of loving-kindness, compassion, understanding and non-discrimination' (Hanh 2002e). Put differently: 'The essence of a Sangha is awareness, understanding, acceptance, harmony and love. When you do not see these in a community, it is not a true Sangha, and you should have the courage to say so' (Hanh 2002b).

The Sangha is a collection of dissimilar people with different needs but functioning together like an organism or a body where each person is needed and there is not judgement between them (Tùng Nghiêm, personal communication, 15 January 2007). When one member suffers, all suffer. When one member experiences joy, all experience joy. When one member suffers, others, who do not have the same problems, can come and help. At Plum Village they believe that the eyes and wisdom of the Sangha are clearer than the eyes and wisdom of the individual members. The Sangha is there to offer wisdom, perspective and insight to those who are in the midst of the disorientation of suffering (Hanh 2002c). This happens, in part, by creating safe places for people to look deeply into the nature of their suffering (Anonymous novice monk, personal communication, 16 January 2007).

The most authentic form of Sangha is created where people live together day in and day out under the same roof and with the same economic resources. There they must learn to live together and to make decisions together (Hanh 2003c). This is what Plum Village is. It is a Buddhist monastery, a Sangha, where the permanent members live in very close proximity, where together they learn to transform sufferings and enjoy life.

Plum Village people recognize that they are many kinds of Sanghas beyond the particular geographic Sangha. After each meal the monastics are taught to say a Gatha, or poem acknowledging some of these other roots. They express gratitude for their parents, teachers, friends and all living beings (Tùng Nghiêm, personal communication, 15 January 2007). Having witnessed the violence associated with the Christianization of Vietnam, Thây does not encourage people to leave their original spiritual tradition. Since he teaches that the Buddha is not a god, he encourages people to keep and to honour their original roots and to take up secondary roots with Buddhism. Honouring their original roots means examining what is the best which has been passed down in that tradition but also the suffering which has been passed down. In the case of parents, I was told how this important practise of nourishing healthy roots can lead to great healing.

The wounds of the past generations, of our ancestors, all their suffering is written in all our cells. By acknowledging it, recognizing it, we can bring healing and justice not only for us, but also for the past generations and also for the next generations because this suffering will not be transmitted anymore, but your happiness and well-being will be transmitted instead. (Anonymous novice monk, personal communication, 16 January 2007)

Part of growing roots and living as a Sangha is to examine your original roots for the suffering and goodness passed down to you. It is possible to nourish the goodness and to transform the suffering into happiness.

At Plum Village they believe that even international political relations should and can operate on the basis of being a Sangha. Thây calls on the UN to transform into a true Sangha. By this he is speaking not of conversion to Buddhism but about the way countries and leaders relate to each other (Hanh 2002c). There are ways of embracing places of suffering with the compassion of the Sangha such that space can be created for healing and transformation of relationships.

If the Sangha is the soil and each member is a seed, then the Sangha is the place where one learns to grow roots.

The practise is, therefore, to grow some roots. The Sangha is not a place to hide in order to avoid responsibilities. The Sangha is a place to practise for the transformation and healing of self and society… In order for us to develop some roots, we need the kind of environment that can help us become rooted. (Hanh 2002b)

Healing justice, then, is about growing roots, finding belonging, learning to respond with compassion to the inevitable conflicts that arise, and being embraced by the support of a community.

Seeing the enemy as brother or sister

Communicate with the people you want to serve, the people who may be criminal. You have to look upon them with the eyes of compassion. They have a lot of suffering, anger and craving and fear in them and they are to be helped. There are many ways that are nonviolent, gentle, and peaceful to help. We have many better weapons than the gun. Mindfulness, gentleness, a smile, compassion. (Hanh 2003g)

This was Thây's advice to correctional officers. See the 'other' not as other or as enemy but as a brother or sister. When we 'other' or distance people, we create the conditions for violence (Tùng Nghiêm, personal communication, 15 January 2007). When we see through the eyes of compassion, we see that we are already connected as brothers and sisters (Hanh 2002c). What is left is to figure out a way to respond as such.

Thây's response to the conflict between Pakistan and India is exactly along these lines. He said, 'The United Nations should tell Pakistan and India that they are friends, they are brothers. They see each other as enemies when really they are already brothers and sisters' (Hanh 2002c). Another example is Thich Nhat Hanh's 2007 visit back to Vietnam which marked his second visit after almost 40 years of exile. During that visit he, together with Plum Village, hosted three requiem masses to work at the healing of the wounds of the Vietnam War. The ceremonies were to ask for healing for all those who had suffered during the war. While some wanted them to focus only on the Vietnamese or only on the Northerners or only on the Southerners, Plum Village's way is to recognize that all of these are brothers and sisters already and so all were acknowledged together, something which has not happened in any official forum in the 32 years since the end of the Vietnam War.

In this way Plum Village tries to nurture the understanding that leads to compassion. They are convinced that the seeds of compassion as well as the seeds of violence are in everyone. Even the one whom we think is most evil has the seeds of goodness within (Hanh 2003a). The task, then, is to help transform people by the practises of loving-kindness and compassion, so that seeds of goodness will grow.

In Vietnam during the war some people threw grenades into the offices of the School of Youth and Social Service (SYSS), killing two workers. Sister Chân Không had to write a eulogy. She chose to address directly those who had killed her friends.

> We cannot hate you, you who have thrown grenades and killed our friends, because we know that men are not our enemies. Our only enemies are the misunderstanding, hatred, jealousy, and ignorance that lead to such acts of violence. Please allow us to remove all misunderstanding so we can work together for the happiness of the Vietnamese people. Our only aim is to help remove ignorance and illiteracy from the country of Vietnam. Social change must start in our hearts with the will to transform our own egotism, greed, and lust into understanding, love,

commitment and shared responsibility for the poverty and injustice in our country. (Cao 1993)

Here it is possible to see how a victim of crime can address the perpetrators of that crime with compassion. By rejecting the need for human enemies she is able to invite all on the path of social transformation.

When speaking to correction officers Thây outlines what he sees as the tasks of corrections officers in relationship to offenders:

Criminals are good people. Water the good seeds in them. Help them to get in touch with the positive elements of life (Hanh 2003d).

Help prisoners to transform, by practising loving-kindness, compassion (Hanh 2003g).

…make their life much more comfortable and joyful. Transform the prison into a place to learn and understand (Hanh 2003g).

Inmates in prison are there to be helped not there to be punished (Hanh 2003f).

See the criminal out of compassion – see them as someone you are trying to help. If you see them as your enemy you are not doing right thinking (Hanh 2003f).

Again these quotations illustrate the basic insight that the criminals are good people who need loving help to become more joyful. A nun explained to me how her ideas of criminals had changed through the practise.

Before I began practising I really saw a criminal as evil and I didn't have understanding for the criminal. I had lots of understanding for the victim but not for the criminal. I couldn't put myself in their shoes. I couldn't understand how a person becomes like this. Through the practise I really see that I am just as capable of doing it… I am just the same as they are. I can see the conditions that created that. It's innocent in a way. I don't want to punish. I think they shouldn't continue down this path but I don't need to punish. (Nhu· Nghiêm, personal communication 17 January 2007)

She also said that prisons should be more like retreat centres so that those who have harmed others can rediscover who they are and how powerfully they are connected to everything else.

In these stories healing justice is about learning to see that you and those you see as enemies are both subject to suffering and in need of compassion. Healing justice is about developing the eyes and hands of compassion so that all beings may be happy, free and living in wellbeing. In the view of Plum Village this is not only a commendable ideal or private faith position, it is practise which can bring about massive changes both in the inner self and in the socio-economic systems of our times.

Healing justice as the blooming of compassion

> Once a practitioner can begin to understand the roots of suffering not only in himself or herself but in the parent or child, compassion blooms for perhaps the first time, and skilful means to achieve reconciliation present themselves. (Lawlor 2002)

In facing the roots of suffering in ourselves and in others compassion can bloom. Plum Village believes that those who have behaved without compassion will not learn compassion from blame, punishment and violence. They will only learn to touch the world with compassion when they have learned to be compassionate with themselves (Tùng Nghiêm, personal communication, 15 January 2007). Here we return to our starting point, coming home to the present. This seems to be the experience of Plum Village. They believe that the survival of the planet depends on such compassion and loving-kindness (Hanh 2002b).

They believe that compassion, rather than violence, is the best means of self-protection (Hanh 2002a). Compassion has a way of facing suffering which can be disarming and transformative. Nearly all of the people I talked to spoke of coming with personal sufferings and over time developing compassion for themselves and for all living beings.

In the context of Plum Village healing justice does not seek some balancing of the scales of pain, or merely the repair of harm. It seeks the blooming of compassion, the deep transformation of societies and persons that happens when sufferings are responded to with the eyes of compassion.

Healing justice as engaging disputes: Bathing in mindfulness

> Give your anger a bath of mindfulness; you will get relief, your anger will lose some of its power. (Hanh 2003f)

It should already be clear that Plum Village's view of healing justice is not aimed first of all at responding to harms or disputes. Their primary focus is elsewhere. Their focus is to not to wait until there are great experiences of suffering, but to move upstream to create the conditions that lead to joy rather than craving or suffering. Therefore, Plum Village tends not to deal with the kinds of conflicts dealt with in the criminal justice system (Tùng Nghiêm, personal communication, 15 January 2007). You could say that their goal is to structure life in such a way that criminal justice systems are not needed. However, it is important to understand how that perspective relates to harms and disputes. Plum Village is clear that each person in the community carries within them the seeds of violence. Working at their own sufferings and living so close together in such a multi-cultural community, harms between people do happen. So how then does Plum Village respond to harms? Give them a bath! Harms need to be cared for, gently held like a baby, acknowledged and soaked in the waters of mindfulness of the community. Plum Village has a number of practises of engaging disputes or sufferings. All of them are various forms of surrounding harm with mindfulness such that it might heal.

One basic assumption of their response to harm is that they need to look deeply at the suffering to locate the causes and roots. Referring to the opening poem and the sea pirate who raped the refugee girl, one monk explained how justice involves such a search to transform the root causes. He said, 'Justice is to work in such a way as to change the conditions where the sea pirate was born, to work with the people there to change the living conditions so that they don't help to create a sea pirate' (Anonymous novice monk, personal communication, 16 January 2007). Such a view comes from the belief that we manifest the suffering that has been given to us through our parents and relations, through our consuming, and through the socio-economic structures which feed our cravings but not our true identity. When someone acts out, it is the task of the community to help the person and the broader community to understand what are the causes – in persons, in community and in structures of society – that led to this behaviour and then to work at transforming the causes. Sorting through this suffering is aided by meditation. I was told the story of a farmer dumping out a bag of mixed seeds and quickly sorting the seeds without any trouble, because the farmer had learned how to recognize and differentiate the seeds. The practises of meditation develop the concentration, awareness and understanding that help the community to sort through the seeds of suffering to see what is really there and what is in need of being transformed (Anonymous novice monk, personal communication, 16 January 2007).

A second feature of their way of responding to harm is their assumption that this suffering has a reasonable explanation which probably has some collective dimensions. Therefore, blame and focusing solely on the individual has no place within their approach. One monk explained this aversion to blame. 'When we blame or punish a person, we identify them with their sufferings and we water the seeds of suffering within them' (Anonymous novice monk, personal communication, 16 January 2007). Another nun explained that their purpose in confronting suffering is 'to reflect love to the other rather than reflecting violence, blame. If the other acts this way because she hasn't experienced love, she needs to have that reflected to her' (Đào Nghiêm, personal communication, 17 January 2007). The focus is on understanding and helping the person to identify, not with blame, but with their true identity.

A third feature of this approach is the focus on helping to nourish that which is positive within the person suffering. To help someone to face and transform the suffering inside of them, much attention must go to building that person up in positive ways. Their practises of responding to harm have a lot to do with building people up.

It is important to note that those I interviewed saw the criminal justice system as quite misguided. It focuses on symptoms rather than root causes, individual blame rather than transforming persons and society, and it makes people identify with their violent acts rather than identify with a more holistic view of themselves and life. Because incarceration is connected to blame, inflicting harm and putting someone into an environment which will surely water the seeds of violence, it seems quite unhelpful to those at Plum Village. They focus on helping the person and the community to understand the nature of the suffering and the nature of their goodness so that they can work to transform into joy root causes of suffering in persons and society.

One of the practises of the community which works at these precepts is called *Beginning Anew*. The community uses the practise every week or two, depending on the hamlet. Individuals also use it whenever they need it. The practise is to listen deeply and to look deeply and honestly at oneself and to create a new beginning in oneself and in one's relationships. Plum Village describes it as a four-part process:

1. Flower watering – This is a chance to share our appreciation for the other person. We may mention specific instances of when the other person said or did something that we had admired. This is an opportunity to shine light on the other's strengths and contributions to the Sangha and to encourage the growth of his or her positive qualities.

2. Sharing regrets – We may mention any unskilfulness in our actions, speech or thoughts that we have not yet had an opportunity to apologize for.

3. Expressing a hurt – We may share how we felt hurt by an interaction with another practitioner, due to his or her actions, speech or thoughts. (To express a hurt we should first water the other person's flower by sharing two positive qualities that we have truly observed in him or her. Expressing a hurt is often performed one-on-one with another practitioner rather than in the group setting. You may ask for a third party that you both trust and respect to be present, if desired.)

4. Sharing a long-term difficulty and asking for support – At times we each have difficulties, and pain arises from our past that surfaces in the present. When we share an issue that we are dealing with we can let the people around us understand us better and offer the support that we really need.

Confronting is not avoided, but it is done gently. In the circle when one member speaks, everyone else has to listen until that member is fully done speaking. The only limitation on this is that the speaker must use loving speech. If the speaker begins to attack or become aggressive, he is invited to stop and take care of his anger and to continue the process at another point (Định Nghiêm, personal communication, 15 January 2007). They believe that this kind of care-filled confrontation can weaken the suffering in the other even as they are being confronted. Further confrontation at Plum Village is not an individual matter. If one is hurting, the whole community is hurting and can come and help. If one is caught in wrong desires or harmful actions, rather than blame, the whole community is asked to reflect on whether or not they too are caught in wrong desires. Knowing that harmful actions don't come out of nowhere, they ask the community to reflect on how they failed to create the conditions for happy living. Even as part of the community is suffering from harm, the rest of the community is asked to cultivate a spirit of loving kindness. When one member suffers, it is important to be surrounded by a compassionate community in which not everyone has the same problem (Hanh 2002b).

Another practise, called *Shining the Light*, also reflects this double role of community as caregiver and as co-responsible. The practise of Shining the Light is the practise of inviting people to shine light on your practise, your way of being. First, you ask a friend to shine light on you and then that person suggests five or so others to ask. This is not a practise of blaming or punishing. It is a practise of reflecting the good qualities and the weaknesses. However the person doing the reflecting is also to ask themselves, 'How have I contributed to this person's weakness and to this person's happiness?' (Hanh and Lawlor 2002). This practise aims to transform the actions of both the asker and the asked. It is done annually over several months during the Winter Retreat as each hamlet brings together all its monks or nuns to shine the light on each monastic. So a nun might sit in a circle with 35 other nuns and hear each of them speak of her strengths and weaknesses they had observed over the past year (Tùng Nghiêm, personal communication, 15 January 2007). Monks and nuns reported that this practise helped them to feel built up and at the same time supported them to work at transforming the suffering still inside of them (Pháp Xả, personal communication, 17 January 2007).

Responding to harm is about finding ways to reduce suffering, to transform anger, to regain freedom, to increase compassion, and to transform the wider environment so that these steps are sustained through time. Those who harm others are not blamed, punished and sentenced to incarceration in unhealthy communities where everyone suffers from similar problems. Rather, those who harm are invited to give their anger a bath. They are invited to participate in looking deeply at the situation to learn more about how this came about and what inner and outer changes are needed. They are challenged to understand how to not feed in the suffering the first place but rather to feed every day the seeds of compassion so that each person can return to one's true self. If they are sentenced, it is to a community of diverse people who will help to care for their anger and their compassion and also will examine themselves for how they contributed to this person's suffering.

What happens when someone just doesn't want to work at things or seems unable to work things out? I was told this does happen (Đinh

Nghiêm, personal communication, 15 January 2007). In such cases they try to follow the same pattern.

> We don't blame them or force them to change. You can't change them but you can change the conditions around them. You can ask what are the conditions that support their living in suffering… You can also water all the positives within that person to help get them to a place where they want to transform their suffering. (Anonymous novice monk, personal communication, 16 January 2007)

The focus is still on not blaming but rather cultivating supportive conditions which water the seeds of compassion within. Another nun told me that in such cases they also practise 'unilateral beginning anew' where one party to the harm works at healing and transforming even if the other is not yet ready to work at their part (Định Nghiêm, personal communication, 15 January 2007).

Plum Village responds to harm by bathing the harmer and the harmed in the mindfulness of the community. This 'bathing' creates the space to understand deeply the suffering that is present, to show love to people who sometimes respond in unloving ways, and to transform the root causes of the suffering of the community and persons involved.

Barriers to healing justice

What would Plum Village suggest are some of the key barriers to this kind of healing justice? I will draw out five themes.

First, individualism. Individualism, they say, lies at the root of our culture and civilization and is seen as the cause of much suffering in the past century (Hanh 2002c). The fruits of individualism are loneliness, the feeling of being cut off, alienation, division, the disintegration of the family, and the disintegration of society (Hanh 2002b). Further, they see the high mobility associated with individualism as leaving many young people 'without roots… They wander around, not quite human beings' (Hanh 2002b).

Second, the five cravings. According to Buddhist teachings, the five cravings are the cravings for wealth, sex, fame and power, food and drink, and sleep (Hanh 1987b). The hunger for these things leads to wrong thinking. However, modern society has the pursuit of these cravings as the basis of its understandings of freedom, liberty and happiness. Much of the West's economic system is structured to search after these cravings.

Consumerism (Đào Nghiêm, personal communication, 17 January 2007), escapism (Mai Nghiêm, personal communication, 18 January 2007) and speed (Như· Nghiêm, personal communication 17 January 2007) are some of the ways that we feed these cravings while at the same time getting farther and farther away from the beauty and suffering inside ourselves and our world. In Buddhist experience these cravings can never be satisfied and always lead to distorted perceptions. These distortions lead to forgetfulness. When we forget the best ways of living we fall into the five cravings and are liable to drown there. Such an environment stops people from practising right mindfulness (Hanh 2002b).

Third, reliance on fear and violence. In too many societies violence is seen as a tool through which one can build safety and suppress unwanted violence. However, Thây sees violence as the inability to look with compassion. It cannot create safety because it does nothing to make the other feel safe (Hanh 2002c). It cannot be used as a tool to suppress unwanted violence because violence cannot be suppressed (Hanh 2003g). They also believe that seeking after cravings creates all kinds of violence in the world. Fear for security and for protecting that which has been acquired through craving also increases violence (Pháp Xả, personal communication, 17 January 2007). Violence, however it is used, feeds the seeds of violence, despair and hatred. Feeding those seeds acts as a barrier to being peace.

Fourth, 'habit-energy'. Habit-energy is the old patterns, patterns of rushing, patterns of responding out of violence or fear, patterns of judging. Habit-energy pulls us back to the old ways of doing things. These ways can be transformed through acknowledging them and speaking to them. But without engaging the old patterns or habit-energy it is not possible to create the response of mindful living.

Fifth, wrong perception/wrong thinking. It is wrong thinking that 'makes you hateful, angry, suffering in self, and makes others suffer' (Hanh 2003g). Wrong thinking is thinking that distorts reality. It is the thinking that flows from not following the wisdoms of non-self, non-discrimination and impermanence. Guilt and blame are two examples of wrong perception which perpetuate violence (Đào Nghiêm, personal communication, 17 January 2007).

Final words

Plum Village offers a case study of a community whose approach to healing justice was born out of their experience of the worst kinds of crime and violence and the structural injustices of intra-national and international political self-interest. Drawing on a 2500-year tradition of Buddhism, their understanding of healing justice is rooted in compassion, understanding and loving-kindness at every step of the process. For them, healing justice is about learning to look deeply into the nature of suffering to find the path to well-being. The well-being of which they speak is not so much focused on responding to injustice or repairing harm. Rather, it is about learning one's true names, or as the opening poem puts it, 'to see that my joy and pain are one... so I can wake up and so the door of my heart can be left open, the door of compassion'. At Plum Village they believe that such compassionate transformation is available to all beings and that all beings on our planets are now dependent on humans rediscovering such ways as the basis for our ecological, sociological and economic ways of being.

Part III – Looking Through the Case Studies

Part III – Broadening the Scope of the
Case studies

Chapter 7

Shared Characteristics of Healing Justice

Personal Peacemaking[6]
Today I shall dream –
of people together,
Loving, sharing, eating, dancing.

And at the end of the day,
When things are much the same,
I shall continue to hope.
I shall remember that the personal
is always political; that inner peace
cannot be separated from wholeness
and health in community;
that small acts of beauty
by small groups of people
still carry the potential
to change the world.

Joy Mead (2003)

Our three case studies of healing justice have brought us into contact
with three very different communities. The communities were selected
in part because they differ on a whole range of criteria: geography, eth-
nicity, language, spiritual tradition. What they each shared, or were said
to share, was a phenomenon of healing justice. Yet on the surface many
elements that were seen to constitute healing justice in one setting were
absent from the others. At Hollow Water, healing justice was wrapped

---

6   Extract taken from 'Personal Peacemaking' in *Making Peace in Practice and Poetry.* Copy-
     right © 2003 Joy Mead.

up with becoming Anishinabe. How could others share this? In the Iona Community, healing justice sometimes included the laying-on of hands in prayer, a practise which was not shared by the other communities. In Plum Village walking meditation and breathing meditation were core practises of healing justice; the others did not mention such practises. Those accustomed to mainline Western styles of justice might feel some sense of disorientation or frustration as our search to touch and taste healing justice has brought us through territory not normally considered relevant to justice, law and dispute resolution.

But has our search identified any coherence to healing? Are these communities experiencing a common phenomenon? At the level of forms and process, these communities differ in significant ways. The task of this chapter is to determine if there were any characteristics or features of healing justice that were shared by these communities. As we look at each community's story and its vision and practise of healing justice, what patterns and themes emerge? Is there a shared logic of healing justice? Do these communities share a theory of how change happens? Another way of looking at this task is to ask what is the geography of healing justice? What territory does it cover? Where and how is it located in the life of the community? These are the questions to which we now turn.

While these communities had important differences, there were also many points of similarity. The poem at the opening of this chapter could have been written by a member of any of the communities. A member of the Iona Community wrote it, but it expresses something of the shared imagination and logic of each of them. This chapter contains a comparative analysis to try to highlight elements of what might be a shared logic or imagination of healing justice. I have tried in this analysis to use the language of healing justice, rather than to switch to some external academic discourse. I have argued from the beginning that healing justice needs to be understood on its own terms and this includes the comparative analysis.

This chapter lifts out common themes of healing justice in three parts. The first part focuses on the particular shared characteristics of healing justice as they relate to five areas: vision, practise, responses to harm, dynamics that sustain and dynamics that act as barriers. Through comparative analysis, I have found characteristics common to each of the three case studies. This section lists these features with some brief explanation but not much elaboration. The goal is to identify the range of common characteristics which are shared between these three communities. Characteristics shared by two but not three communities are not included here.

The second part of this chapter takes a broader, more integrated perspective, to identify the major distinguishing features of healing justice as they relate to the kinds of relationships that sustain healing ways of justice. This section moves the discussion of the common features to greater depth. It builds on the comparative analysis and points towards some of the major finds of this research.

The third part of this chapter explore features of what we could call the logic or imagination of healing justice. It argues that such a shared imagination does exist and therefore it tries to put some handles on this imagination.

Shared characteristics of healing justice visions

These shared characteristics are like little dots in a much larger picture. They are pin points where the communities' imaginations converge and the phenomenon of healing justice emerges. My hope is that by correctly identifying these little pinpoints, a new picture will emerge. Perhaps it is like the connect-the-dot pictures that my daughters sometimes play with. The dots by themselves can be confusing. Their meaning only emerges when connected. But the dots give my daughters the courage and the means to draw pictures in ways they previously thought were not possible.

Healing justice vision acts as paradigm or imagination of a community

In each of the communities healing justice was not a discrete act or realm of activity that could be divided from other realms. It was the imagination that undergirded everything else. Healing justice was the whole system working together so that healing, politics, spirituality, work, geography, non-violent action, ecological peacebuilding and responding to harm all co-existed in a life-giving way. Thus, all of their practise was healing justice.

Healing justice vision uses compassion rather than violence as the basis of security

In different ways, each community moved away from violence and towards compassion as the basis of security. In the Iona Community, we saw it in their commitment to active non-violence and nuclear pacifism. In Hollow Water it was a movement away from incarceration. In Plum Village it was in their first mindfulness training concerning not supporting killing. Each community moved away from violent means as a basis of security. Each community moved towards an engaged kind of compassion as the means for developing a secure order.

Healing justice vision embodies sacred teachings in ways of being

For these communities, the spiritual (which co-exists with the physical) was the very source of healing. To be Anishinabe, to be Christian, to be a little Buddha – this was the focus of these communities. By embodying peace, love, life and truth as a way of being, the communities reflected their sacred teachings with each step rather than seeing them as end products which could be attained by different means. For them there was no way to healing justice. Healing justice was the way.

Healing justice vision sees through the lenses of interconnection and wholeness

In Hollow Water people talked of the laws of interconnection and wholeness. In the Iona Community people saw the whole world as Christ's: 'in him all things hold together' (Colossians 1:17, NIV). In Plum Village they used the language of inter-being. Each community approached life through a web of interconnectedness and saw healing justice as recovering wholeness, balance and interconnected relationship.

Healing justice vision responds to the innate goodness and the need for healing in all of life

For each of the communities, healing justice arose as they responded respectfully to the innate goodness of the 'Other.' For them, any step which acknowledged the gifts of life was healing justice, whether the respectful response was offering tobacco to Creator at Hollow Water, walking meditation at Plum Village or singing praises of God within the Iona Community.

Healing justice vision recognizes you are the land

Healing justice, for these three communities, dissolved the separation between human and non-human. For them the land was as much a part of healing justice as people. The land was also innately good, reflecting interconnection and wholeness. This kind of healing justice did not just extend the values of social justice to the environment. It saw the Earth as both giver and receiver of healing justice, as teacher, facilitator and recipient.

Healing justice vision creates space for learning your true identity

For each of these communities healing justice was about learning their true name. Knowing who they were was about responding to the knowledge that you were interconnected with the whole world. Your true identity included your self-image and the rejection of your individual self. It was about learning how you were connected and to whom, how you differed from others and how you were similar, and what kinds of suffering and gifts had been passed down to you.

Healing justice vision uses a logic of community

For these three communities healing justice was a returning home to community. Rather than the logic of individualism which asks only 'what I have done', 'what I will get from this', their healing justice was immersed in the logic of community. This logic extended the timeframe from individuals to generations. In situations of harm their concern was not just with the impact on direct victims but also with ways of structuring life so that no harm would come to anything, whether human or non-human.

Healing justice vision moves beyond repairing harm to structuring life in such a way as to cultivate joy

In Hollow Water the people talked of Living the Good Life. The Iona Community talked of the Kingdom of God. At Plum Village it was the Pure Land of the Buddha. In each case these concepts were not distant ideas or faraway places attained after death. These were ways of living life most fully and joyfully in the present. For them healing justice was embodying the good life.

Healing justice vision cultivates an economics of healing justice

Each community saw that the current economic system of their country was not based in healing justice ways and therefore militated against it at each step. The communities were clear that an alternative economics was needed, even if they were less clear on what that would look like. In

Hollow Water people spoke of nation building and developing an economic base such that they did not have to be dependent on government. The Iona Community had committed themselves to action for economic justice and promotion of just and peaceful social, political and economic structures throughout the world. At Plum Village people spoke about transforming the habits of nourishing themselves with consumerism and the American dream. They called for the cultivation of an economics of healing justice based not on greed but need, not on individualism but on ecological and community-based sustainability.

Shared characteristics of healing justice practises
Healing justice enters into brokenness and seeks transformation
These communities found healing justice and continued to practise it by staying transformatively present to the brokenness in the world. At Hollow Water their brokenness was the brokenness of sexual abuse, alcoholism and colonialization. In the Iona Community it was the brokenness of those left behind by industrialization and expanded to include many others who had been marginalized by church or society or both. At Plum Village their burden was the immense suffering for the people of Vietnam through the Vietnam War and continuing today. These communities practised healing justice by staying present to and becoming engaged in these sufferings.

Healing justice transforms your own suffering, violence and complicity
Practitioners of healing justice did not stand outside violence, suffering and harm. At each community they were working at transforming their own suffering, violence and complicity in the causes of violence. Rather than externalizing violence and blaming it on others they worked to touch it in themselves. The social change of healing justice arose from their own hearts. Here inner healing and outer healing co-existed. Each community had practises which supported its members to do this ongoing work of transforming their own suffering, violence and complicity.

Healing justice builds community
Each community saw 'building community' as one of the most important practises of healing justice. Community was the end and the means of healing justice. Hollow Water and Plum Village are geographic

communities whereas the Iona Community members share some time in geographic community but live dispersed around the world. Even as other pressures militated against them, these groups built community. They believed that there was something in the human spirit that needed healthy, supportive community. Much of their day-to-day practise of healing justice was taken up in the tasks of building community.

Healing justice engages social change by cultivating gift-based and needs-based social structures

In Hollow Water it was the clan system. In the Iona Community it was sanctuary and at Plum Village it was cultivating healthy environments. In each case they spoke of transforming social structures by creating places where each person's needs were met, where each person was needed, and where each had responsibilities for the care of others. Each community saw healing justice as something that could interrupt and disturb the dominant social structures and, at the same time, create a basis for some kind of alternative.

Healing justice enacts practises to cultivate sacredness

Whether dancing, singing, praying, walking or sitting, each community was full of practises and ceremonies to cultivate sacredness. Each community saw all of life as sacred, either a gift from God or Creator, or as something which was innately miraculous. Healing justice is living life as a response to sacredness. It is a way of life awakening to sacredness and creating sacred relationships.

Healing justice performs everyday life activities from a healing justice perspective

Each community focused on everyday life as the primary location of healing justice activity. When Hollow Water said that their ceremonies could not be separated from everyday life, they meant that there were ways to move through everyday life activities respectfully. When visitors went for a course to an Iona Community centre, they were expected to participate in washing, cleaning and cooking because it was in these everyday activities that healing justice was experienced. When Plum Village spoke of doing everything in mindfulness, they were finding healing justice ways of moving through everyday life activities.

Healing justice lets nature do its work

Each of these communities placed itself in a particular relationship with the Earth, which reflected its sense of healing justice. At Hollow Water Black Island days, the Wilderness Therapy programme and the traditional ceremonies nurtured this relationship. In the Iona Community it was the island centres. At Plum Village each hamlet was designed to be in beautiful relationship with the Earth. All communities tried to be close enough to listen to the Earth and to see their impact on it. Healing justice was practised by being in right relationship with the Earth.

Healing justice educates and disciples into healing justice perspectives

Each community practised healing justice through a long journey of learning. The movement in Hollow Water really only got off the ground when a group of 12 people committed to a two-year process of learning and experimenting with sexual abuse healing. The Iona Community started as an alternative way of educating clergy and continues to run courses open to all at their Island centres. Plum Village also runs courses throughout the year, partly to be open for 'outsiders', but also for their own monastics. Healing justice is practised by ongoing processes of learning, discovering, applying and further learning.

Shared characteristics of healing justice response to harm

Healing justice nurtures local facilitators

Both Hollow Water and the Iona Community said, 'We are not the healers.' For them, it was Creator or God who heals. Their job was to facilitate healing. At Plum Village, people were very quick to say, 'You can't force healing.' They also worked to facilitate but not to force healing justice. Underneath this goal of facilitating healing was a principle that local people responded to their own conflicts. Hollow Water fought for years for the right to respond to harm in their own ways. Healing justice happened through nurturing local facilitators.

Healing justice listens to the voices of brokenness

Each community had ways to let harms surface and be acknowledged in a caring way. Creating safety and space for those who had been harmed, or even for those who had harmed others, to come and speak about that harm was a very important part of healing justice. Each community had created mechanisms to surface conflict and to listen carefully to the stories of those who had experienced harm. All communities recognized that the path of healing justice had to do with compassionate listening to the broken.

Healing justice recognizes the enemy as a brother or sister

Healing justice responses to harm were rooted in a basic insight that the enemy was also a brother or sister. Hollow Water recognized that both the victim and the victimizer were family members who needed to be treated as such. The Iona Community worked to include the marginalized as brothers and sisters. Plum Village began even their response to international conflicts with this basic insight, 'You are brothers already.' Healing justice worked because it fostered the connection and responsibility of family, and not because it suspended the rights of citizens.

Healing justice creates space for those involved in a harm to meet in a circle

Whether through a Sentencing Circle at Hollow Water, a circle of respectful dialogue in the Iona Community or a Beginning Anew circle at Plum Village, each community had found ways of creating space for those involved in a harm to meet in a circle. Space was given to hear the full story, to respond to the other and to find a new way forward.

Healing justice expands the circle

Each community offered a series of expanding circles in which harms were addressed. This offered added support while, at the same time, providing more resources to confront denial and to cultivate joyful living. By expanding the circle to include more of the community, these communities reflected a concept of healing justice in which the health and harm of one person was not separate from the health and harm of the community. When the communities were given opportunity for input, they sometimes saw that they too needed to take responsibility and to be transformed.

Healing justice shifts focus from symptoms to root causes

Each of the communities learned to investigate the roots of any particular harm. Treating symptoms without addressing root causes did not make sense to any of them. As they searched for root causes, they searched many sources. Their searches sometimes took them into the structures of their own community, or to international politics or to ecological relations. Their healing justice looked to the broad environment to find root causes of harms. Taking responsibility for these root causes was not solely the task of individuals but of families, communities, and various other social structures.

Healing justice broadens the horizon of time to be considered for harms

In Hollow Water this was expressed as the principle of looking back and looking forward seven generations to understand the current situation and what should be done. The Iona Community, working with offenders, required understanding of the initial causes of offending. In Plum Village people spoke of how the wounds (and gifts) of your ancestors were passed down to you and were present in your every cell.

They refused to limit healing justice to the logic of incidents and opened the horizon of time so as to more fully understand and transform the patterns, structures and relationships which led to any particular harm.

Healing justice creates conditions to break the patterns of unhealthy relationships by creating conditions for healthy relationships

Hollow Water spoke of this in terms of rediscovering the kinds of social structures they had before they had need of jails. The Iona Community's Jacob Project (Scotland) did this by working with ex-offenders to change their lifestyle into the conditions for healthy living. Plum Village said that the basis of their whole practise was to recognize and to do the things that led to health and to recognize and to avoid the things that did not. Healing justice helped persons and communities to understand the unhealthy patterns which led to harm and to cultivate the kind of relationships which embodied healing justice.

Healing justice conducts ceremonies and feasts

In each community healing justice responded to harm through ceremonies and feasts. Whether it was going to the sweat lodge in Hollow Water, intercessory prayer in the Iona Community or Formal Beginning Anew in

Plum Village, these communities found ways of coming together, drawing on their particular spiritual traditions and through them engaging more deeply with each other and the world around them. Feasting played a large role in healing justice. Eating together allowed them to share basic elements which sustained life.

Healing justice works even when people are denying responsibility

Because the healing justice communities did not see the individual victimizers as the sole source of harm, they could work with victimizers even while they were denying responsibility for the harms. The communities worked to change the conditions around the victimizers, helped them to touch their own innate goodness and to strengthen the positive relationships around them, and thus drew them out of denial. The community saw they could unilaterally take responsibility for their parts in creating the conditions of harm.

Healing justice 'sentences' people to a loving community where they can heal

In Hollow Water sentencing sometimes involved wilderness therapy or spending time camping with the community at Black Island Days. The Iona Community took young offenders into their community at Camas, and through the Jacob Project (Scotland) they worked with them to find housing and work. At Plum Village I was told prisons should be like retreat centres, designed to cultivate healthy relationships and to show prisoners how they were connected to everything else. In all cases victimizers were 'sentenced' to the community. Healing justice was practised by giving people every resource to heal and to become a healing resource to the rest of the community.

Shared characteristics of dynamics that sustain healing justice

Healing justice is sustained by sacred teachings and culture

Each community said that their visions and practises of healing justice were sustained by their sacred teachings and sacred practises. Exactly what that meant differed from community to community. In Hollow Water, it included reviving the place of Elders, of women and of their original language as they tried to find a social structure more in line with the original teachings about Creator. In the Iona Community, it included daily prayer, Bible reading and accountability for time and money as they tried to incarnate Jesus' way of being in the world. In Plum Village, it meant daily practises of sitting meditation, breathing meditation and eating meditation as they learned to awaken the Buddha within. In each case, the sacred teachings and cultures acted as a vision, a practise and a sustaining dynamic of healing justice. These communities all expected to find healing justice in people who did not participate in their community. They also believed that for them to sustain this orientation towards healing justice they needed to be in right relationship with their own spiritual traditions.

Healing justice is sustained by facing suffering

To sustain healing justice you have to be in a compassionate relationship to those who are suffering. While some other ways of justice are sustained by the ability to make others suffer, healing justice in the communities that I witnessed was sustained by staying compassionately present to the suffering of all. Healing justice did not try to hide suffering away, or to escape suffering by moving to some kind of separate 'spiritual' plane of existence. These communities believed that a necessary component of well-being was to find yourself in the heart of ill-being. Facing the roots of suffering in the self and the world helped to create the conditions for joy to bloom.

Healing justice is sustained by staying close to the earth

These communities saw it as their responsibility to care for the Earth; but they also saw the Earth as a teacher. The Earth taught the ways of healing justice. In fact, the Earth in some ways defined healing justice, for what happened to the Earth happened to people. Harming the Earth led to a lack of wholeness and suffering. Respecting the vast network of relationships within the Earth led to balance and health. Right relationship with the Earth was needed to sustain healing justice.

Healing justice is sustained by living in small caring communities

Living in community reflected the vision of healing justice even as it was a vehicle of healing justice. The common claim was that over time a living caring community helped its members to let go of fear and greed.

Through the caring community each person could rediscover their true identity. Hence, it was not accidental that examples of healing justice were found among them. For them the community, not the individual or the state, was the primary unit of understanding. They did not suggest that the community had the right to inflict suffering on the persons within it. The community was there to help persons to heal, but the community also needed healing. This socio-structural change in orientation was embedded in their understanding of healing justice and was sustained by its community-rooted practise.

Healing justice is sustained by the special roles of women and children

In different ways women and children played key roles in the development and sustaining of healing justice at each community. In Hollow Water it was the mothers and grandmothers who initiated and sustained their movement. When they grew weary the children stepped in and gave motivation through their challenges. The Iona Community learned over time that fully opening up to women and children was an important aspect of their healing justice practise. At time of writing they have a female leader and a whole youth section as part of the structure of their organization. Plum Village rejected the patriarchy under-girding much of Vietnamese Buddhism. Nuns at Plum Village were respected as Buddhas. Children at Plum Village also had a unique role in awakening the rest of the community to the ways of healing justice.

Healing justice is sustained by local communities taking responsibility back into their own hands

Healing justice was sustained by these local communities taking responsibility for their own healing paths. Each community recognized that the one-size-fits-all approaches to justice, whether state, restorative or healing justice, simply did not work. Healing justice took root in particular communities. What it looked like in one context needed to be different from what it looked like in the next because the contexts were different. In Hollow Water this happened through the establishment of the CHCH programme. In the Iona Community this happened by their focus on indigenizing movements of faith and in their critiques of government for being too distant from the communities they represented. In Plum Village it was most evident in the ways engaged Buddhism related to the communist, non-communist and American governments. It was also evident in their focus on rooting Buddhism in different cultures. Healing justice meant responsibility had to be taken back by local communities.

Healing justice is sustained by forming new partnerships with Western systems

Healing justice was sustained by forming new partnership with Western state systems. What I saw in Hollow Water was such a partnership. The Iona Community also found many ways of partnering with the state system to work at healing justice with those who were incarcerated or recently released from that system. Plum Village had a long history of working with agencies like UNESCO. They also spoke to justice professionals about healing justice ways of doing their work. These communities partnered with the state on the basis of the needs of the community and not on behalf of the state.

Healing justice is sustained by ongoing education and discipleship in healing justice

Healing justice was sustained in the communities because of their ongoing orientation towards learning and change. Whether it was the Return to Spirit trainings at Hollow Water or courses offered by the Iona Community or Plum Village, these communities were engaged in the ongoing tasks of describing, practising, debating and transforming their healing justice orientations. Bringing people together over time to learn about healing justice created a mechanism for change even as it created the relational capacity to engage more deeply in healing justice.

Healing justice is sustained by organizing like a movement not an institution

For each of these communities it was important to organize as a movement or as an organism rather than an institution. Hollow Water saw itself as a healing movement not a healing project of the community. The Iona Community believed that the tendency of institutions to preserve themselves was one of the biggest blocks to healing justice. For them organizing as a movement was a recognition that they must not structure themselves so that they would last forever. Plum Village believed the Sangha should organize like an organism or a body where members needed each other and there was no judgment between them. Organizing in this fashion was contrasted with hierarchical, bureaucratic and institutional ways of organizing.

Healing justice is sustained by being accountable to the community
Accountability to the community was a key to sustaining healing justice. When such accountability was missing in Hollow Water the momentum of the healing movement was lost. For the Iona Community accountability was a key part of their community rule. In Plum Village we saw it in the bi-weekly practise of reviewing and reciting the mindfulness training. Healing justice was not a possession such that once you had it you always had it. Healing justice required the constant attention and nurturing of the conditions that reminded people how to cultivate such a justice.

Healing justice is sustained by recognizing the value of other spiritual traditions
Healing justice was sustained by engaging in interfaith relationships. Each community was keen to share from and about their spiritual tradition, but they did not believe that everyone needed to be like them. Hollow Water worked with both Christians and traditional people. The Iona Community was active in both interdenominational and interfaith discussions. In an attempt to find a different path from the mixing of violence and Christian conversion witnessed in Vietnam, Plum Village encouraged people to always honour their original spiritual roots. They, too, were engaged in interfaith dialogue. These interfaith relationships sustained healing justice by creating the space for members of the communities to recognize the 'other' as brother and to remind themselves not to hold on to their own practises too tightly.

Shared characteristics of dynamics that act as barriers to healing justice

Healing justice suffers when 'internal' harms are not dealt with
Surprisingly, some of the barriers to healing justice came from those who advocated such a practise. Healing justice had not come from distant professionals. It had come from community members who were also in the process of healing. When those members consistently lacked integrity, the healing justice movement was challenged. The ways in which healing justice advocates treated themselves and others sometimes were the most significant barriers to healing justice. When communities lost trust in the advocates of healing justice, the community withdrew its participation and healing justice ceased to be a holistic community movement. This

did not mean that advocates of healing justice had to be blameless, but the character of those involved was important. They had to be willing to return to a healing path when harms occurred. They had to learn to reflect healing justice at work in their relationships with others.

Healing justice suffers when advocates seek reproduction mode or desire for permanence

Each community spoke of the danger of the reproduction mode and the desire to keep structures alive forever. In Plum Village they spoke of this in terms of the lens of impermanence. This lens which through everything was seen in a state of change was the basis of right thinking. These communities saw institutionalization of their ways as more of a barrier than an effective way to share their understandings of justice. Being a holistic community movement and an imagination, healing justice could not be imposed or treated as a process of a project or a system.

Healing justice suffers when wrong notions of power emerge

Each community suggested that notions of hierarchical power served as barriers to healing justice. They identified this kind of power in different ways. The Iona Community spoke of it in terms of a desire to impose on others. Hollow Water and Plum Village saw danger even in notions of equality. To them, equality was too often the mid-point between two strongly hierarchical positions of power: inferiority and superiority. They were not seeking a balancing of negatives. Imposing healing justice through such notions led to problems. We saw very clearly that as Hollow Water shifted to a more hierarchical leadership structure, momentum for healing justice declined.

Healing justice suffers when guilt and shame take over

Each community showed an aversion to some practises of guilt and shame. In Hollow Water they saw guilt and shame as barriers that did not allow the person to grow. The Iona Community was formed, in part, in response to the shame those in poverty were made to feel. In Plum Village the urge to blame others was seen as evidence of wrong thinking and a barrier to healing. These communities were not afraid to confront those who harmed others, but they were clear that the purpose of such confrontation was to cultivate healing and friendship, not guilt and shame. When guilt and shame became the means and the ends, healing justice was distorted.

Healing justice suffers when forgetfulness becomes common

Each community saw forgetfulness as a key barrier to healing justice. In Hollow Water the tendency to forget the Creator and not give thanks was seen as a danger. In Plum Village people pointed to forgetfulness as not being aware of the present in what you were doing as you were doing it, thus potentially causing great suffering. In the Iona Community this danger of forgetfulness was seen in their focus on the importance of accountability for learning about, and relating to, God and also for the ways their lives (time and money) reflected healing justice. In all of these communities, healing justice was seen as impaired by people's tendency to forget their true identity.

Healing justice suffers when certain aspects of mainstream Western culture are valued

The communities identified some aspects of mainstream Western culture as barriers to healing justice. These included values like individualism, consumerism and capitalism. Each of these was identified as a root of much suffering. In Plum Village people spoke of them as factors that fed the seeds of violence in people every day. The communities saw these aspects of Western culture as ways of structuring and imagining which fed violence rather than healing justice. For them healing justice acted as the basis for life. Healing justice was a paradigm which could transform these economic, political and ideological systems which lead to violence.

Major features of healing justice: sustaining right relationships

That we can find 46 common characteristics between these three communities strongly suggests that we are dealing with similar phenomena which can be grouped under the name of healing justice. Hollow Water worked out a logic of healing justice in relation to sexual abuse, colonialism and a return to their traditions. I saw the same logic reflected in the way the Iona Community related to those who suffered from urban industrialization and in the way they attempted to recover a Christian identity rooted in the co-existence of healing, peace and justice. I also saw this logic in Plum Village as they related to war, Buddhist renewal and particular ways of being peace. A common logic of healing justice was practised in relation to crime, de-colonialization, spiritual renewal, structures of economics and military combat. The ability to generalize about healing justice is somewhat limited by the fact that this study focuses on only three case studies. I have not argued that I have identified all the significant variations of healing justice that are demonstrated in these three cases. Further study of other communities with a healing justice practise may reveal other significant characteristics of healing justice which I have missed or not clearly highlighted here. This research is not finished. However, the fact that healing justice has been practised by different groups around the world in such diverse and challenging applications suggests there is a robust vitality in healing justice which deserves further attention.

In this section I will outline six distinguishing features of how these communities increased and sustained a set of social, spiritual and ecological relations which encouraged healing justice rather than more punitive forms of justice.

Having the right relationship with Spirit is the first feature of these healing justice communities. The right relationship with Spirit, as observed in this comparative study, involved nurturing a sense of the innate sacredness of all Creation, drawing on the laws of interconnectedness and wholeness, seeing the enemy as a brother or sister. For these communities healing justice is not a secular or humanistic act if secular and humanistic imply some separate existence, not related to Spirit. Doing the work of justice is facilitating the work of Spirit. Healing justice is a spiritual and physical activity. The Spirit is the source of this sense of justice. Each community had a sacred view of all of Creation. This created particular ways of engaging in harms. The 'harmer' could not simply be seen as offender, enemy or other. The one who harmed was also a brother and sister. The one who harmed also had the same sacred character as the ones being harmed. That people learn to live in unsacred ways was not justification to treat them in further unsacred ways, but rather motivation to remind them of their sacred identity. Justice and law was not about keeping the savage from doing evil, but about helping the wounded to remember their true names, their identities based on a sacred web of relationships. Sacredness seemed to have a relational character in which all of creation was seen as woven together. In this way, 'laws of interconnection' formed the imagination of both what healing justice was and the means of cultivating it. Thus, right relationship with Spirit meant that healing justice was more about cultivating the conditions of the engaged peace of living the Good Life and not primarily about crime or primarily about harm. It is about living in a good way with the Spirit and therefore cultivating the conditions for life to flourish. It seems that healing justice is not possible without a right relationship to Spirit.

Having the right relationship to the Earth is the second distinguishing feature of healing justice. In the three communities the right relationship with Earth was not based on ownership, control or resource manipulation as in the landowner model. Nor was it based primarily on the avoidance of the harmful impact of people, as in the environmental law model. Rather, for healing justice, right relationship with the Earth involved seeing the Earth as a gift and as a teacher and seeing oneself as part of the Earth. This was quite different from popular notions of 'nature' which seem to mean 'not human', thus creating a dualism of nature and humanity where all too often nature is understood to be beautiful, but humans are harmful. In these case studies communities understood that having the right relationship with the Earth influenced social, spiritual and economic relationships. For example each community saw capitalism as a problematic eco-political system because it is based in an unjust relationship with the Earth. This in turn creates unjust relationships within and between people. In healing justice the right relationship with the Earth means that justice is extended to the *whole* Earth, including all people.

Their healing justice practises involved mindful walking, touching the earth, sweats, fasts in the bush and regular time in the outdoors. These practises had healing value, in part because they placed participants in close enough relationship to the land that they might learn something about their identity and how they were connected to the whole Earth. Being close to the Earth was a key method of healing justice while at the same time articulating a goal of healing justice. That is to say that addressing harms in healing justice could well involve taking responsibility for a bad relationship with land. In these communities, and in healing justice, there is little distance between personal transformation in 'nature' and working at global transformations of socio-economic structures. The right relationship with Earth, a learning–listening relationship, led to and sustained efforts at both kinds of changes.

Having the right relationship with those who are suffering is the third defining feature of healing justice. These communities started on their path towards healing justice by opening themselves to an awareness of the suffering around them. They continued to sustain and practise their notion of healing justice by staying present to the suffering of others. Suffering was not just a matter to be resolved and forgotten.

In healing justice understandings those who are suffering draw our attention to the patterns and structures of life which advantage some people and disadvantage others. Staying present to suffering means learning friendship, compassion and even self-care, as the suffering of others often stirs our own anger and fear. However, for those who suffer, blame and guilt will not help them to grow. Staying present to suffering also means learning to engage and transform the systems and patterns which breed the conditions of suffering. Again, suffering, like the relationship with the Earth, sustains a robust notion of justice which extends well beyond dispute resolution or repairing harm.

For these communities, being in right relationship with those who are suffering also included being in right relationship to their own suffering and their own complicity in the suffering of others. Each community refused to externalize or project their own violence on others, as in the case of scapegoat theories of violence (Girard 1997). They saw themselves as complicit in violence, as injured persons and as people in the process of healing themselves. Healing justice did not come from impartial experts or neutral third parties. It came from people who were themselves complicit in violence and on a healing path. These dynamics lead to a justice not focused on blame and punishment but on supporting people to keep rediscovering a healing path of justice.

Having a collective orientation is the fourth distinguishing feature of healing justice. The communities argued that there is something about individualism that leads inherently towards a punitive kind of justice. They also argued that a collective orientation of a particular kind could lead to a more healing kind of justice. In Hollow Water, when the individual formed the basic frame of reference and the courts tried to establish guilt, then justice was reduced to heaping guilt on the individual. Alternatively, in healing justice the logic of interdependent relationships looked at the whole system to understand the ways in which the whole system encouraged or enabled such harming behaviour. The goal was to take responsibility for harms, in part by transforming the system so that such behaviour was not encouraged in the first place. However the logic of interdependent relationships was not just about harm. Learning from the

Earth, all of our relationships were seen to be in a state of interdependent flux. Although harm to one element affected many, so did increasing the capacity for joy. Healing justice worked to transform persons and systems in ways that increased life for all.

Some will argue that since Western societies no longer have communal orientations healing justice is impossible. This is a challenge I pick up in the next chapter. Here it is important to note that in these case studies their collective orientations were created or reinvigorated from a very low level of collectivity. Hollow Water had to recover their sense of community and their identity and even the knowledge of their sacred traditions. The Iona Community was started in part because a more community-oriented perspective on faith was missing from their church experience. Plum Village is a collection of exiles and new friends partnering to create a new community. In each case, these communities did not have a pre-existing close community, but rather created it in response to a recognition that it was lacking. The collective, identity-based elements of healing justice were learned.

The fifth distinguishing feature of healing justice is that healing justice means are employed to achieve healing justice ends. Each of the communities argued that confrontations of violence required ways of moving and engaging that were themselves not violent by nature. They also argued that justice was not primarily about control and order. In fact, at times justice or, at least, healing justice unsettled and disrupted notions of order, control and being settled. Theologian Chris Huebner agrees and declared that this is precisely the capacity that concepts of Christian peace must have and sorely lack (Huebner 2006). From the case studies we can see that when healing justice looks at the need to transform patterns and structures of relationships, it becomes more of an untamed or wild sense of justice than a domesticated one. It is willing to challenge notions of order and control just as it is able to confront and transform the advocates of healing justice who are, of course, still complicit in violence. The end goal of healing justice is a respect for, and a cultivation of, the innate goodness in all, both us and them, friend and enemy, human and earth, physical and spiritual. The means are the same. And thus the dualism of most approaches to justice is somehow dissolved. Healing justice assumes that when harms happen, and they will, what is needed is healing, not punishment, blame or shame. Healing is needed for victim and victimizer, but the need might also include community, society, nation, international relationships and ecological relations. Maintaining the state order is not the goal. The goal is to nurture the conditions in which people will bloom like a flower, and will live the good life. This requires a kind of watering, a cultivating of the positive conditions of growth. It also involves risk, a willingness to die and a willingness to let go of the status quo and to change. Using healing justice means to achieve healing justice ends includes all of these factors and more.

The final distinguishing feature of healing justice is that it uses harms as an opportunity to unfold a healing justice paradigm. I have emphasized throughout this study that healing justice is not merely a way of responding to harm but is a paradigm or a way of imagining the world. For these communities their responses to harm were sometimes the entry point into exploring an alternative paradigm or imagination. Hollow Water started to respond to sexual abuse and found themselves on the path to recovering Anishinabe identity. The Iona Community started making connections with Polmont Young Offenders Institution and found themselves working through the Jacob Project Scotland at issues of lifestyle change. Plum Village used harms to remind the community how to water the flowers in each person and how to walk in such a way as to cultivate a kind of mindfulness. It is possible to start with harms and move towards discovering and rediscovering a personal and collective identity based in compassionate relationship with the Spirit and all the Earth. From this perspective 'state citizenship' is a narrow and potentially problematic identity marker. Healing justice, especially in the Hollow Water example, includes the possibility of transforming even notions of state and of citizenship. Healing justice begins with harms and moves almost seamlessly to cultivating an alternative paradigm. Because it is not merely a reflection of state justice, but actually draws on alternative sources, it has the potential to be a very interesting dialogue partner for both Western state systems and the restorative justice movement. The next chapter explores further just what healing justice could offer in such dialogues.

Major features of healing justice: logic of shared imagination of healing justice

The first part of the chapter addressed points of connection or common characteristics of healing justice. The second part of the chapter focused more generally on the kinds of relationships necessary to sustain a healing way of justice. In the final section, I try to outline some of the shared imagination or logic of healing justice. Each of these three summaries of the chapter are overlapping attempts to put words around what these three communities share as it pertains to healing justice. My impression has been that the area of greatest overlap is not common processes but a shared imagination. In this section, I identify six basic logics of healing justice. Previously I have contrasted these logics with the logic and geography of crimebut for now it is important to find ways of naming the logic of healing justice that emerged from listening to these communities.

1. Logic of land and Spirit

Healing justice does not begin with states and institutions. Healing justice, as practised by these communities, begins and ends with the Spirit and the land. For each of these communities healing justice came from a journey into old wisdom teachings. They trace this justice to the heart of and gift from the Creator. Each community had a different name and understanding of this Spirit. However, all communities argue that if one wants to create and sustain a healing kind of justice one needs to be in a particular relationship with Spirit and land.

Both Spirit and land push a sense of justice beyond the individual orientation and beyond the state orientation. In fact this kind of justice is not primarily about social control but more about cultivating a life that acknowledges and responses to the gift, beauty and fragileness of life.

When the land becomes a teacher of justice, the goal is to find wholeness by finding common connection. The goal of justice is more to (re) discover a sustainable and good balance in the local community than it is to impose a hierarchical state order on distant lands.

2. Logic of transforming patterns

When one begins with a broad view of justice, as something sacred, as something reflected in the logic of the Earth which involves balance, harmony and wholeness, then it follows that the procedures of justice involve transforming relationships and patters within the whole system. This does not follow the typical logic of rules and procedures. Here justice is a creative act of staying close to those who suffer as they demonstrate, like canaries in a mine, those aspects of the environment which lead to harm rather than healing. The logic of transforming patterns is one that seeks to understand the root causes and conditions of harm and to break the unhealthy patterns that lead to such harm. It intimately links the episode of harm to the structures, patterns and relationships that encourage such harm. This logic expands the horizon of time and widens the relevant who. Where criminal justice focuses on the offender, healing justice focuses on the whole community – present, past and future. Rather than dealing with incidents it sees patterns, generations and structures. Rather than primarily blaming individuals it responds to harm as on opportunity to transform the whole community.

3. Logic of cultivating the conditions of loving-kindness
Rather than a kind of justice rooted in responding to harms (the logic of problem responsiveness) healing justice is rooted in the logic of cultivating the conditions of loving-kindness. This logic of justice does not wait for harm or for symptomatic episodes. It seeks at all points to cultivate the conditions for loving-kindness. In Johann Galtung's terminology this not a justice based in negative peace (the absence of peace) but by positive peace (the presence of peace) (Galtung 1969). This logic sees healing justice as an exploration of the kind of social, economic and political conditions that do not lead to harm but to loving-kindness. This logic is interested in how to organize a community in such a way as to lead to joy. When harm happens, this logic does not focus all of its attention to the negative. It believes that demonstrating loving-kindness is the way of awakening those who have forgotten how to act in such a way. The logic of cultivating the conditions of loving-kindness then has a double goal: to avoid the environments that cause harm while at the same time cultivating the environments that lead to the fullness of life.

4. Logic of finding true identity
Rather than labelling victims, offenders and professional helpers, healing justice seeks to reveal to each person their true names. Inspired by watching land and Spirit, one's true names are about how it is that we are connected to 'others'. Those who have forgotten how to act as good relatives need to be reminded of what it is to be a good relation. Those who suffer harm are often seen as one who is out of balance – in danger of forgetting their essential natures, their true names. The logic of finding

true names means that justice must create space to explore identify and to rediscover how all things are connected. This logic does not try to create good by telling people they are essentially bad. Rather it tries to awaken the compassion for the other by teaching about one's true nature and the nature of our mutual interdependence. This logic assumes that those who live in forgetfulness of these things need to be surrounded by a caring community that will help them remember who they are. These communities do not have a single universal process as this kind of logic seeks to understand identity both in its particularity and interconnectedness.

5. Logic of interdependent relationships

Clearly healing justice is not a logic that turns on individual autonomy. It is a logic of interdependent relationships. Because all things are seen as essentially interconnected, responsibly and accountability are understood communally. Rather than blaming the individuals, this logic moves to understand how it is that families, villages and countries raise the kind of people who harm others. At the same time this logic focuses on transforming those same sets of relationships to cultivate healing justice. This logic of interdependent relationships is different from the logic of states. This logic gives preference to locally based and locally driven harms responses over state-based and state-driven ones. It is interested in transforming the whole collective – in its memory, its structures, its relationships and its patterns of behaviour. This logic of interdependent relationships sees healing justice as creating community – creating social, economic and political structures – rooted in a healing perspective.

6. Logic of healing for all

This logic sees healing as the interpretative framework for justice. Rather than punishment, it sees healing as both the means and ends of justice. While healing justice is not always a justice free of punishment, punishment does not become the main interpretative framework. Healing justice is rooted in a justice that respects the sacredness of each person and believes that all can heal. This logic of healing then does not rely so heavily on punishment and violence as a last resort. This logic sees the world as constantly engaged in processes of change and consistently open both to change towards healing and change towards harm. The logic of healing for all sees harms as an opportunity to work at healing for all involved – the ones harmed and the ones harming. It also works to transform the family, the socio-economic and ecological structures. The logic of healing for all returns us to the logic of Spirit and land, in whom all find their true identity.

We can see here that healing justice covers different territory than criminal justice. It has a different geography and a different logic. Based on the common patterns outlined above we could contrast the logic of crime and the logic of healing justice as follows.

Table 7.1 Contrasting the Logics: Criminal Justice and Healing Justice	
Criminal Justice	**Healing Justice**
Logic of states and institutions	Logic of Creator and Creation
Logic of rules and processes	Logic of transforming patterns (the sacred)
Logic of problem-responsiveness	Logic of cultivating loving-kindness
Logic of nouns	Logic of finding true identity
Logic of individual autonomy	Logic of interdependent relationships
Logic of punishment and violence	Logic of healing for all

Previously I have tried to draw out in more detail the logic of geography of the criminal justice system and how that contrasts with a healing justice logic (Sawatsky 2008). Here I have tried to outline some of the features of the logic or geography of healing and simply wish to point to some of the ways they contrast and are in tension with the main stream logics of criminal justice.

Conclusion

While the communities differed in many ways, the substance, strategy and place of healing justice within these three communities had many common characteristics. There seemed to be a shared logic of healing justice even if the processes of healing justice differed.

Each aspect of my tentative definition of healing justice seemed to be well borne out by the actual case studies.

Healing justice is:

a collective paradigm or imagination, usually drawing on an ancient wisdom tradition, that seeks to find ways of surviving together:

> ➤ by structuring life so that means reflect the end of respect for life and

> ➤ by treating harms as opportunities to transform suffering and root causes of harm and, at the same time, to cultivate conditions of respectful living within the interrelated aspects of self, other, community/ies, social structures, environment and Spirit.

There are, of course, other ways to summarize the heart of healing justice. Healing justice is about nurturing particular kinds of relationships with Spirit, Earth, those who suffer and the collective. It is about discovering the horizon of joy, compassion and love. This kind of justice is about rediscovering who you are and about cultivating the kinds of environments that every day will feed such compassion.

Very likely a different researcher would have highlighted somewhat different aspects of these communities. By verifying the case studies with the communities, and by rooting the comparative analysis in the content of the approved case studies, I have confidence that the characteristics I have presented are more than my imagination and bias and were true reflections of each community. Moreover, as these case studies examined the interplay between visions, practises and sustaining dynamics, I am confident that these case studies represent not the aspirations, the distant ideals, but the operational praxis of the community. The case studies represent what happens on the ground.

These findings present compelling evidence that healing justice does exist, and that it does have some coherence, at least for these three communities, even across the divides of culture, spiritual tradition, language and geography.

Having seen that healing justice does exist in small pockets around the world, and that there is a consistent pattern to this sense of justice, we now turn to what the meaning of these findings might be for three groups: those practising healing justice, those in the field of restorative justice and those interested in Western forms of governance.

Chapter 8

Taking Healing Justice Seriously

Reconciliation[1]

We are waking up to our history
from a forced slumber
We are breathing it into our lungs
so it will be part of us again
It will make us angry at first
because we will see how much
you stole from us
and for how long you watched us suffer
we will see how you see us
and how when we copied your ways
we killed our own.

We will cry and cry and cry
because we can never be the same again
But we will go home to cry
and we will see ourselves in this huge mess
and we will gently whisper the circle back
and it will be old and it will be new.

Then we will breathe our history back to you
you will feel how strong and alive it is
and you will feel yourself become a part of it
And it will shock you at first
because it is too big to see all at once

---

[1]   Taken from *Nation to Nation: Aboriginal Sovereignty and the Future of Canada* edited by J. Bird, L. Land, M. Macadam and D. Engelstad. Published by Public Justice Resource Centre. Copyright © Tababodong 2002.

and you won't want to believe it
you will see how you see us
and all the disaster in your ways
how much we lost.

And you will cry and cry and cry
because we can never be the same again
But we will cry with you
and we will see ourselves in this huge mess
and we will gently whisper the circle back
and it will be old and it will be new

(Tababodong 2002).

Introduction

This poem by a Canadian Aboriginal author highlights some of the ways healing justice might be taken seriously. The poem opens the book *Nation to Nation: Aboriginal Sovereignty and the Future of Canada.* It addresses the process by which nation to nation dialogue might evolve between First Nations and Canada. To me, it highlights a number of aspects of healing justice and of my journey into healing justice.

Taking healing justice seriously requires creating places where communities can 'wake up to our history, from a forced slumber'. Aboriginal peoples are starting to wake up and see how colonialization, assimilation and the resource demands of capitalism have forced them into a deep slumber. They have forgotten who they are. They have lost the ways they traditionally used to survive, heal, adapt and flourish. When forced to copy foreign ways, it killed their own. And now waking up is not easy. It is an experience of anger, injustice and shock. But the response is not to attack or even to first transform the state that forced this slumber. Their response is to go home, to cry together and to learn to whisper the circle back. The Hollow Water community's story is surely such a story. Their goal is not to return to some golden age in the past, but to create the space to engage such that, 'it will be old and it will be new'.

As Aboriginal people rediscover who they are, they are discovering many beautiful and valuable resources within their culture and traditions. Some have articulated this rediscovery as healing justice.

But it is not just Aboriginal people who are waking up from a forced slumber. We see in Plum Village a community organized in such a way

245

that people might wake up, be mindful and engage the whole world with compassion. Here the forced slumber comes in part through the trauma of the Vietnam War and in part through the pressures of modern society. They, too, speak of needing to rediscover one's true identity, of needing to 'breathe it into our lungs' and of learning to go back home to gently whisper the circle back. They recognize that in our world it is often easier to live in forgetfulness than mindfulness. They try to identify practises which can sustain an awakened, mindful and engaged way of being.

In the Iona Community we also see this sense of waking up from a forced slumber, a slumber brought about by industrialization and by theologies which separate spiritual from political and action for justice from the prayers of the people. They, too, speak of needing to learn their true names, about seeing how they are connected to the world and about learning to start with the innate goodness of all creation rather than the original sinfulness of human beings.

In these communities healing justice is discovered through a process of going home to weep together. Taking healing justice seriously for them is not first and foremost about adapting the state system. Taking healing justice seriously is first about finding spaces for communities to wake up, to see the ways they have been forced asleep, to feel how much they have lost and to learn that copying foreign ways all too often kills local ways. The communities in this study have created and are creating such space.

According to the poem, change to the larger society comes as:

> we will breathe our history back to you
> you will feel how strong and alive it is
> and you will feel yourself become a part of it.

For me, this was what happened in travelling between these communities. They breathed their history into me and I could feel how alive it was and I could feel myself becoming a part of it. However, learning this new *geography of healing justice* is not easy. I saw that modern communities around the world could respond to harms, not with punishment, blame and fear, but with trying to offer help, healing and transformation. I found a sense of justice not rooted in administering pain but in cultivating joy. I found that healing justice was not a romantic aspiration but was a practical reality practised by diverse communities around the world. Soon hard questions about my own traditions emerged or, as the poem says: 'you will see how you see us and all the disaster in your ways'.

Have the Western state systems of justice forced us into a slumber? Not just Aboriginal people, but all people. Is restorative justice part of a new awakening or just another form of slumber? As we have copied colonializing ways, did it kill our own? Do we have a history, an identity, a people that we can go back home to and learn to cry together and to gently whisper the circle back? What might it look like for different nations to come together to see ourselves in this huge mess and to gently whisper the circle back in ways that are 'old and new'?

The task of this final chapter is to try to unpack some of these questions as we point towards ways of taking healing justice seriously.

Before working at the application of healing justice it is necessary to make a few comments on just how such application should happen. There are two extreme application models we must avoid. On the one hand is the *wholesale conversion model*. This model is applied by inviting people to leave their previous world and step into the world of one of these communities. Equally to be avoided is the rejection of the idea of healing justice on the basis that 'their' world is too different from 'our' world. These are different responses to the same faulty assumption. Both assume a dualism and separation between the realm of healing justice and everything else. We might say, 'These communities are so community-oriented or spiritually-oriented that they violate the basic values of the modern world and there is nothing we can learn from each other.' Or we might say 'Criminal justice is so based in violence that the only way to learn from healing justice is to drop everything and join one of these communities.' Both perspectives assume a dualistic view within a logic of wholesale conversion. While conversion is a mode of application used by these communities, it is not their primary mode. As we saw in the case studies and in the common features, healing justice is not based on dualism of them/us, violence/peace, Spirit/non-Spirit. These communities believe that their practises have to be sustained by larger cultural dynamics, but they do not believe that others need to become like them in order to learn from them. Moreover, although they reject the conversion model as the primary model of application, they do not reject a learning model. Each community believes that others can learn something from them. The conversion model is the extreme of too much change or, perhaps, change of the wrong kind when it is used as the only model of application.

The other extreme we need to avoid could be called the *pluck-and-choose model* of application. Adam Crawford called it butterfly collecting

(Crawford 2002). In this model you simply pluck and choose whatever you desire from the practises and visions of healing justice. This model usually avoids either the calls for structural change or the calls for changes of heart and, instead, focuses on exotic processes which would be introduced to and, perhaps, imposed on others. I have already offered a critique of this model in Chapters 1 and 2. From our case studies we see that the vision and practises of healing justice are sustained by particular kinds of relationships and structures. Merely adapting a healing justice practise without engaging in wider change does not necessarily mean that such a practise will be used in healing justice ways. This is the extreme of too little change or, perhaps, change of the wrong kind. This model cannot be totally disregarded. In fact the communities in this study encourage trying their practises. At Plum Village people will tell you that if you mindfully enjoy three breaths, you can receive some healing right away. The Iona Community are happy to share their songs, which they believe are part of the 'new ways to touch the hearts of all' (The Iona Community n.d.-c). An Elder at Hollow Water told me that their sacred teachings are not unique to the Anishinabe and the principles could be incorporated when systems are renewed to meet a community's needs. So we see again each community suggesting that others can learn from them. We also see that the pluck-and-choose model can be a means of application, but it must not be the primary means. When we pluck-and-choose, we are the ones who decide. Most often we choose that which has some connection with our pre-existing frame of reference. Such choices tend to reinforce our existing paradigm without giving sufficient space to see what the application might look like from the original viewpoint, from the perspective of the communities.

In brief, how we apply the meaning of healing justice is a challenge. There is a strong suggestion from the communities themselves that there are meanings which could be applied. There is also serious inadequacy in following the easiest models of application, the conversion model and the pluck-and-choose model.

If healing justice is to be taken seriously it must be accepted on its own terms. The ways in which we apply healing justice to existing knowledge and practise must be consistent with healing justice itself. Some may take the task of application as primarily responding to the possible objections to healing justice. It is too community-oriented, it is too Spirit-oriented, it ignores the rights of the individual and leads to loss of autonomy to name a few. These objections should not be disregarded, but neither should they be the primary lens of understanding or the primary guide of application. That would miss the opportunity to see how the cases of healing justice themselves guide the process of exploring how healing justice could be taken seriously in other contexts.

This chapter explores how healing justice could be taken seriously, first, by identifying various overlapping interests of healing justice, criminal justice and restorative justice. It is important to begin with what is shared between these various approaches. Next, I point toward ways that healing justice expands the horizons of criminal justice and restorative justice. In other words I will try to draw attention to how healing justice moves in ways and in spaces not normally occupied by criminal justice and restorative justice. I will then address some of the challenges to taking healing justice seriously and will conclude by highlighting the kinds of questions that the fundamental assumptions of healing justice raise for Western conceptions of justice, restorative justice and for communities which already have some form of healing justice practise.

Overlapping interests of healing justice, criminal justice and restorative justice

One of the central, albeit modest, claims of this research is that healing justice exists. I made this argument in the previous chapter. Each community had a different conception of healing justice, but we witnessed enough points of comparison to conclude that we were seeing a similar phenomenon in each community. So then the modest claim that healing justice exists was expanded to say that healing justice existed in three different communities, countries, language groups and ethnic groups. This extension of the claim was merely a reflection of the methodology of the research. The goal was to find three communities that differed significantly on the grounds stated above but that appeared to share a phenomenon of healing justice. Implicit in these claims was the suggestion that it was valuable for others to be aware of these case studies, as they represented ways small communities could live out a sense of healing justice within the modern world.

However, as we move from being aware of cases of healing justice toward locating healing justice within the jurisdictions of criminal justice and restorative justice, it is important to understand the various points of connection between them. Here it is helpful for us to understand common functions. Comparing dissimilar systems on the basis of forms rather than functions often leads to an inability to see how these divergent forms might share a similar function. The strategy of focusing on functions before forms has been used in law (Llewellyn 1940), theology (Lindbeck 1984), art (Greenough 1947), architecture (Lambert 1993), peacebuilding (Lederach 1995) and, of course, sociology (Durkheim 1982).

One of the purposes and functions of healing justice is that it seeks to create and sustain peaceful and just relationships among peoples. Part of this goal is to prevent the suffering of others. There are connecting points here, of course, with the functions of law and of restorative justice. Karl Llewellyn's (1940) law-jobs theory argues that there are certain functions, or law-jobs, that any group needs to work at so that they can survive as a group. He identifies four functions of law which he sees as operational in groups as diverse as Western legal professionals and Cheyenne Indians. One function relates to organizing life in such a way as to prevent the harm of others. Sometimes in Western societies this takes the form of regulatory frameworks (Adams and Brownsword 2007) but the function and goal is the prevention of harm through advocating particular norms of behaviour. In restorative justice we also see interest in building up particular kinds of social relationships. Howard Zehr claims that one of the pillars of restorative justice is that it promotes engagement or participation (Zehr 2002b). Others point toward how restorative justice is intended to build and normalize particular kinds of social relationships which could be called peaceful and just (Braithwaite 2003b; Dyck 2000; Sullivan and Tifft 2001). Healing justice, criminal justice and restorative justice seem to share an understanding that law and justice somehow must function to prevent harms and to build towards more just relationships. Some of the overlapping features dissipate as each field defines these terms but we can identify this as an area of functional overlap.

Healing justice seeks to find ways of responding to harms that build a more just and peaceable future. Karl Llewellyn sees this as the first function of law; law must provide some mechanism for settling disputes. Another of Howard Zehr's pillars of restorative justice is the focus on harms (Zehr 2002b). A second area of functional overlap, then, is harm-response or dispute settlement.

Healing justice seeks to find ways of doing justice that engage basic human needs and human nature. Legal theories also tend to see law as needed to engage and sometimes protect us from our basic human nature.

To be clear healing justice and many legal theories disagree as to the essential characteristics of that nature and those needs. However, they share the idea that justice somehow must function to engage the basic nature of humanity. More and more scholars and practitioners of restorative justice advocate the idea that restorative justice is a way to address the basic needs of those involved (Maxwell and Morris 2006; Sullivan and Tifft 2004; Zehr 2002b). So a third area of functional overlap is the development of socio-cultural systems responsive to basic human needs and natures.

At the level of how law and justice are meant to function, healing justice has significant overlap with some conceptions of restorative justice and some more general Western conceptions of law. This overlap is not complete, but neither is it insignificant. Western law discourses share with healing justice an interest going well beyond dispute resolution and extending to peaceable social relations. Restorative justice and healing justice share much in spirit although the application of restorative justice tends to be much more narrowly focused on harms-response. Major differences notwithstanding, we can see substantial areas of overlap at the level of socio-cultural function. Healing justice, criminal justice and restorative justice share some of their *raison d'être*, purpose of being.

Expanding the horizon of criminal justice and restorative justice

In the previous section I made the modest claim that healing justice exists. The remainder of this chapter focuses on a much more significant and far reaching claim: the existence of healing justice challenges some of the basic assumptions of Western understandings of the nature of justice in general and criminal justice in particular. One of the ways healing justice challenges many Western conceptions of justice is by directly challenging some of its basic assumptions regarding human nature, the nature of justice, the role of punishment, the role of the state and the role of the individual. These challenges will be picked up later. In this section I explore some of the ways that healing justice extends the horizon of criminal justice and restorative justice, highlighting what healing justice offers which might be surprising and new in these other fields.

Here I return to the major features of healing justice as outlined in the previous chapter, the six distinguishing features of how these communities increased and sustained a set of social, spiritual and ecological relationships which encouraged healing justice. They included:

1. Nurturing the right relationship with Spirit.

2. Nurturing the right relationship to the Earth.

3. Nurturing the right relationship with those who are suffering.

4. Nurturing a particular kind of collective orientation.

5. Employing healing justice means to achieve healing justice ends.

6. Using harms as an opportunity to unfold a healing justice paradigm.

Most of these features do not figure strongly in Western approaches to law or in restorative justice. However, this research suggests that each is vital to sustaining the relationships that can support healing kinds of justice. If we are interested in the possibility that justice can be more than a retributive or punitive experience, this research provides reason to pause and consider how these features, if put into practise, might transform our understandings of justice. Put more strongly, this research suggests that without these features a system may be 'doomed' to a punitive approach to justice. In this view, a mere changing of processes such as is advocated in much restorative justice will not sustain a healing approach to justice. It will be mere tinkering unless the changes also engage the challenges of the six features of healing justice.

Of these distinguishing features, some have been considered but, by and large, the following ones have been rejected by mainstream Western approaches to justice and law: (1) right relationship to spirit, (4) collective orientation and (5) means–ends consistency. These will be picked up later.

However, some of these features simply represent a different horizon of justice and a different way of moving within justice. Take our relationship with the Earth. The main mode of relating to Earth in much of the Western legal tradition is through ownership as reflected in property law. Karl Renner, the Austrian legal theorist, studied the social function of institutions like property law (Renner 1949). He claims that the right of property ownership is the right to power in the private interest, or the right to dominate. Indeed, in capitalist societies the legal systems include comprehensive rules concerning private property since the economic system is based on acquiring private wealth (Harris 2007). So there is a sense of owning land that is quite different from the kind of relationship with the Earth practised in the three communities in this study. Restorative justice tends not to address any issues of land, with the exception of some indigenous groups who do work at taking people 'on the land' as part of their justice work. Generally, outside a dominion–ownership paradigm, theories of justice have done little direct thinking on the role of the land in sustaining a particular orientation to justice. For example John Rawls' influential *Theory of Justice* (1999) is silent on this topic. So is almost all the literature in restorative justice and criminal justice. However, for the three communities in this research, relating well with the land was both a sustaining force behind healing justice and a way to practise healing justice. When the land becomes teacher it can offer reorientation to those who have been disorientated by harm. It can also provide models for social and cultural organizing and transforming which build on natural cycles of life, death and change.

In Western societies the discourses most related to this linking of land and justice are the relatively recent ones on ecological senses of justice. These emerged in the 1960s–1970s. Richard Lazarus in *The Making of Environmental Law* (2004) argues that while environmental law affects most things people do today, it only came into force in the 1970s. The United Church of Canada adopted its first policy concerning the protection of the integrity of creation as part of its peace and justice platform in 1977 (United Church of Canada n.d.). The UN Stockholm Conference on the Human Environment in 1972 was the first significant international gathering related to the harmful impact of human activities on the environment. Within criminology, green criminology (focus on crimes against the environment) has emerged only in the last few years (Carrabine 2004). Attention to the relationship between the Earth and justice is fairly new. However, climate change has directed much attention to relationship to land as a justice issue. Healing justice also highlights this but goes beyond a stewardship relationship (us taking care of the land) to cultivating healing and teaching relationships with the land where both land and humans can experience healing.

Having a right relationship with those who are suffering is also a major practise and sustaining dynamic of healing justice. Indeed, restorative justice has also tried to re-establish a central role for the response to harms for victim, offender and community. It tries to work first hand with the people who are suffering rather than focusing primarily on the institution whose rules have been broken. Restorative justice advocates understand this to be a corrective to the absence or invisibility of these groups within the modern criminal justice processes. Western societies tend to hide away those who are suffering, building hospitals for the sick, funeral parlours for the dead, prisons for the criminals and 'old folks' homes for the elderly. Western societies tend to export their conflicts to experts: the doctor for the physically ill, the priest or pastor for the spiritually ill and the psychologist for the mentally or emotionally ill. These are particular cultural features not shared by all societies. Western societies, despite what could be called a fixation on justice as pain, do not want to stay in close relationship with those who are in pain. The communities in this study see such tendencies as problematic. Communities need to respond to their own harms. But communities also need to be in close relationship with those who are suffering in the community. Here I refer both to those suffering from harms (or what is typically called crime) and those suffering from the structural violence of systems which were not designed to help them to meet their needs and to flourish. Staying in right relationship with those who are suffering sustains a healing way of justice because it encourages the search, not only for ways to work at personal healing, but also collective and structural healing. Socio-cultural transformation is part of healing justice in a way that it is not typically part of criminal justice or even restorative justice. The Western justice systems are the dispute mechanisms of Western states, and are designed to make those systems work better. Healing justice, however, does not assume a state model and assumes that the status quo of socio-cultural relationships is part of what is causing the suffering in the community. By staying in right relationship with those who are suffering healing justice moves beyond merely responding to harms and works to transform the whole system. Restorative justice typically has worked to hear the voices and needs to those who suffer – the victim, the offender and the communities – but has struggled to use that awareness to transform the whole system.

Using harms to unfold a healing justice paradigm also names spaces and ways of moving which are outside the normal geography of criminal and restorative justice. Anthony Duff claims that punishment should be seen as a way of communicating a public message to a citizen about the moral framework of the state (2001). He sees punishment as a forceful means of communication designed to serve the goals of repentance, reform and reconciliation (Duff 2001). This sounds similar to the themes of healing justice. However, there is a critical difference. Although Duff uses harms as a starting point the paradigm which he unfolds is one of state authority. For Duff, it is important that the state rather than the community is the instrument of this justice. In his words 'There is also, of course, good reason for the law itself to discourage, or in extreme instances to count as criminal, such informal kinds of punishment, since they are all too likely to be misdirected or excessive' (Duff 2001). Restorative justice is vague as to what paradigm it tries to unfold with its justice practises. Its close proximity to the state system, sometimes means that it reflects the same logic as the state (Sawatsky 2006). The question for restorative justice is, what does it intend to restore? It surely does not restore the state of the relationship before the harm happened. But what does it intend to restore? Social and psychological safety so that people can live without trauma within the current system? Some biblical sense of right relations or *shalom*, as Zehr speaks of it (Zehr 1990a)? Something else? Each of the communities in the study of healing justice had ways of naming and identifying what they sought to heal or restore. Those needing healing justice included persons but also the community, the nation, and their relationship with land and with Spirit. To work towards these healing goals the processes of responding to harms had to work at transforming the originating causes of harm and cultivating the conditions of healing justice. For them the means and the goal of justice was the abundance of joy, living the good life or being peace. Justice was not primarily an experience of punishment but one of (re)discovering one's true names. These dynamics are also largely absent from much of the discourse on criminal justice and restorative justice.

In the previous section I tried to highlight the overlap of healing justice with criminal justice and restorative justice. Here I have argued that some of the major features of healing justice draw attention to aspects of justice which are typically unexamined in the fields of criminal justice and restorative justice.

Difference and points of tension

In this section I want to take up some of the major features of healing justice which are, or at least appear to be, in direct contradiction with mainline Western understandings of justice. For many Westerners these aspects of healing justice are the most challenging. In the historical development of Western justice some versions of these features were considered and discarded as the praxis of modern justice 'progressed'.

On 'secular' justice and the spiritual roots of healing justice

Rooting a sense of justice or law within a religion or a spiritual tradition is not new. While the current Western legal traditions tend to emphasize social, political and economic factors to the exclusion of spiritual ones, there is a long tradition through the centuries of drawing on Spirit as a basis of justice or law. Harold Berman's *Law and Revolutions* (1983) traces the influence on the Western legal tradition of the revolutions of the eleventh to fifteenth centuries. Revolutions, he argues, are mostly religious. In *Law and Revolution II* (2003) he picks up the argument, examining the sixteenth and seventeenth centuries but mostly focusing on the Protestant Reformation. Mixing religion or Spirit and a sense of justice is not new, says Berman.

However, the way healing justice does this mix differs markedly from many of the past attempts. Take the Protestant Reformation as an example. From his Christian understandings Martin Luther advocated a violent kind of justice as a response to evil. Luther's Two Kingdom theology is full of various separations: fallen/redeemed, City of Man/ City of God, sinner/saint, flesh/spirit, visible/invisible, earthly righteousness and heavenly righteousness. These separations were fed by a very low view of humans. In Luther's view most people had not received the gift of salvation, were 'totally depraved', 'savage' and 'wild beasts' (Luther 1958). As Witte comments, Luther saw 'law as a thick chain or harness designed to keep savage sinners under some measure of control and to keep society in some semblance of order' (Witte 2003). Here we can see an example of a notion of justice and law which draws on spiritual traditions but not in ways that lead to a healing kind of justice. This illustrates how the wrong relationship to Spirit can lead to dehumanization and violence such as was experienced by these communities. From the standpoint of healing justice, one of the problematic assumptions of this 'wrong' view of Spirit and justice is that it begins with a very low view of humanity. This low view of humanity seems to accompany approaches to justice which are rooted in Spirit but with violent results. Long before Luther, early Christian theories of the atonement developed a theology of justice as punishment (Gorringe 1996). The satisfaction atonement theory, developed by Anselm of Canterbury in the eleventh century, claims that God's judgment demands punishment for human sin, which is the basic condition of all people, according to the theory of original sin. God's justice is meted out as punishment for sin. Jesus is then interpreted as one who quenches God's thirst for punishment by giving himself, the only innocent one, to be killed for the sake of the sins of the world. Eventually the state takes the place of God, judging others and meting out pain. The church sanctions the government as carrying out God's work on earth. And Jesus is neutered – taken out of the political domain – leaving the church to save souls while the state tends to people's physical sins. In Buddhist contexts the storyline is different. However, there are similar attempts to baptize violence and punishment as a tool of the spiritual community, often in partnership with some form of state government. Robert Florida tells of this Buddhist history of violence (2004). Lawrence Keeley's controversial research suggests that many Aboriginal groups used extreme violence in both internal and inter-tribal relations (1995). In each case a spiritual view rooted in a low view of humanity creates a violent kind of justice. Healing justice is rooted in Spirit and that rootedness in Spirit leads these communities to treat humans (and in some cases all living beings) as sacred, with capacity to be healed, to belong, to be essentially needed. Rupert Ross noted this in Aboriginal communities and named it an ethic of original sanctity (1992).

On individualism, autonomy and the collective aspects of healing justice

Another point of contention for some is the communal or collective nature of healing justice. Despite a very long tradition, collective orientations are at odds with much of the political theory of Western governance. The criminal justice system, for example, comes out of a political philosophy which is based in notions of the autonomous self. Criminal law scholar Andrew Ashworth writes, 'One of the fundamental concepts in the justification of criminal laws is the principle of individual autonomy – that each individual should be treated as responsible for his or her own behaviour' (2006). Another legal scholar, William Wilson, agrees, saying that autonomy is 'a fundamental, yet challengeable, premise' underlying the whole operation of criminal law (1998).

Healing justice challenges the basic premise of individual autonomy. Communities in this research identified individualism as a barrier to healing justice. Their healing justice turned on the logic of interdependent relationships rather than the logic of individual autonomy. At the same time we saw that these three communities operated within the modern world. These communities were created and developed partly in resistance to the individualistic culture; they were not pre-existing communities with thick communal tendencies. These communities are developing ethics of responsibility for actions. As these are communal ethics, this responsibility extends not just to persons but to whole communities.

The presence of collective notions of justice challenges the assumption that justice and law is primarily the concern of the state. Generally, in more individualistic societies, the state sees itself as having been given the consent of the individuals to govern for the common good. The state claims a monopoly on law and justice as part of its claim to be the only authority to administer violence (Weber 1965). However, others believe that states claim this monopoly on addressing conflicts because communities need such conflicts to grow strong, and states see strong communities as a challenge to its authority and ability to control (Christie 1977; Dickson-Gilmore and La Prairie 2008). However the state often tells the story as one of needing to step in to save the population from vigilant community justice. In these stories communities can not be trusted, except to revert to violence.

In any case, the assumption of many is that any new ideas about justice, be it restorative justice (Aertsen, Daems and Robert 2006) or healing justice, must be institutionalized into the state system. However, from the standpoint of the communities in this study, the desired situation is far more confusing. Part of what makes healing justice work is that it is not an individualistic, state-oriented system of justice as applied to all in one universal fashion. The state is not the main actor in healing justice. Communities are.

On justice as punishment and the ends–means consistency
The idea that peaceable ends can only be cultivated by peaceable means (another major feature of healing justice) is also very old, but it is not very common in contemporary Western societies. Both progressive social reformers and conservatives within Western legal traditions have argued

that administering pain is an essential means to achieving justice (Ashworth 1998; Beccaria 1963; Bentham 1830; Duff 2003; Hart 1968; Kant 1887). While some of these reformers fought for the rights of slaves, women, and prisoners, each of them assumes, in different ways, that justice as punishment is a kind of necessary evil. While some advocates of the kind of punishment name it as a necessary evil, many articulated the benefits, some even seeing it as part of the healing path. Plato saw pain and punishment as a 'cure' for the unhealthy mind (2008). Simone Weil saw as 'a vital need for the human soul' that it showed 'respect' and had the capacity to bring someone back inside the law (1998). The idea that punishment is an essential condition for justice is widespread through multiple layers and generations of society.

However, most societies have seen such a punishment justice as problematic and open to all sorts of abuses. As this sense of justice necessarily includes the state threatening and inflicting injury or pain on its citizens, many tools have been developed to justify and to limit the excess of punishment. The Just Deserts 'school' was started as a way to limit (not prohibit) the state's ability to punish. Its theorists and reformers have introduced a number of tools to temper the kinds, forms and amounts of punishment handed down by the state. These tools include:

➤ *proportionality* – The directive to punish only as much as that particular offender deserves and no more.

➤ *parsimony* – Andrew Ashworth describes parsimony as the principle 'that the court should always impose the least punititive measure available, since punishment is an evil in itself' (1998).

➤ *impartiality* – In Western justice impartiality has often meant that neutral third party professionals like judges are needed to make sure all parties are treated fairly, and that the particular identity of any one person does not unduly affect the processes.

These tools are designed to temper justice because justice is seen as inherently painful (and therefore, some argue, violent). They see and treat justice as a disease, helpful in small dosages (like an immunization shot) but potentially deadly in large ones.

The history of law and justice in Western society is in significant part a history of punishment. This history is typically told as a movement from the brutality of unbridled local vengeance towards a more humane, ordered and state-run system of justice (Rancourt and Fourier 1999). While this is a contested story (Boulding 2000; Ehrenreich 1997; Foucalt 1977), we can see that even under the 'more humane' justice of the state, justice still is equated to, or pursued by means of, pain and punishment. The current 'tough on crime' policies of many Western states represent another influence on Western justice. This is not a move toward a more humane justice, but towards a more punitive kind of justice (longer sentences, less judicial discretion, less early parole, more incarceration and fewer alternative measures). Garland (2001) argues that such a trend is characteristic of late modern societies where criminal justice becomes politicized (led by politicians trying to get votes) but where nearly all political parties advocate the same 'tough on crime' policies despite all of the historical, empirical and anecdotal evidence that such approaches cannot work.

The basic assumption running through all these influences within Western justice (the popular understanding of the history of punishment, the tools of proportionality, parsimony and impartiality to temper punishment and the current return to 'tough on crime' policies) is that justice requires pain and punishment. The essence of justice is the infliction of pain.

These case studies, however, call into question this basic assumption so broadly shared. In fact the cases demonstrate a justice based in healing, not punishment, or pain, or some lesser evil. They demonstrate a justice that is more about learning who you are than about impartiality, more about touching the abundance within Earth than about imposing proportional pain, more about cultivating the conditions that lead to joy, than about limiting the 'excess' of punishment. I have articulated these as a means–ends consistency. Western justice systems assume the need to suspend normal ethical behaviours (treating people with respect, compassion, non-violence) and to engage in behaviour (justice as pain and punishment) which if it happened in some other sphere of society might be considered criminal. Healing justice does not make this same move. It assumes that those who behave as if they have no family do not need to be locked up with other criminals but actually need their family to come and surround them and help them find a way forward (Yazzie and Zion 1996).

Challenging the notions of Western societies over reliance on punishment is not new. Paul Redekop, a restorative justice scholar, recently wrote a book on changing paradigms from punishment to restorative discipline (2008). He sees no room for punishment in our society. Scholars in Aboriginal justice have for a long time been challenging the notion that justice must include pain and punishment (McCaslin 2005c). The penal abolition movement is founded on the premise that our societies have the ability and need to do away with prisons as our response to crime (Morris 1995). This study adds to those arguments, not purely from the standpoint of theory, but also from the standpoint of practises, of living communities who are already living different ways.

On the role of violence within healing justice

It is important to understand the ways this research challenges this notion of justice as pain or punishment. Healing justice is not the practise of a vision of justice purified of all violence. It is practised and sustained by the ongoing work of inner healing. It comes from those who recognize that they have been and in some ways still are complicit in violence. For these communities violence is not depicted as some foreign external evil with which we must do battle, as is presented to us in the so-called 'war on crime'. We only need to look at ourselves to see and touch violence. Seeing violence as existing in each person is different from condoning it as a means of justice. These case studies have demonstrated three communities with notions of justice in which justice co-exists with healing. These communities demonstrated that harms of all sorts could be responded to without punishment as a necessary ingredient. In fact, it could be argued that their kinds of healing justice did more to further the taking of responsibility and the creating of community safety because they did not orient themselves towards punishment.

Punishment was not completely absent from these case studies. Hollow Water's partnership with the criminal justice system still held the threat of jail for those who failed to work with the community to complete a healing contract. The Iona Community partnered with the penal system itself in developing relationships with young people who had been incarcerated. However, those who use the presence of such punishment and violence to whitewash the dominant orientation of justice as punishment have not understood the practises and visions of these communities.

Although someone may argue that penal justice is preferable to healing justice, this research demonstrates that at least there is a choice to be made. Penal justice is not the only way. Violent justice is not the only way. These communities demonstrate that justice need not reflect the characteristics of injustice. Whether people and communities find the ways of healing justice compelling or not is separate from the point I am making. Although many forces have colluded and agreed that justice is about pain and punishment, the communities in this research present us with choices and options. They do not offer a path that is free of violence, but they do offer options in which justice is more about the support to heal than the demand for punishment, more about seeking an abundance of joy than balancing the scales of pain.

Clearly healing justice presents some major challenges to those within mainline Western imaginations of justice. The basic features of healing justice challenge and perhaps offend some of the basic values of Western life. However, healing justice is a justice that is found within the modern world. While the history of Western punishment sees itself as moving towards more humane ways of justice, healing justice takes a few giant leaps in such a direction. Therefore it is challenging to mainline notions of Western justice, but it also builds on areas of common concern, and it does so in ways that some advocates of restorative kinds of justice may find compelling.

How target audiences might take healing justice seriously

Taking the fundamental assumptions of healing justice seriously has been the focus of this whole chapter. A first step to taking healing justice seriously is correctly locating the geography of healing justice in relation to the geography of crime and the geography of restorative justice. I have offered some ways of locating this by pointing to areas of overlapping interests, areas of expanding horizons and areas which directly challenge these other geographies. The remainder of this chapter highlights the kinds of questions this research raises for three audiences: communities with a practise of healing justice, advocates of restorative justice and those involved in Western governance. My hope at the outset of this research was that its findings might help us to ask more interesting, helpful questions. These questions arise, not from within the normal discourse on justice and law, but from the assumptions of communities which have some kind of active practise of healing justice and which come from diverse places around the world. By asking questions, I wish to point towards the kinds of research and soul searching left to do. But I am also asking questions to create the room for a multiplicity of answers arising from different groups in different places. Since healing justice was practised in different forms in different places, any attempt at applying healing justice must leave room for similar diversity.

Research implications for communities which practise healing justice

The three case studies where we found healing justice all came from faith or spiritual communities. We saw that their sacred traditions functioned as a source, a practise and a sustaining dynamic of healing justice. However, as we are most painfully aware, the presence of sacred teachings does not necessarily mean the presence of healing justice. In fact it is often spiritual communities that have been leading advocates for more violent forms of justice, both domestically and internationally. This research raises the question as to why these communities sometimes turn towards violent justice and at other times towards a kind of healing justice. What makes Hollow Water different from some of the pre-colonial violent Aboriginal groups (Keeley 1995)? What makes the Iona Community different from the Christian colonial empires of the last 600 years? What makes Plum Village different from the long heritage of violent Buddhist communities in parts of Japan, Thailand, Tibet or Sri Lanka (Florida 2004)?

Advocates of healing justice based in sacred traditions must wrestle with the ways their traditions have too often provided the justifications of more violent forms of crime control by supporting the dominant political power interests (Bianchi 1994; Gorringe 1996; Hadley 2005).

Christianity, my own tradition, provides an number of troubling examples. Since the 1400s there have been 14 major empires (Austro-Hungarian, Belgian, British, Danish, French, German, Italian, Japanese, Ottoman, Portuguese, Russian, Spanish, Swedish and United States), all based in violent ways. Twelve of these have self-identified as Christian. Over hundreds of years Christianity has both influenced, and been influenced by, various violent partnerships with various states. The partnerships led to the establishment of penal justice systems but more broadly included the goals to civilize, colonialize and Christianize the world. I have previously highlighted six features of Christianization which led to this kind of violence:

➤ equating a good Christian with a good citizen

➤ offering an authoritarian and hierarchical understanding of Christianity and of the individual's relationship to the universe

➤ developing a theology to justify violence

➤ believing that the truth can be owned by one group

➤ separating of spiritual and physical

➤ building missionary zeal to make the world Christian (Sawatsky and Sawatsky, forthcoming).

These points are, of course, open to debate and need more elaboration than there is space for here. My point is that by the way healing justice draws on sacred traditions it critiques and transforms features of these traditions which have been dominant for hundreds and, perhaps, thousands of years.

This research suggests that there are offsetting features of spiritual traditions which lead to healing justice. On the basis of the shared characteristics of healing justice, these might include:

➤ *recognizing you are the land* – Rather than building allegiances to the state, healing justice practitioners seem to find their home within a common connection with land. Such an approach moves beyond humanizing and anthropomorphic senses of justice. Having a compassionate relationship with land is part of healing justice.

➤ *seeing through the lens of interconnection* – While authoritarian and hierarchal understanding of religion seem to be part of a feature of violent expressions of faith, seeing through the lens of interconnection offers a different orientation to power, the nature of change and even the object of change.

➤ *educating and discipling in healing justice and compassion, rather than in violence as a basis of security* – Healing justice does not try to find ways of justifying violence to achieve justice, nor does it find roots in the shame-and-blame paradigm. Healing justice is about an orientation towards learning to assist everyone in the process of finding his or her true identity, which is tasting compassion.

➤ *treating enemies as brothers and sisters and recognizing the innate goodness of others* – Healing justice is not something that can be owned or used to lord it over others. It comes as gift. It comes from the insight that in some way we are all related. Deeper paths of transforming open up by treating others as family rather than by treating them as less than human.

➤ *seeing through the lens of wholeness* – Rather than separating the spiritual and physical realms, healing justice is cultivated by seeing and practising wholeness.

➤ *creating space for people and communities to learn their true identity* – Rather than trying to impose one way of being (for instance, 'making the world Christian') this kind of healing justice works to put responsibility back into the hands of local communities.

By contrasting features of Christianization with features of healing justice, I am trying to demonstrate some of the range and depth of the potential application of these findings. I am also trying to demonstrate a limitation in application, namely, that one can not simply advocate for a return to sacred teachings without doing that in ways which also reflect the vision and practises of healing justice. Healing justice can be used to examine and transform sacred traditions themselves, which for hundreds and even thousands of years have sometimes expressed themselves in violent and oppressive ways. Each of the communities in this study is engaged in such activity. Hollow Water is engaged in (re)discovering the resources of pre-colonial times. The Iona Community is finding its theology and place, in part, by a careful return to some of the Celtic understanding of the sixth century. Plum Village, too, is engaged in reinterpreting Vietnamese Buddhism, finding resources through the centuries, even drawing on and updating some of the original writings of the Buddha going back 2500 years. Healing justice communities are sustained by sacred teaching, but they find renewal by engaging and transforming the dominant features of those traditions which have so often lead to violence and oppression.

More research and reflection is needed by communities that practises healing justice to understand both the tendencies to violence and the tendencies to healing justice within their traditions. Some of this is already under way (Alfred 1999; Loy 2003; Snyder 2001) but much more is needed. It may be that the common characteristics of healing justice, highlighted in the previous chapter, could provide a starting point for investigation. We need not look for similar forms of healing justice (although some may be present). Instead, good research must look to see if there are elements within particular traditions which function in the same way as the common characteristics of healing justice.

More research is also needed into communities which practise healing justice. Would a similar study with three different communities reveal similar patterns or would different patterns or common characteristics emerge? Ideally research would bring these communities together to speak to each other about healing justice. What would those conversations reveal?

Applications of healing justice to Western systems of governance

The question is not how we institutionalize processes of healing justice into the state system, as some in restorative justice have asked. *Institutionalizing Restorative Justice* (Aertsen *et al.* 2006) offers a collection of essays mostly in that vein. We saw in our study of the common characteristics of healing justice that both institutionalization and the desire for permanence so common within institutions served as barriers to healing justice. If modern states want to take the implications of healing justice seriously they should start by cultivating the kinds of relationships which sustain more healing ways and avoiding the kinds of relationships which act as barriers to it. States could ask themselves how they could support a set of social relationships which lead to more healing ways. Here I return to the major features of healing justice outlined in the previous chapter. I use them to point towards the kinds of questions this research raises for Western systems of governance.

1. Transform the ways we relate to the Earth

When we are connected to the environment in the wrong way we become more violent. When we are connected in good ways we nurture the capacity for healing justice. The research strongly suggests this conclusion. What is different about this research is that it argues that the ways we relate to the Earth influences not just matters of environmental sustainability, but also matters of justice sustainability, harm prevention and the ability to live the good life. These case studies argue that humans have a need to connect and listen to the Earth. When this need is blocked anti-social and cruel action follows. The implications of this insight are tremendous. How could prisons be redesigned to assist all of the people in them to reconnect with the healing and beauty of the Earth? How can cities be designed to create space for people to touch the Earth, to grow or raise their own food and to see both their impact of the environment and the impact of the environment on them? How could global economic relationships be structured to encourage and support sustainable local relationships with the Earth? Taking healing justice seriously includes restructuring our relationship with the land. This has implications in every sphere.

2. Draw on the sacred as a source of healing justice

Each of the communities in this study saw the sacred or spiritual as a key source of its notions of healing justice. Most Western states tend to see things spiritual as irrelevant to notions of justice. On the other end of the continuum, some Western states see themselves as states of a particular religion. The communities in this study argue for neither the irrelevance nor the institutionalization of spirituality. They do argue that spirituality is a core source of healing justice. The Hollow Water case, which works in partnership with the government, demonstrates one model where the government is freed from both the need to argue for the irrelevance of spirituality or for the need for the government to proclaim a state religion. Nevertheless the government finds a way to support a local community engaged in working at Creator's Law. More research and more experimentation are needed in how states can encourage a justice rooted in spiritual sources.

3. Transform the justice system

I have argued that many of the developments in Western criminal justice have been based on models of justice as punishment. Can the system be reworked from another perspective? The New Zealand 1989 Young Persons and their Families Act is an interesting example of law which is based on promoting positive principles rather than providing the preset mechanisms and processes for compliance. This law consists of eight principles which must be respected at every stage of the legal proceedings. These principles have to do with strengthening families, meetings the victims' needs, and avoiding the criminal system.

Perhaps this example opens up the possibility of lawmakers cultivating a more positive view of justice. Perhaps governments could work with local groups to develop principles of healing justice which could then be enacted into law as a guide for every step of responding to harms. This research suggests some key principles for consideration:

> ➤ The justice system should comprise structures to support the healing of offenders, victims and communities at every step. From the making of laws to the enforcing of laws, from determining what happened to determining what should be done one of the primary principles must be supporting the healing of offenders, victims and communities.

➤ Measures dealing with offending should aim first to understand why harms take place — roots, patterns, intentions, unmet needs. Such measures should then institute both personal and structural changes required to avoid environments which lead to harm and to cultivate environments which lead to responsibility and joy.

➤ The healing of victims should be a key goal of justice. Justice measures should aim to meet their needs which include the needs for loving communities and space to (re)discover their true identity.

➤ Where sentencing is needed, offenders should be sentenced to loving communities who will assist them in (re)discovering their true identity.

➤ Justice measures which feed the seeds of violence and shame within victims, offenders or communities should be replaced by measures which aim to water the seed of compassion within each.

➤ Funding should be diverted from the costly court and incarceration systems and should be reallocated in ways that strengthen local communities. Can we create a restorative economic strategy where incidents of harm (e.g. rape) flag the need and economic resources to work at healing both the needs of those involved in the incident and the needs of the community or village? Can we create restorative economic strategies so that we can direct funds to strengthen community, such that we stop raising sea pirates capable of rape? Government funding strategies should not create the conditions which breed violence but rather create the conditions for people to develop strong, compassionate identities.

These seem to be some of the implications of this research for the justice system. I say 'seem to be' because from a healing justice perspective the communities themselves will need to work out the implications of their approach.

4. Support the growth of small communities
Are cities so large that it is not possible to be caring? Do city planning and urban migration patterns contribute to a spirit of punishment and

penal justice by breaking down the kinds of social relationships which cultivate more healing approaches to justice? The communities in these case studies recognized that healing justice requires an examination of basic social structures. Healing justice requires particular kinds of social spaces or environments which are conducive to healing ways of being in the world. In Hollow Water the hope of some was that the clan system and the traditional ceremonies would help to create such a social structure. Zen Buddhism includes the practise of arranging homes and communities within the natural environment in ways that are conducive to healing and peace. One member of the Iona Community has written a book which reflects theologically on 'built environments' (Gorringe 2002). Each of the communities had some sense that what they believed about healing justice affected the kinds of social arrangements they encouraged. Governments could take responsibility in town-planning and zoning requirements to encourage elements which seem to be connected to more healing ways of being, elements such as close connection to land, small communities, and use of local sustainable building materials which reflect a care of, and a listening to, the Earth.

Research implications for restorative justice

The case studies in healing justice are valuable to restorative justice (and to state justice) because they are an alternative paradigm, not defined by the imagination of the state. These cases can help to deepen and broaden the scope of restorative justice. For example, restorative justice has challenged the state's focus on crime as the breaking of rules. In its place, restorative justice proposes a focus on 'repairing harm'. Ruth Morris and the transformative justice movement have in turn challenged restorative justice for being too incident-focused, waiting for harm to be done and then focusing on harm. She says that rather than starting by focusing on the incident of crime or harm, transformative justice focuses on the causes of crime (Morris 2000). The cases of healing justice we have studied have similarities with this orientation. However, their beginning point has more to do with causes of joy than the causes of crime.

This widening and deepening of the horizon of justice brings different challenges and participants to the circle. Although restorative justice has struggled to move beyond a case-incident orientation (what I have called a tertiary care orientation), the communities which practise healing justice seem to move easily between the needs of persons, the transformation of socio-economic systems and the place of land in justice. Healing justice challenges restorative justice to move beyond repairing harm. These communities reveal that justice is about understanding the root causes of suffering and joy. It is about cultivating the environments and conditions which lead to joy and compassion. It is about acknowledging gift, not simply trying to control or bring order.

I believe the shared characteristics offer very clear and practical challenges to the restorative justice movement. I have recast them as key questions which could be a guide for theoretical and practical development. They would be good starting points for further research. By focusing on the shared characteristics of responding to harms, I do not wish to contribute to the confusion so strongly ingrained in Western cultures that justice is mostly about responding to harms. Part of the challenge of the shared characteristics of healing justice is that such a justice has very positive aspects which can be worked out in the context of everyday life, not just as we respond to harms. I focus here on harms, because this is a starting point of restorative justice and a way to illustrate the kinds of applications which could happen within restorative justice as the rest of the shared characteristics are also explored for their meaning.

> *Healing justice communities nurture local facilitators.* As restorative justice moves more and more towards trained and certified facilitators of encounters, are local community facilitators again being sidelined by a new breed of conflict specialists?

> *Healing justice communities listen to the voices of brokenness.* How can restorative justice proactively create mechanisms to surface stories of harm and victimization? Restorative justice has largely waited for harms to surface through state mechanisms and case referrals and then has tried to deal with victims and offenders in restorative ways. How can restorative justice move in advance of the state system, surfacing harms, perhaps even harms not defined as crimes?

> *Healing justice communities recognize the enemy as a brother or sister.* As professionalism creeps into restorative justice there is a temptation to treat the people who are involved in harms as 'clients', 'participants' or 'stakeholders'. How could restorative justice practitioners encourage the practise of seeing and perhaps even educating those whom they work with that they are brothers and sisters already? As states move more and more to policies of

public humiliation of ex-offenders by systems like public notifi-
cations, could restorative justice offer some form of alternative
based on recognizing the enemy as a brother or sister?

➤ *Healing justice communities create space for those involved in a harm to
meet in a circle.* This is an area of focus and strength of restorative
justice. However, could restorative justice move further upstream
and hold 'pre-emptive peacebuilding circles'? These communities
hold circles before major harms take place as a means to surface
smaller harms, to build trust and to work at long-term aspects
of healing justice rather than being caught in a short-term crisis
mode. How could restorative justice facilitators use their strength
and experience in creating space for people to meet in a circle to
move upstream and work at the long-term aspects of building
restorative justice in communities?

➤ *Healing justice communities expand the circle.* Some practises of restorative justice always include steps to expand the circle while
others almost never expand the circle. How could the restorative
justice movement develop the capacity to know when and how to
widen the circle of participants? Furthermore, restorative justice
has sometimes allowed the community a very limited role in supporting the victim and the offender. These communities expand
the circle, not only to draw on further supportive resources, but
also to encourage historical–structural analysis (looking at patterns) and to examine if there are ways in which the community
needs to take responsibility and change. How could restorative
justice see itself as a vehicle for transforming communities and
structures?

➤ *Healing justice communities shift focus from symptoms to root causes.*
Much restorative justice practise focuses mainly on the harm and
its impact on the victim. Perhaps in trying to be victim-centred,
restorative justice has also become symptom-centred. Indeed victims must have an important role in restorative justice. Listening
to their stories and meeting their needs is an important part of
both restorative and healing justice. But it is not the whole story.
Harming behaviour comes out of somewhere. It usually has multiple causes. How could restorative justice work to transform the
causes and conditions which lead to a particular harm?

➤ *Healing justice communities broaden the horizon of time to be considered for harms.*How could restorative justice move beyond the logic of incidents and open up the horizon of time so as to more fully understand and transform the patterns, structures and relationships which led to any particular harm? When stories are shared in restorative justice encounters they tend to focus on the harm and its impact. Is there also a way of creating opportunity to look through the generations to see if a particular harm is part of a larger pattern for which transformation is also needed? What if every restorative justice encounter had to follow the Hollow Water practise of considering seven generations into the past for causes and seven generations into the future for wise impacts of current decisions?

➤ *Healing justice communities create conditions to break the patterns of unhealthy relationships by creating conditions for healthy relationships.* What are the politics of restorative justice? What are the creative ways of arranging society so that it is restorative, healthy and just? What are the positive conditions and causes that bring about restorative justice?

➤ *Healing justice communities conduct ceremonies and feasts.* What would restorative justice look like if it was open to the possibility that the Spirit was the source of healing? I don't mean bracketing the current processes with prayer at the beginning and ending of a session. Rather, how can restorative justice participants touch what some say is the very source of healing and allow their imaginations and their every step be transformed by such an encounter? This is the function of ceremonies in the communities which practise healing justice. For instance, since feasting is a key part of this activity, what would happen if restorative justice saw feasting together as potentially part of a restorative encounter?

➤ *Healing justice communities work even when people are denying responsibility.* Restorative justice has been very strongly formed by the notion that restorative measures need voluntary participation. This notion leaves a vacuum when victims or victimizers do not voluntarily participate. By default, the state deals with the vacuum and takes cases if people are denying responsibility. Each of the communities which practise healing justice finds ways of working even if people are denying responsibility. How can restorative justice work when people are denying responsibility? How can restorative justice confront denial by changing the conditions which surround victimizers in denial? How can restorative justice encourage a community to take responsibility even when one member of the community is denying personal responsibility?

➤ *Healing justice communities 'sentence' people to a loving community where they can heal.* How can restorative justice develop increased capacity to surround the harmed and the offender in loving communities where they can heal? How can restorative justice help shift the huge financial resources available for incarceration to resources for helping to support loving communities? How can restorative justice direct such resources to the transformation of broken harming communities into more loving ones?

These are the kinds of questions this research raises. Such questions are not entirely new to restorative justice. Theoreticians have touched on the edges of many of them. However, these challenges come not from scholars and theoreticians. They come from the lives of three very different communities which are already engaged in healing justice and already have responses to these questions. They can not be discarded as rhetorical or idealistic. If the restorative justice movement were to take these questions seriously, we would see many divergent forms of justice emerge, united by a restorative or healing imagination.

Final words

This research has been an exploration of the nature of healing justice. I found examples of healing justice practised in diverse communities around the world and selected three of them. In comparing these cases I discovered that there was a broad basis of similarity between them. Healing justice, at least as found in these three communities, has commonalities in vision, is practised through strategies which have similarities and is critically dependent on certain kinds of relationships and structures. We can say with confidence that healing justice exists even in the modern world. The implications of this healing kind of a justice are far-reaching and cross-disciplinary. For those who wish restorative justice to be a meaningful alternative and for those who believe current criminal justice approaches are not good enough, this research provides a glimmer of hope. The hope is not so much the hope of finding a satisfying alternative theory of justice, but the hope of knowing that healing justice is already being practised around the world.

The communities in this study have been my teachers helping me to see a horizon of justice which beautifully confounds some of the basic premises of what I had been taught in my study of criminal, restorative and social justice. I thank them for opening up different ways of seeing and being and I acknowledge that I am yet a toddler, barely learning to walk in the ways of healing justice.

The reader should not be misled. Healing justice comes from senses of beauty, compassion and deep peace and embodies them. Some might find this appealing. However, healing justice gains its power by entering into the painful sufferings of the world. It is not an easy path. It does not come simply. The communities and people I met were not perfect. They struggled as the way forward that had seemed so promising became obscured. They were also joyful, but their joy did not come from trying to escape suffering. Their joy came from knowing that they could stand in the midst of suffering and not be ashamed, fearful or vengeful. The more they learned to see with the eyes of compassion, the more they understood of the depths of suffering. Healing justice leads to joy in the midst of suffering.

Those who expect justice to control suffering and to deal with suffering so that they do not have to would do well to stay far away from healing justice. It will surely disappoint.

Those who wish to pursue healing justice are invited to do so in ways that embody healing justice. There is more that we do not understand about healing justice than what we do understand. More research is needed but, even more important than research, more demonstration plots of healing justice are needed for us to understand it better.

This study demonstrates that healing justice exists. It offers an outline of its common features, as I understand them through three case studies. However, change is in the nature of healing justice and of these communities. Healing justice is not something fixed that we can hold on to and control. It is more of a wise imagination for how to live in the world. Healing justice comes as a gift. It disappears or recedes when not treated as such. It is my hope that this study has contributed to healing justice in ways which respect healing justice. I believe that these case studies have great implication for those with the capacity to listen.

References

Aboriginal Corrections Policy Unit (1997) *The Four Circles Of Hollow Water: Ojibwa Circle, Offender Circle, Victim Circle, Hollow Water Circle.* Ottawa: Solicitor General Canada Aboriginal Corrections Policy Unit.

Adams, J. and Brownsword, R. (2007) *Understanding Contract Law.* London: Sweet & Maxwell.

Aertsen, I., Daems, T. and Robert, L. (eds) (2006) *Institutionalizing Restorative Justice.* Cullompton: Willan.

Alfred, G. R. (1999) *Peace, Power, Righteousness: An Indigenous Manifesto.* Don Mills, Ontario: Oxford University Press.

Alper, B. S. and Nichols, L. T. (1981) *Beyond the Courtroom: Programs in Community Justice and Conflict Resolution.* Lexington, MA: Lexington Books.

American Friends Service Committee (1971) *Struggle for Justice. A Report on Crime and Punishment in America, Prepared for the American Friends Service Committee.* New York: Hill & Wang.

Amstutz, L. S. and Mullet, J. H. (2005) *The Little Book of Restorative Discipline for Schools: Teaching Responsibility, Creating Caring Climates.* Intercourse, PA: Good Books.

Ashworth, A. (1998) 'Deterrence.' In A. Hirsch and A. Ashworth (eds) *Principled Sentencing: Readings on Theory and Policy.* Oxford: Hart Publishing.

Ashworth, A. (2006) *Principles of Criminal Law.* Oxford: Oxford University Press.

Austin, R. (1993) 'Freedom, responsibility, and duty: ADR and the Navajo Peacemaking Court.' *Judges' Journal 8,* 11.

Badali, J. (1999). 'Healing, restorative justice ultimately builds a safer society. *Anglican Journal.* Accessed at http://www.anglicanjournal.com/125/09/oped01.html, 22 July 2008.

Barnett, R. (1977) 'Restitution: a new paradigm of criminal justice.' *Ethics 87,* 4, 279-301.

Battiste, M. A. and Henderson, J. Y. (2000). *Protecting Indigenous Knowledge and Heritage: A Global Challenge.* Saskatoon: Purich Publishers.

Bazemore, G. and Schiff, M. (2004) 'Paradigm muddle or paradigm paralysis? the wide and narrow roads to restorative justice reform (or, a little confusion may be a good thing).' *Contemporary Justice Review 7,* 1, 37–57.

Bazemore, S. G. and Umbreit, M. S. (2001) *A Comparison of Four Restorative Conferencing Models.* Washington, DC: US Dept. of Justice, Office of Justice Programs, Office of Juvenile Justice and Delinquency Prevention.

Beccaria, C. (1963) *On Crimes and Punishments.* Indianapolis, IN: Bobbs-Merrill.

Bell, J. L. and Maule, G. (1986) *A Touching Place: Songs for Worship from the Iona Community.* Glasgow: Wild Goose Publications.

Bentham, J. (1830) *The Rationale of Punishment.* London: Robert Heward.

Berman, H. J. (1983) *Law and Revolution: The Formation of the Western Legal Tradition.* Cambridge: Harvard University Press.

Berman, H. J. (2003) *Law and Revolution II: The Impact of the Protestant Reformations on the Western Legal Tradition.* Cambridge: Harvard University Press.

Bianchi, H. (1994) *Justice as Sanctuary: Toward a New System of Crime Control.* Bloomington, IN: Indiana University Press.

Boers, A. P. (1992) *Justice that Heals: A Biblical Vision for Victims and Offenders.* Newton, KA.: Faith and Life Press.

Bohannan, P. (1957) *Justice and Judgment among the Tiv.* London: Oxford University Press.

Borofsky, R. and Albert, B. (2005) *Yanomami: The Fierce Controversy and What We Can Learn from It.* Berkeley, CA: University of California Press.

Boulding, E. (2000) *Cultures of Peace: The Hidden Side of History.* Syracuse, NY: Syracuse University Press.

Bradney, A. and Cownie, F. (2000) *Living without Law: An Ethnography of Quaker Decision-making, Dispute Avoidance and Dispute Resolution.* Aldershot: Dartmouth.

Braithwaite, J. (1989) *Crime, Shame, and Reintegration.* Cambridge: Cambridge University Press.

Braithwaite, J. (1997) 'Assessing an Immodest Theory and a Pessimistic Theory.' In M. Tonry (ed.) *Crime and Justice, Vol. 25: An Annual Review of Research.* Chicago: University of Chicago Press.

Braithwaite, J., Dolinko, D. and Tonry, M. (1999) 'The future of punishment.' *UCLA Law Review 46,* 6, 1719–1940.

Braithwaite, J. (2001) 'Restorative justice and a new criminal law of substance abuse.' *Youth & Society 33,* 2, 227–248.

Braithwaite, J. (2002) *Restorative Justice and Responsive Regulation.* New York: Oxford University Press.

Braithwaite, J. (2003a) 'Restorative Justice and a Better Future.' In E. McLaughlin, R. Fergusson, G. Hughes and L. Westmarland (eds) *Restorative Justice: Critical Issues.* London: Sage Publications.

Braithwaite, J. (2003b) 'Restorative Justice and Social Justice.' In E. McLaughlin, R. Fergusson, G. Hughes and L. Westmarland (eds) *Restorative Justice: Critical Issues.* London: Sage Publications.

Braithwaite, J. and Pettit, P. (2000) 'Republicanism and Restorative Justice: An Explanatory and Normative Connection.' In J. Braithwaite and H. Strang (eds) *Restorative Justice: Philosophy to Practise.* Burlington: Ashgate Publishing.

Braithwaite, J. and Strang, H. (2000) *Restorative Justice: Philosophy to Practise.* Aldershot: Ashgate.

Braithwaite, J. and Strang , H.(2001) *Restorative Justice and Civil Society.* Cambridge and Melbourne: Cambridge University Press.

Breton, D. and Lehman, S. (2001) *The Mystic Heart of Justice: Restoring Wholeness in a Broken World.* West Chester, PA: Chrysalis Books.

Buckman, R. and Sabbagh, K. (1993) *Magic or Medicine?: An Investigation of Healing and Healers.* London: Macmillan.

Burgess, R. (2000a) 'The Ministry of Healing in the Life and Worship of the Church.' In R. Burgess and K. Galloway (eds) *Praying for the Dawn.* Glasgow: Wild Goose Publications.

Burgess, R. (2000b) 'Weeping for Cities and Working for Justice.' In R. Burgess and K. Galloway (eds) *Praying for the Dawn.* Glasgow: Wild Goose Publication.

Burgess, R. and K. Galloway (2000) *Praying for the Dawn: A Resource Book for the Ministry of Healing.* Glasgow: Wild Goose Publications.

Bushie, B. (1997a) 'CHCH reflections: Burma.' Aboriginal Corrections Policy Unit (eds) *Four Circles of Hollow Water.* Ottawa: Solicitor General Canada Aboriginal Corrections Policy Unit.

Bushie, B. (1997b) 'Hollow Water circle: a personal reflection.' Aboriginal Corrections Policy Unit (eds) *Four circles of Hollow Water.* Ottawa: Solicitor General Canada Aboriginal Corrections Policy Unit.

Bushie, B. (1997c) 'W'daeb-awae': the truth as we know it.' Aboriginal Corrections Policy Unit (eds) *Four Circles of Hollow Water.* Ottawa: Solicitor General Canada Aboriginal Corrections Policy Unit.

Bushie, B. (1999) 'Community holistic circle healing: a community approach.' *Building Strong Partnerships for Restorative Practises Conference,* Burlington, Vermont.

Bushie, J. (1997) 'CHCH reflections: Joyce.' Aboriginal Corrections Policy Unit (eds) *Four Circles of Hollow Water* Ottawa: Solicitor General Canada Aboriginal Corrections Policy Unit.

Cao, N. P. (1993) *Learning True Love: How I Learned and Practised Social Change in Vietnam.* Berkeley, CA: Parallax Press.

Carrabine, E. (2004) *Criminology: A Sociological Introduction.* London and New York: Routledge.

Cayley, D. (1998) *The Expanding Prison: The Crisis in Crime and Punishment and the Search for Alternatives.* Toronto: House of Anansi Press.

Chappell, D. W. (1999) *Buddhist Peacework: Creating Cultures of Peace.* Somerville, MA: Wisdom Publications in association with Boston Research Center for the 21st Century.

Christie, N. (1977) 'Conflict as property.' *British Journal of Criminology 17,* 1, 1–5.

Christie, N. (1981) *Limits to Pain.* Oslo: Universitetsforlaget.

Church Council on Justice and Corrections of Canada (2001) 'Connecting the dots: final report on healing justice education forms.' Church Council News.

Churchill, C. (1933) *GOTHAM. Poems (1933).* London: The King's Printers.

Clayton, M. and Williams, A. (2004) *Social Justice.* MA, Mass.: Blackwell Publishing.

Comaroff, J. L. and Roberts, S. (1981) *Rules and Processes: The Cultural Logic of Dispute in an African Context.* Chicago: University of Chicago Press.

Community Holistic Circle Healing Hollow Water (1996). 'Hollow Water First Nation position on incarceration.' In Church Council on Justice and Corrections (Canada) (eds) *Satisfying Justice: Safe Community Options that Attempt to Repair Harm from Crime and Reduce the Use or Length of Imprisonment.* Ottawa: Church Council on Justice and Corrections (Canada).

Compton, R. and Jones, T. S. (2003) *Kids Working It Out: Strategies and Stories for Making Peace in Our Schools.* San Francisco: Jossey-Bass.

Conley, J. M. and O'Barr, W. M. (1993) 'Legal anthropology comes home: A brief history of the ethnographic study of law.' *Loyola of Los Angeles Law Review 27,* 41–49.

Consedine, J. and Bowen, H. (1999) *Restorative Justice: Contemporary Themes and Practise.* Lyttelton, NZ: Ploughshares Publications.

Cooley, D. (1999) *From Restorative Justice to Transformative Justice: A Discussion Paper*. Ottawa: Law Commission of Canada.

Cormier, R. B. (2002) *Restorative Justice: Directions and Principles: Developments in Canada*. Ottawa: Solicitor General Canada.

Cousins, M. (2004) 'A Haudensoaunee approach to justice.' *Justice as healing 9*, 1.

Couture, J. (2001a) 'Comments on Hollow Water community healing.' In *Mental Health of Indigenous Peoples*. Montreal: McGill University.

Couture, J. (2001b) *A Cost-Benefit Analysis of Hollow Water's Community Holistic Circle Healing Process*. Ottawa: Solicitor General Canada.

Couture, J. E. and Couture, R. (2003) *Biidaaban: The Mnjikaning Community Healing Model*. Ottawa: Public Safety and Emergency Preparedness Canada.

Coward, S. (2000) *Restorative Justice in Cases of Domestic and Sexual Violence: Healing Justice? Directed Interdisciplinary Studies*. Ottawa, Carlton University.

Crawford, A. (2002) 'The State, Community and Restorative Justice: Heresy, Nostalgia and Butterfly Collecting.' In L. Walgrave (eds.) *Restorative Justice and the Law*. Cullompton: Willan Publishing.

Crawford, A. and Clear, A. (2003) 'Community Justice: Transforming Communities through Restorative Justice.' In E. McLaughlin, R. Fergusson, G. Hughes and L. Westmarland (eds) *Restorative Justice: Critical Issues*. London: Sage Publications.

Creswell, J. W. (1998) *Qualitative Inquiry and Research Design: Choosing among Five Traditions*. Thousand Oaks, CA: Sage Publications.

Creswell, J. W. (2003) *Research Design: Qualitative, Quantitative, and Mixed Methods Approaches*. Thousand Oaks, CA: Sage.

Crocker, D. A. (2001) 'Can there be healing through justice?' *Responsive Community 11*, 2, 32–42.

Daly, K. (2003) 'Mind the Gap: Restorative Justice in Theory and Practise.' In A. Hirsch, J. Roberts, A. Bottoms, K. Roach and M. Schiff (eds) *Restorative Justice and Criminal Justice*. Oxford: Hart Publishing.

De Vaus, D. A. (2001) *Research Design in Social Research*. London: Sage Publications.

Denzin, N. K. (1978) *The Research Act: A Theoretical Introduction to Sociological Methods*. New York: McGraw-Hill.

Dickie, B. and MacDonald, J. (2000) *Hollow Water*. Montreal: National Film Board of Canada.

Dickson-Gilmore, E. J. and La Prairie, C. (2005) *Will the Circle be Unbroken?: Aboriginal Communities, Restorative Justice, and the Challenges of Conflict and Change*. Toronto: University of Toronto Press.

Dignam, J. (2003) 'Towards a Systemic Model of Restorative Justice: Reflections on the Concept, its Context and the Need for Clear Constraints.' In A. Hirsch, J. Roberts, A. Bottoms, K. Roach and M. Schiff (eds) *Restorative Justice and Criminal Justice: Competing or Reconcilable Paradigms?* Oxford: Hart Publishing.

Dirks, N. B. (1992) *Colonialism and Culture*. Ann Arbor, MI: University of Michigan Press.

Drewery, W. (2004) 'Conferencing in schools: punishment, restorative justice, and the productive importance of the process of conversation.' *Journal of Community & Applied Social Psychology 14*, 5, 332–344.

Duff, A. (2001) *Punishment, Communication, and Community*. Oxford: Oxford University Press.

Duff, A. (2003) 'Probations, punishment and restorative justice.' *Harvard Journal 42*, 2, 181–197.

Durkheim, É. (1982) *The Rules of Sociological Method*. New York: Free Press.

Durocher, R. (2002) 'Offenders and Restorative Justice' (lecture), University of Winnipeg & Menno Simons College.

Dyck, D. (2000) 'Reaching toward a structurally responsive training and practise of restorative justice.' *Contemporary Justice Review 3*, 3, 239–265.

Edelstein, L. (1943) *The Hippocratic Oath, Text, Translation and Interpretation*. Baltimore, MD: Johns Hopkins Press.

Ehrenreich, B. (1997) *Blood Rites: Origins and History of the Passions of War*. New York: Metropolitan Books.

Elder Hanlon, T. (1999) 'Circle justice: An ethnographic study.' MA thesis, Department of Sociology, University of Lethbridge AB, Canada.

Fattah, E. A. (2002) 'From Philosophical Abstraction to Restorative Action, from Senseless Retribution to Meaningful Restitution: Just Deserts and Restorative Justice Revisited.' In E. Weitekamp and H.-J. Kerner (eds) *Restorative Justice: Theoretical Foundations*. Cullompton: Willan Publishing.

Ferguson, R. (1998) *Chasing the Wild Goose: The Story of the Iona Community*. Glasgow: Wild Goose Publications.

Florida, R. (2004) 'Buddhism and violence in modernity.' In D. Hawkin (eds.) *The Twenty-first Century Confronts its Gods: Globalization, Technology and War*. New York: State University of New York Press.

Forrester, D. B. (1997) *Christian Justice and Public Policy*. Cambridge: Cambridge University Press.

Foucault, M. (1977) *Discipline and punish: the birth of the prison*. London: Allen Lane.

Four Directions International (2001) *Mapping the Healing Experience of Canadian Aboriginal Communities: Site Visit Report for Hollow Water Community Holistic Circle Healing Process*. Cochrane, Ontario. Four Directions International.

French, R. R. (2002) *The Golden Yoke: The Legal Cosmology of Buddhist Tibet*. Ithaca, NY: Snow Lion Publications.

Froestad, J. and Shearing, C. (2007) 'Conflict Resolution in South-Africa: A Case Study.' In G. Johnstone and D. W. Van Ness (eds) *Handbook of Restorative Justice*. Cullompton: Willan Publishing.

Galloway, K. (2000) 'Justice as Healing.' In R. Burgess and K. Galloway (eds) *Praying for the Dawn: A Resource Book for the Ministry of Healing* Glasgow: Wild Goose Publications.

Galloway, K. (2004) *The Dream of Learning Our True Name.* Glasgow: Wild Goose Publications.

Galtung, J. (1969) 'Violence, peace and peace research.' *Journal of Peace Research 6,* 3, 167–191.

Garland, D. (2001) *The Culture of Control: Crime and Social Order in Contemporary Society.* Chicago: University of Chicago Press.

Geertz, C. (1973) *The Interpretation of Cultures: Selected Essays.* London: Fontana.

Ghosananda, M. (1992) *Step by Step : Meditations on Wisdom and Compassion.* Berkeley, CA: Parallax Press.

Giddens, A., and Birdsall, K. (2001) *Sociology.* Cambridge: Polity Press.

Gilligan, J. (2001) *Preventing Violence.* New York: Thames & Hudson.

Girard, R. (1977) *Violence and the Sacred.* Baltimore, MD: Johns Hopkins University Press.

Gluckman, M. (1969) 'Concepts in the comparative study of tribal law.' In L. Nader (ed.) *Law in Culture and Society.* Chicago: Aldine.

Gorringe, T. (1996) *God's Just Vengeance: Crime, Violence, and the Rhetoric of Salvation.* Cambridge and New York: Cambridge University Press.

Gorringe, T. (2002) *A theology of the Built Environment: Justice, Empowerment, Redemption.* Cambridge: Cambridge University Press.

Government of Canada (2008) *Schedule 'N': Mandate for Truth and Reconciliation Commission.* Accessed 5 June 2008 at http://www.residentialschoolsettlement.ca/SCHEDULE_N.pdf.

Greenough, H. (1947) *Form and function: remarks on Art.* Los Angeles, CA: University of California Press.

Hadley, M. L. (2001) *The Spiritual Roots of Restorative Justice.* Albany: State University of New York Press.

Hadley, M. L. (2005) 'Spiritual Foundations of Restorative Justice.' In D. Sullivan and L. Tifft (eds) *Handbook of Restorative Justice.* London: Routledge.

Hallowell, A. I. (1955) *Culture and Experience.* Philadelphia, PA,: University of Pennsylvania Press.

Hamilton, A. C. (2001) *A Feather, Not a Gavel: Working Towards Aboriginal Justice.* Winnipeg, MB: Great Plains Publications.

Hanh, T. N. (1967) *Vietnam: Lotus in a Sea of Fire.* New York: Hill and Wang.

Hanh, T. N. (1987a) *Being Peace.* Berkeley, CA: Parallax Press.

Hanh, T. N. (1987b) *The Sutra on the Eight Realizations of the Great Beings: A Buddhist Scripture on Simplicity, Generosity, and Compassion.* Berkeley, CA: Parallax Press.

Hanh, T. N. (1991) *Peace is Every Step: The Path of Mindfulness in Everyday Life.* New York: Bantam Books.

Hanh, T. N. (1992a) *Breathe! You Are Alive: Sutra on the Full Awareness of Breathing.* London: Rider.

Hanh, T. N. (1992b) *Touching Peace: Practising the Art of Mindful Living.* Berkeley, CA: Parallax Press.

Hanh, T. N. (1993) *Call Me by My True Names: The Collected Poems of Thich Nhat Hanh.* Berkeley, CA: Parallax Press.

Hanh, T. N. (1995) *Zen Keys: A Guide to Zen Practise.* London: Thorsons.

Hanh, T. N. (1998) *Fragrant Palm Leaves: Journals, 1962–1966.* Berkeley, CA: Parallax Press.

Hanh, T. N. (2001) *Anger: Wisdom for Cooling the Flames.* New York: Riverhead Books.

Hanh, T. N. (2002a) *Be Free Where You Are.* Berkeley, CA: Parallax Press.

Hanh, T. N. (2002b) 'Go as a Sangha.' In T. N. Hanh and J. Lawlor (eds) *Friends on the Path.* Berekley, CA: Parallex Press.

Hanh, T. N. (2002c) 'Spirituality in the Twenty-first Century.' In T. N. Hanh and J. Lawlor (eds) *Friends on the Path.* Berkeley, CA: Parallax Press.

Hanh, T. N. (2003a) In 'Compassion is Our Hope: Practising to Reduce Violence in Society.' *Protecting and Serving without Stress or Fear.* Green Lake, WI: Plum Village Productions.

Hanh, T. N. (2003b) *Finding Our True Home: Living in the Pure Land Here and Now.* Berkeley, CA: Parallax Press.

Hanh, T. N. (2003c) *I have Arrived, I am Home: Celebrating Twenty Years of Plum Village Life.* Berkeley, CA: Parallax Press.

Hanh, T. N. (2003d) 'I have Arrived, I am Home: Dharma Talk.' In *Protecting and Serving without Stress or Fear.* Green Lake, WI: Plum Village Productions.

Hanh, T. N. (2003e) *Joyfully Together: The Art of Building a Harmonious Community.* Berkeley, CA: Parallax Press.

Hanh, T. N. (2003f) 'Mindfulness of Anger: Embracing the Child Within'. In *Protecting and Serving without Stress or Fear.* Green Lake, WI: Plum Village Productions.

Hanh, T. N. (2003g) 'Right Thinking: The Code of Law' In *Protecting and Serving without Stress or Fear.* Green Lake, WI: Plum Village Productions.

Hanh, T. N. (2005). 'Creating Our Environment: Building a Foundation of Stability and Peace'. *Colors of Compassion 2005: Healing Our Families, Building True Community,* Escondido, CA: Plum Village Productions.

Hanh, T. N. (2007) *For a Future to be Possible: Buddhist Ethics for Everyday Life.* Berkeley, CA: Parallax Press.

Hanh, T. N. and J. Lawlor (2002) *Friends on the Path: Living Spiritual Communities.* Berkeley, CA: Parallax Press.

Hanh, T. N. and Monks and Nuns at Plum Village (2007) *Chanting from the Heart: Buddhist Ceremonies and Daily Practises.* Berkeley, CA: Parallax Press.

Harland, A. (1996) 'Towards a Restorative Justice Future.' In B. Galaway and J. Hudson (eds) *Restorative Justice: International Perspectives.* Monsey, NY: Criminal Justice Press.

Harris, P. (2007) *An Introduction to Law*. Cambridge: Cambridge University Press.

Hart, H. L. A. (1968) *Punishment and Responsibility*. Oxford: Clarendon Press.

Harvey, J. (1987) *Bridging the Gap: Has the Church Failed the Poor?* Edinburgh: Saint Andrew Press.

Hauerwas, S. (1981) *A Community of Character: Toward a Constructive Christian Social Ethic*. Notre Dame, IN: University of Notre Dame Press.

Henderson, J. S. k. j. Y. (1995) 'Exploring justice as healing.' *Justice as Healing 1*, 1, 1–4.

Henderson, J. S. k. j. Y. and McCaslin, W. (2005) 'Exploring Justice as Healing.' In W. McCaslin (eds.) *Justice as Healing: Indigenous Ways*. St Paul, MN: Living Justice Press.

Herman, J. L. (1997) *Trauma and Recovery*. New York: Basic Books.

Herman, J. L. (2003) 'The mental health of crime victims: Impact of legal intervention.' *Journal of Traumatic Stress 16*, 2, 159–166.

Hollow Water Community Holistic Circle Healing (1995) 'The Sentencing Circle: Seeds of a community healing process.' *Justice as Healing* (Winter).

Hopkins, B. (2004) *Just schools: A Whole School Approach to Restorative Justice*. London: Jessica Kingsley Publishers.

Huebner, C. (2006) *A Precarious Peace: Yoderian Explorations on Theology, Knowledge and Identity*. Scottdale, PA: Herald Press.

Hume, D. (2004) 'Of Justice.' In M. Clayton and A. Williams (eds) *Social Justice*. Oxford: Blackwell Publishing: 32–45.

Jackson, M. (1992) 'In search of pathways to justice: alternative dispute resolution in Aboriginal communities.' *University of British Columbia Law Review*, special edition, 147–238.

Jackson, M. and Rubin, J. (1996) *Report of the Royal Commission on Aboriginal Peoples: Bridging the Cultural Divide*. Ottawa: Canada Communication Group.

Johnston, B. H. (1976) *Ojibway Heritage*. Toronto: McClelland and Stewart.

Johnston, D. and Sampson, C. (1995). *Religion, the Missing Dimension of Statecraft*. New York: Oxford University Press.

Johnstone, G. (2002) *Restorative Justice Ideas, Values, Debates*. Cullompton: Willan.

Johnstone, G. (2004) 'How, and in What Terms, should Restorative Justice be Conceived?' In H. Zehr and B. Toews (eds) *Critical Issues in Restorative Justice*. Monsey, NY: Criminal Justice Press.

Johnstone, G. and Van Ness, D. W. (2007) 'Meaning of Restorative Justice.' In G. Johnstone and D. W. Van Ness (eds) *Handbook of Restorative Justice*. Cullompton: Willan Publishing.

Judah, E. H. and Bryant, M. (2004) *Criminal Justice: Retribution vs. Restoration?* Binghamton, NY: Haworth Social Work Practise Press and Haworth Pastoral Press.

Kant, I. (1887) *The philosophy of Law: An Exposition of the Fundamental Principles of Jurisprudence as the Science of Right*. Edinburgh: T. & T. Clark.

Keeley, L. H. (1995) *War before Civilization*. New York and Oxford: Oxford University Press.

King Jr, M. L. (1967). 'Nomination letter to The Nobel Institute concerning Thich Nhat Hanh.' Accessed on 20 October, 2008, at www.hartford-hwp.com/archives/45a/025.html.

Kvale, S. (1996) *Interviews: An Introduction to Qualitative Research Interviewing*. Thousand Oaks, CA: Sage Publications.

Lajeunesse, T. (1993) *Community Holistic Circle Healing: Hollow Water First Nation*. Ottawa: Corrections Branch, Solicitor General Canada, Ministry Secretariat.

Lajeunesse, T. (1996) *Evaluation of the Hollow Water Community Holistic Circle Healing Project*. Ottawa: Solicitor General Canada.

Lambert, S. (1993) *Form Follows Function? Design in the 20th Century*. London: Victoria & Albert Museum.

Lane, P., Bopp, M., Bopp, J. and Morris, J. (2002) *Mapping the Healing Journey: The Final Report of a First Nation Research Project on Healing in Canadian Aboriginal Communities*. Ottawa: Solicitor General Canada.

Large, N. (2001) 'Healing justice.' *Alberta Views* (May/June), 20–25.

Lawlor, J. (2002). 'Sharing the Path.' In T. N. Hanh and J. Lawlor (eds) *Friends on the Path*. Berkeley, CA: Parallex Press.

Lazarus, R. J. (2004) *The Making of Environmental Law*. Chicago: University of Chicago Press.

Lederach, J. P. (1995) *Preparing for Peace: Conflict Transformation across Cultures*. Syracuse, NY: Syracuse University Press.

Lederach, J. P. (2005) *The Moral Imagination: The Art and Soul of Building Peace*. New York: Oxford University Press.

Lee, G. (1996) 'Defining traditional healing justice.' *Justice as Healing 1*, 4.

Lee, G. (1997) 'The newest old gem: family group conferencing.' *Justice as Healing 2*, 2.

Legge, M.J. (1995) 'Multidialogical Spiraling: Healing and Justice in Feminist Theology and Ethics.' In *Gender, Genre and Religion: Feminist Reflections*. Waterloo, ON: J. Morry and E. Neumaier-Dargyay (eds) Wilfred Laurier Press for Calgary Institute for the Humanities.

Lewinski, S. v. and Hahn, A. v. (2004) *Indigenous Heritage and Intellectual Property Genetic Resources, Traditional Knowledge and Folklore*. London: Kluwer Law International.

Lewis, A. (1995) 'Truth and healing.' *New York Times* (16 January) 17.

Lindbeck, G. A. (1984) *The Nature of Doctrine: Religion and Theology in a Postliberal Age*. Philadelphia, PA: Westminster Press.

Lindon, R. and Clairmont, D. (1998) *Making it Work: Planning and Evaluating Corrections and Healing Projects in Aboriginal Communities*. Ottawa: Ministry of the Solicitor General of Canada, Government of Canada.

Llewellyn, K. N. (1940) 'The normative, the legal and the law-jobs: the problem of juristic method.' *Yale Law Journal 49*, 8, 1355–1400.

Llewellyn, K. N. and Hoebel, E.A. (1941) *The Cheyenne Way: Conflict and Case Law in Primitive Jurisprudence*. Norman, OK: University of Oklahoma Press.

Locke, J. (2004) 'Of Property.' In M. Clayton and A. Williams (eds) *Social Justice*. Oxford: Blackwell.

Loy, D. (2001) 'Healing Justice: A Buddhist Perspective.' In M. L. Hadley (eds.) *The Spiritual Roots of Restorative Justice*. New York: Albany University of New York Press.

Loy, D. (2003) *The Great Awakening: A Buddhist Social Theory*. Boston, MA: Wisdom.

Luther, M. (1958) *Luther's Works ... Edited by Jaroslav Pelikan*. Saint Louis, MO: Concordia Publishing House.

MacCallum-Paterson, M. (1988) *Toward a Justice that Heals: The Church's Response to Crime*. Toronto: The United Church Publishing House.

Macdonald, L. O. (1999) *In Good Company: Women in the Ministry*. Glasgow: Wild Goose Publications.

Macleod, G. F. B. M. o. F. (1955) *The Place of Healing in the Ministry of the Church*. Glasgow: Iona Community.

MacRae, A. and Zehr, H. (2004) *The Little Book of Family Group Conference: New Zealand Style*. Intercourse, PA: Good Books.

Macy, J. (2007) *World as Lover, World as Self: Courage for Global Justice and Ecological Renewal*. Berkeley, CA: Parallax Press.

Maine, H. J. S. (1906) *Ancient Law: Its Connection with the Early History of Society, and its Relation to Modern Ideas*. London: John Murray.

Malinowski, B. (1926) *Crime and Custom in Savage Society*. New York: Harcourt, Brace.

Manson, M. (1994) 'Justice that heals: native alternatives.' *Canadian Lawyer* (October), 28.

Marshall, C. D. (2001) *Beyond Retribution: A New Testament Vision for Justice, Crime, and Punishment*. Grand Rapids, MI amd Cambridge: William B. Eerdmans Publishers.

Marshall, M. (2003) 'Healing the body, healing the spirit, healing the community.' *Reviews in Anthropology 32*, 4, 315–325.

Martin, M. (1999) 'From criminal justice to transformative justice: the challenges of social control for battered women.' *Contemporary Justice Review 4*, 415–436.

Maxwell, G. M. and Morris, A. (2001) *Restorative Justice for Juveniles: Conferencing Mediation and Circles*. Oxford: Hart Publishing.

Maxwell, G. and Morris, A. (2006) 'Meeting Human Needs: The Potential of Restorative Justice.' In A. J. W. Taylor (ed.) *Justice as a Basic Human Need*. New York: Nova Science Publishers.

Maxwell, J. A. (2005) *Qualitative Research Design: An Interactive Approach*. London: Sage Publications.

McCaslin, W. (2005a) 'Healing in Rough Waters.' In W. McCaslin (ed.) *Justice as Healing: Indigenous Ways*. St Paul, MN: Living Justice Press.

McCaslin, W. (2005b) 'Reweaving the Fabrics of Life.' In W. McCaslin (eds.) *Justice as Healing: Indigenous Ways*. St Paul, MN Living Justice Press.

McCaslin, W. D. (2005c) *Justice as Healing: Indigenous Ways*. St Paul, MN: Living Justice Press.

McCold, P. (2006) 'The Recent History of Restorative Justice: Mediation, Circles and Conferencing.' In D. Sullivan and L. Tifft (eds) *Handbook of Restorative Justice: A Global Perspective*. New York: Routledge.

McIlhagga, K. (2000) 'The Church's Healing. Ministry.' In R. Burgess and K. Galloway (eds) *Praying for the Dawn: A Resource Book of the Ministry of Healing*. Glasgow: Wild Goose Publications.

McLaughlin (2003) *Critical Issues in Restorative Justice*. London: Sage Publishing.

Mead, J. (2003) 'Personal Peacemaking.' In *Making Peace in Practice and Poetry*. Glasgow: Wild Goose Publications.

Meaden, B. (1999) *Protest for Peace*. Glasgow: Wild Goose Publications.

Megivern, J. J. (1997) *The Death Penalty: An Historical and Theological Survey*. New York: Paulist Press.

Melton, A. P. (2001) 'Indigenous justice systems and tribal society.' *Justice as Healing 6*, 1.

Mercredi, O. (2001) 'Concluding Remarks'. *Conference on Restorative Justice*, Winnipeg, Centre for Excellence in Restorative Justice and Reconciliation.

Miles, M. B. and Huberman, A. M. (1994) *Qualitative Data Analysis: An Expanded Sourcebook*. Thousand Oaks, CA: Sage.

Mill, J. S. (1884). *A System of Logic, Ratiocinative and Inductive*. London: Longmans.

Miller, B. G. (2001) *The Problem of Justice: Tradition and Law in the Coast Salish World*. Lincoln, NE: University of Nebraska Press.

Monks and Nuns at Plum Village (2003) *How to Enjoy Your Stay in Plum Village: An Introduction to Plum Village*, Berkeley, CA: Parallax Press.

Monteith, W. G. (2000) 'Service of Prayers for Healing of the Iona Community: A Historical and Theological Perspective.' In R. Burgess and K. Galloway (eds) *Praying for the Dawn: A Resource Book of the Ministry of Healing* Glasgow: Wild Goose Publications.

Monture-Angus, P. (1995) 'The Existing System Can't Be Indigenized.' (conference) *Restorative Justice: Four Community Models*, Saskatoon, Saskatchewan 17 and 18 March unpublished.

Moore, B. (1967) *Social Origins of Dictatorship and Democracy. Lord and Peasant in the Making of the Modern World*. London: Penguin.

Morris, R. (1995) *Penal Abolition, the Practical Choice: A Practical Manual on Penal Abolition*. Toronto: Canadian Scholars' Press.

Morris, R. (2000) *Stories of Transformative Justice*. Toronto: Canadian Scholars' Press.

Morrison, B. (2002) *Bullying and Victimisation in Schools: A Restorative Justice Approach*. Canberra: Australian Institute of Criminology.

Morrow, D. (2000) 'Where there is Injury... Hope for Healing in Northern Ireland.' In R. Burgess and K. Galloway (eds) *Praying for the Dawn*. Glasgow: Wild Goose Publications.

Morton, T. R. (1957) *The Iona Community Story*. London: Lutterworth Press.

Muhly, E. J. P. (2001) 'Transformative or restorative justice.' *State of Justice 3*.

National Film Board of Canada (2000) *Hollow Water*. Montréal: National Film Board of Canada.

Newell, J. P. (2004) *Each Day & Each Night: Celtic Prayers from Iona*. Glasgow: Wild Goose Publications.

Nguyen, T. T. (ed.) (1997) *History of Buddhism in Vietnam. Cultural Heritage and Contemporary change. Series III, Asia; v. 1*. Washington, DC: Council for Research in Values and Philosophy.

Nixon, W. (1997) *Legal Anthropology*. Accessed on 20 October 2006 at www.indianna.edu/~wanthro/legal.htm.

O'Connell, T. (1998) 'From Wagga Wagga to Minnesota.' In Conferencing: A New Approach to Wrongdoing Proceeding of the First North American Conference on Conferencing. Real Justice, online. Accessed 20 October 2008 at www.iirp.org/library/nacc/nacc_oco.

Pavlich, G. (2005) *Governing Paradoxes of Restorative Justice*. London: GlassHouse Press.

Pavlich, G. (2006) 'Restorative Justice and its Paradoxes.' *VOMA Connections 22*, 1, 14.

PBS Nova Online (2001) *The Hippocratic Oath Today*. Accessed 22 July 2008 at http://www.pbs.org/wgbh/nova/doctors/oath_today.html.

Peachey, D. (2003) 'The Kitchener Experiment.' In G. Johnstone (ed.) *Restorative Justice Reader*. Cullpmpton: Willan.

Pennell, J. and Burford, G. (2000). 'Family Group Decision Making and Family Violence.' In G. Burford and J. Hudson (eds) *Family Group Conferencing: New Directions in Community-centred Child and Family Practise*. New York: Walter de Gruyter.

Pepi, C. L. O. H. (1997) 'Children without childhoods: A feminist intervention strategy utilizing systems theory and restorative justice in treating female adolescent offenders.' *Women & Therapy 20, 4, 85–100*.

Plato (2008) *Laws 10*. Oxford and New York: Clarendon Press.

Plum Village delegation (2006) 'Buddhism responding to the needs of the 21st century.' *World Buddhist Forum*, Hangzhou, China. Accessed 22 July 2008 at http://www.plumvillage.org/general/Buddhism%20Responding%20to%20the%20Needs%20of%20the%2021st%20Century.pdf.

Posey, D. A. and Dutfield, G. (1996) *Beyond Intellectual Property: Toward Traditional Resource Rights for Indigenous Peoples and Local Communities*. Ottawa: International Development Research Centre.

Pranis, K., Stuart, B. and Wedge, M. (2003) *Peacemaking circles: From Crime to Community*. St Paul, MO: Living Justice Press.

Pratt, J. (1996) 'Colonization, Power and Silence: A History of Indigenous Justice in New Zealand Society.' In B. Galaway and J. Hudson (eds) *Restorative Justice: International Perspectives*. Monsey, NY: Criminal Justice Press.

Presser, L. and Gaarder, E. (2000) 'Can restorative justice reduce battering? some preliminary considerations.' *Social Justice 27*, 1, 175–195.

Rancourt, D. and Fourier, M. (1999) *Punishments*. Princeton, NJ: Films for the Humanities & Sciences.

Rashani. (1991) *The Unbroken*. Accessed 20 October 2008 at www.rashani.com/retreats/index.html.

Rawls, J. (1999) *A Theory of Justice*. Oxford: Oxford University Press.

Redekop, P. (2008) *Changing Paradigms: Punishment and Restorative Discipline*. Waterloo, ON: Herald Press.

Renner, K. (1949) *The Institutions of Private Law and their Social Functions*. London: Routledge.

Roach, K. (2000) 'Changing punishment at the turn of the century, restorative justice on the rise.' *Canadian Journal of Criminology 42*, 3, 249–279.

Roberts, S. (1979) *Order and Dispute: An Introduction to Legal Anthropology*. New York: St Martin's Press.

Roche, D. (2001) 'The evolving definition of restorative justice.' *Contemporary Justice Review 4*, 3–4, 341–353.

Ross, R. (1992) *Dancing with a Ghost: Exploring Indian Reality*. Markham, ON: Octopus Books.

Ross, R. (1995) 'Aboriginal community healing in action: the Hollow Water approach.' *Justice as Healing* (Spring).

Ross, R. (1996) *Returning to the Teachings: Exploring Aboriginal Justice*. Toronto: Penguin Books.

Ruether, R. R. (1996) *Women Healing Earth: Third World Women on Ecology, Feminism, and Religion*. Maryknoll, NY: Orbis Books.

R. v. Proulx, SCC 5, [2000] 1 S.C.R. 61.

Ryan, J. (1995) *Doing Things the Right Way: Dene Traditional Justice in Lac La Martre, N.W.T.* Calgary: University of Calgary Press.

Saleh-Hanna, V. (2000). 'Penal abolition, an ideological and practical venture against criminal (in)justice and victimization.' MA thesis, Criminology. Simon Fraser University, Burnaby, British Columbia.

Sawatsky, J. (2003). 'Restorative values: where means and ends converge.' 6th International Conference on Restorative Justice, Vancouver, British Columbia.

Sawatsky, J. (2005) 'Peacebuilder as healer: Lessons from ancestral wisdom and healing traditions in Fiji.' *Peace Research: The Canadian Journal of Peace Studies 37*, 2.

Sawatsky, J. (2006) 'The geography of crime, the geography of healing justice and the ambivalence of restorative justice.' *Restorative Directions Journal 2*, 2b.

Sawatsky, J. (2008) 'Rethinking restorative justice: When the geographies of crime and of healing justice matter.' *Peace Research: The Canadian Journal of Peace and Conflict Studies 39*, 1.

Sawatsky, L. and J. Sawatsky (forthcoming) 'Colonialization and Christianization.' In J. Ross (ed.) *Encyclopedia of Religion and Violence*. Armonk, NY: M.E. Sharpe.

Shefsky, J. (2000) *A Justice that Heals*. Chicago: Window to World Communications.

Singer, R. G. (1979) *Just Deserts: Sentencing Based on Equality & Desert*. Cambridge, MA: Ballinger Publishing.

Sivell-Ferri, C. (1997) 'The Ojibwa Circle: Tradition and Change.' Aboriginal Corrections Policy Unit (eds) *Four Circles of Hollow Water*. Ottawa: Solicitor General Canada Aboriginal Corrections Policy Unit.

Skocpol, T. (1979) *States and Social Revolutions: A Comparative Analysis of France, Russia and China*. Cambridge: Cambridge University Press.

Smith, L. T. (1999) *Decolonizing Methodologies: Research and Indigenous Peoples*. London: Zed Books.

Smith, R. J. (2000) 'Casualties – US vs NVA/VC'. Accessed 23 July 2008, at http://www.rjsmith.com/kia_tbl.html.

Smith, T. W. (2001) *Revaluing Ethics: Aristotle's Dialectical Pedagogy*. New York: State University of New York.

Snyder, T. R. (2001) *The Protestant Ethic and the Spirit of Punishment*. Grand Rapids, MI: W.B. Eerdmans.

Staub, E. (2004) 'Justice, healing and reconciliation: how the People's Courts in Rwanda can promote them.' *Peace & Conflict: Journal of Peace Psychology 10*, 1, 25–32.

Steven, H. (1990) *Roger: An Extraordinary Peace Campaigner*. Glasgow: Wild Goose Publications.

Strang, H. (2002a) *Victim Participation in Restorative Justice*. Oxford: Oxford University Press.

Strang, H. (2002b) *Repair or Revenge: Victims and Restorative Justice*. Oxford: Oxford University Press.

Sullivan, D. and Tifft, L. (2001) *Restorative Justice: Healing the Foundations of Our Everyday Lives*. Monsey, NY: Willow Tree Press.

Sullivan, D. and Tifft, L. (2004) 'What are the Implications of Restorative Justice for Society and Our Lives?' In H. Zehr and B. Toews (eds) *Critical Issues in Restorative Justice*. Monsey, NY: Criminal Justice Press.

Sullivan, D. and Tifft, L. (2006) *Handbook of Restorative Justice: A Global Perspective*. London and New York: Routledge.

Tababodong, R. (2002) 'Reconciliation.' In J. Bird, L. Land, M. Macadam and D. Engelstad (eds) *Nation to Nation: Aboriginal sovereignty and the Future of Canada*. Toronto: Irwin Publishing.

The Iona Community (1991) *The Iona Community Worship Book*. Glasgow: Wild Goose Publications.

The Iona Community (1996) *What is the Iona Community?* Glasgow: Wild Goose Publications.

The Iona Community (2001a) *Iona Abbey Worship Book*. Glasgow: Wild Goose Publications.

The Iona Community (2001b) *The Iona Community: Today's Challenge, Tomorrow's Hope*. Glasgow: Wild Goose Publications.

The Iona Community (2006) *The Iona Community* (brochure). Glasgow: Wild Goose Publications.

The Iona Community (2007) *Members 2007* (booklet). Glasgow: Wild Goose Publications.

The Iona Community (n.d.-a) 'About the community.' Accessed 23 July 2008 at http://www.iona.org.uk/community/main.htm.

The Iona Community (n.d.-b) 'Iona youth.' Accessed 23 July 2008 at http://www.iona.org.uk/youth/main.htm.

The Iona Community (n.d.-c) 'Our worship.' Accessed 23 July 2008 at http://www.iona.org.uk/OurWorship.php.

The Iona Community (n.d.-d) 'The Rule of the Iona Community.' Accessed on 23 July 2008 at http://www.iona.org.uk/community/issues.htm.

Thorsborne, M. (1998) 'Justice as healing in a small Australian town.' *Justice as Healing 3*, 2.

Tierney, P. (2001) *Darkness in El Dorado: How Scientists and Journalists Devastated the Amazon*. New York: Norton.

Toews, B. and Zehr, H. (2003) 'Ways of Knowing for a Restorative Worldview.' In E. Weitekamp and H.-J. Kerner (eds) *Restorative Justice in Context: International Practise and Directions*. Cullompton: Willan.

Umbreit, M. (1989) 'Violent Offenders and their Victims.' In M. Wright and B. Galaway (eds) *Mediation and Criminal Justice: Victims, Offenders and Community*. London: Sage Publishing.

Umbreit, M. (1994) *Victim Meets Offender: The Impact of Restorative Justice and Mediation*. Monsey, NY: Criminal Justice Press.

United Church of Canada (n.d.) 'Ecology.' DOI: www.united-church.ca/ecology, accessed 20 October 2008

United Nations Department of Economic and Social Affairs (2004) *Searching for Innovations in Governance and Public Administration for Poverty Reduction*. New York: United Nations.

Van Ness, D. W. (1986) *Crime and its Victims: What We Can Do*. Downers Grove, IL: InterVarsity Press.

Van Ness, D. W. (1997) Legislating for restorative justice. Drafting juvenile justice legislation: An International Workshop. Cape Town South Africa 4–6 November.

Van Ness, D. W. (1998). 'Restorative justice: international trends'. Paper presented at Victoria University Wellington, NZ, 7 October 1998. Also available at www.restorativejustice.org/resources/docs/vanness13.

Van Ness, D. W. (2002) 'Creating Restorative Systems.' In L. Walgrave (ed.) *Restorative Justice and the Law* Cullompton: William.

Van Ness, D. W. and Strong, K. H. (1997) *Restoring Justice.* Cincinnati, OH: Anderson Publishing.

Van Ness, D. W. and Strong, K. H. (2002) *Restoring Justice.* Cincinnati, OH: Anderson Publishing.

Van Ness, D. W. and Strong, K. H. (2006) *Restoring Justice: An Introduction to Restorative Justice.* Cincinnati, OH: Lexis-Nexis/Anderson Publishing.

Von Hirsch, A. and Committee for the Study of Incarceration (1976) *Doing Justice: The Choice of Punishments.* New York: Hill and Wang.

Wachtel, T. (1997) *Real Justice.* Pipersville, PA: Piper's Press.

Warry, W. (1998) *Unfinished Dreams: Community Healing and the Reality of Aboriginal Self-government.* Toronto: University of Toronto Press.

Weber, M. (1965) *Politics as a Vocation.* Minneapolis, MN: Fortress Press.

Weber, M. (1985) *The Protestant Ethic and the Spirit of Capitalism.* London: Unwin Paperbacks.

Weil, S. (1998) 'The Need for Roots.' In P. Loptson (ed.) *Readings on Human Nature.* Peterborough, ON: Broadview Publishers.

Weitekamp, E. (1993) 'Restorative justice: towards a victim oriented system.' *European Journal of Criminal Policy and Research 1,* 70–93.

Weitekamp, E. (2003) 'The history of restorative justice.' In G. Johnstone (ed.) *A Restorative Justice Reader.* Cullompton: Willan.

Wexler, D. B. and Winick, B. J. (1996). *Law in a Therapeutic Key: Developments in Therapeutic Jurisprudence.* Durham, NC: Carolina Academic Press.

Willging, J. (1996) 'The power of feminine anger in Marie De France's "Yonec" and "Guigemar".' *Florilegium 14,* 123–135.

Willis, J. S. (2003) *A Lifetime of Peace: Essential Writings by and about Thich Nhat Hanh.* New York: Marlowe & Company.

Wilson, W. (1998) *Criminal Law: Doctrine and Theory.* London: Longman.

Witte, J. J. (2003) 'Between sanctity and depravity: Law and human nature in Martin Luther's two kingdoms.' *Villanova Law Review 48,* 727–763.

Wright, M. (1991) *Justice for Victims and Offenders: A Restorative Response to Crime.* Milton Keynes: Open University Press.

Wright, M. (2002) 'The paradigm of restorative justice.' *VOMA Connections* (Summer), 1–7.

Wright, M. (2005) 'Book review: governing paradoxes of restorative justice.' Accessed 23 July 2008 at http://www.restorativejustice.org/editions/2005/nov05/bookreview.

Yazzie, C. J. R. (2005) 'Justice as Healing: The Navajo Response to Crime.' In W. McCaslin (ed.) *Justice as Healing: Indigenous Ways.* St Paul, MO: Living Justice Press.

Yazzie, R. (1995) 'Healing as Justice: The American Experience.' *Justice as Healing 1,* 1.

Yazzie, R. and Zion, J. (1996) 'Navajo Restorative Justice: The Law of Equality and Justice.' In B. Galaway and J. Hudson (eds) *Restorative Justice: International Perspectives.* Monsey, NY: Criminal Justice Press.

Yin, R. K. (1993) *Applications of Case Study Research.* London: Sage Publications.

Yoder, J. H. (1972) *The Politics of Jesus.* Grand Rapids, MI: Eerdmans.

Yoder, P. B. (1987) *Shalom: The Bible's Word for Salvation, Justice, and Peace.* Newton, KA: Faith and Life Press.

Zehr, H. (1985) *Retributive Justice, Restorative Justice.* Elkhart, IN: MCC US Office of Criminal Justice.

Zehr, H. (1990a) *Changing Lenses: A New Focus for Crime and Justice.* Scottdale, PA and Waterloo, Ontario: Herald Press.

Zehr, H. (1990b) *Mediating the Victim/Offender Conflict: The Victim Offender Reconciliation Program.* Akron, PA: Mennonite Central Committee.

Zehr, H. (1994a) 'Justice that heals: the practise.' *Stimulus 2,* 3, 69–74.

Zehr, H. (1994b) 'Justice that heals: the vision.' *Stimulus 2,* 3, 5–11.

Zehr, H. (1997a) 'Restorative justice: the concept.' *Corrections Today 59,* 7, 68–70.

Zehr, H. (1997b) 'Restoring justice: envisioning a justice process focused on healing – not punishment.' *The Other Side 33,* 5, 22–27.

Zehr, H. (2002a) 'Journey to Belonging.' In E. Weitekamp and H.-J. Kerner (eds) *Restorative Justice: Theoretical Foundations.* Cullompton: Willan.

Zehr, H. (2002b) *The Little Book of Restorative Justice.* Intercourse, PA: Good Books.

Zion, J. (1997) 'Punishment versus healing: how does traditional Indian law work?' *Justice as Healing 2,* 3.

Subject Index

Author Index